GERTRUDE STEIN

HER LIFE AND WORK

Gertrude Stein by Picasso, 1906

Metropolitan Museum of Art

GERTRUDE STEIN

HER LIFE AND WORK

---

by

ELIZABETH SPRIGGE

ILLUSTRATED

HARPER & BROTHERS PUBLISHERS

NEW YORK

CONTENTS

ILLUSTRATIONS

Gertrude Stein by Picasso   *frontispiece*

ACKNOWLEDGMENTS

I AM indebted to Miss Alice Toklas for permission to quote from the works of Gertrude Stein, and to Mr. Carl Van Vechten, Miss Stein's Literary Executor. He has also kindly allowed me to use many passages from his correspondence with Gertrude Stein, most of it hitherto unpublished.

I also wish to make grateful acknowledgment to the Yale University Library for permission to work in the Gertrude Stein Collection of the Yale Collection of American Literature and to make use of manuscripts, photographs and other material. And particularly to Mr. Donald C. Gallup, its curator. Also to the Bancroft Library of the University of California at Berkeley for allowing me to transcribe parts of Mrs. Amelia Stein's diaries.

My thanks are also due to the Metropolitan Museum of Art in New York for the reproduction of the Picasso portrait of Gertrude Stein, and to the Baltimore Museum of Art for the reproductions of Picasso's portrait of Leo Stein, the Cézanne 'Bathers' and Marie Laurencin's 'Group of Artists'. To Monsieur Daniel-Henry Kahnweiler and the Galerie Louise Leiris for the Portrait of Kahnweiler and 'Head' by Picasso. And to Mrs. Walter A. Haas for the Matisse 'Femme au Chapeau'. Also to Sir Francis Rose for his painting 'Bilignin Across the Valley'.

I wish to express warm gratitude to the following individuals and organizations for invaluable help during the preparation of this biography in the form of hospitality, advice, information, introductions, gifts and loans of books, facilities and permission to use material:

Baron d'Aiguy, Mr. Newton Aiken, The American Library in Paris, Mrs. C. W. and Lynne Anderson, Mrs. Sherwood Anderson, Mr. George Antheil, Mrs. Esther Arthur (Murphy), Mrs. Helen K. Bachrach, Mrs. George Pierce Baker, Miss Natalie C. Barney, Mr. Alfred H. Barr Jnr., Mr. Joseph H. Barry, Miss Sylvia Beach, Mr. J. W. Beckman, Mrs. Sybille Bedford, Mr. Bernard

Berenson, Mrs. Adelyn D. Breeskin, Mr. John L. Brown, The Carnegie Library in Pittsburgh, Monsieur Jean Cocteau, Madame Jeanne Coppell, Mr. and Mrs. E. E. Cummings, Mrs. Alexander Dean, Mrs. William del Vallé, Mr. Norman Donaldson, Miss Katherine Dudley, Moya Dyring, Mr. A. D. Emmart, Miss Selma Erving, Miss Janet Frisbee, Mr. David Gascoyne, Mrs. Harry Phelan Gibb, Miss Rosamond Gilder, Professor Cabell Greet, Mr. Robert Bartlett Haas, Mrs. Walter A. Haas, Mr. Philip Hall, Dr. Edith Hamilton, Mr. Johan Hamburger, Miss Allanah Harper, Professor James Hart, Mr. Joseph Hone, Mr. Lindley Hubbell, Monsieur Georges Hugnet, Mr. and Mrs. Jacobs, Mrs. Victor Jelenko, Mr. Newell Jenkins, Mrs. Maria Jolas, Monsieur Daniel-Henry Kahnweiler, Karskaya, Mrs. Samuel J. Lanahan, Mrs. Madeline Langworthy, the late Marie Laurencin, Virginia Leirens, Madame Y. J. Lejeune, Mrs. Emanuel S. Leopold, Mr. David Lewis, Miss C. Lounsbery, Mrs. Mabel Dodge Luhan, Jan Marfyak, Mr. Robert McAlmon, Mr. Henry McBride, Mrs. Charles Mendenhall, Mr. Addison M. Metcalf, Mrs. Methol, Mr. Lamont Moore, Dr. Grace L. McCann Morley, Miss Ruth Napier, *The New Yorker*, Mr. St. John Nixon, Mr. Albert E. Norman, Professor and Mrs. Wallace Notestein, Madame Fernande Olivier, Mrs. Osorio, Mr. and Mrs. John R. Pappenheimer, Mr. Norman Holmes Pearson, Monsieur Jean Pernollet, Mr. Fritz Peters, Madame Picabia, Mr. Daniel Raffel, Mrs. Gertrude S. Raffel, The Registrar of Radcliffe College, Mrs. Stanley B. Resor, Monsieur H. P. Roché, Mr. and Mrs. W. G. Rogers, Sir Francis Rose, Miss Annette Rosenshine, Dr. Marion Ross, Dr. Ernest Sachs, Miss Dorothy Sands, Mr. William Saroyan, Miss Marion Saunders, Mrs. K. Sprigge, Mr. Daniel Stein, Mrs. Julian S. Stein, Mr. Donald Sutherland, Mrs. Louise Taylor, Mr. Pavel Tchelitchew, Mr. Virgil Thomson, Miss Mabel Foote Weeks, Mrs. Marjorie Wells, Mr. William Whitehead, Mr. Thornton Wilder, Mrs. Katherine S. Wilson, Mr. Edmund Wilson, Miss Leila Wittler, Miss Roberta Yerkes.

Due acknowledgment is also made to the following publishers: Messrs. W. H. Allen & Co. Ltd.; B. T. Batsford Ltd.; The Exposition Press; Farrar, Straus & Cudahy; M. Fridberg, Harcourt, Brace & Co.; William Heinemann Ltd.; The Hogarth Press; Houghton

Mifflin Co.; Alfred A. Knopf, Inc.; John Lane the Bodley Head; John Lane Company; Random House; Rinehart & Co. Inc.; Charles Scribner's Sons; Martin Secker & Warburg Ltd.; Librairie Stock; Paul Theobald; Yale University Press.

PREFACE

By 1946, when Gertrude Stein died in Paris at the age of seventy-two, she had achieved an ambition, 'I always wanted to be historical, from almost a baby on'.

She had become one of the century's most talked about authors and if only a few of her books were widely read she had influenced a large number of writers, including Hemingway and Thornton Wilder, and was quoted by thousands of people who had never read her at all.

Both as artist and as woman Gertrude Stein has always been a subject of controversy. Ridiculed on the one hand she is acclaimed on the other as the creator of a literary style that has set its mark on twentieth-century prose and poetry, one of the first stream-of-consciousness novelists and an original thinker with psychological and philosophical ideas rooted in the conceptions of William James, under whom she studied, but bearing new fruits. Brought up in California and going East to finish her education, early in the twentieth century she settled in Paris with her brother, Leo Stein, and made France her home for the rest of her life. At once they began buying contemporary pictures; they discovered Picasso, he and Gertrude became close friends and as the Cubist movement was born she found an exciting affinity between the aims of the visual artists and what she wanted to do with words. The Stein collection of contemporary pictures soon became famous and she encouraged many young painters who were greatly impressed with her wisdom. Yet there are people who say that all her unconventional writing is nonsense and that she knew nothing at all about art.

Opinions of her personality differ as widely. She had enormous vitality, an unfailing zest for living and a searching interest in human beings which, expressed in a candid gaze, a compelling voice and hearty laughter, gave her great magnetism. In early days people used to go to her house to see the pictures, but later they went for herself; and she knew an enormous number of interesting contemporaries in every field. Most men and women found her enchanting company, but to a few she seemed merely eccentric and self-centred; for many she had great humour, others found in her none at all. Those closest to her bear witness to a great gift for friendship, but there was also, to borrow one of her titles, a 'history of having a great many times not continued to be friends.'

I did not know Gertrude Stein myself. I had read her autobiographical books with interest and amusement, *Three Lives* with pleasure and *Picasso* with admiration and joy. Then in 1947 I came across Carl Van Vechten's *Selected Writings of Gertrude Stein*[1] and had my first experience of her more idiosyncratic writing. Some of it was unintelligible to me, but I liked the fugal repetitions and subtle variations, particularly in some of the *Portraits*, which at once seemed to me Cubist in construction. In 1948 I chose Gertrude Stein's Resistance play *Yes Is For A Very Young Man* for production by a small London theatre group of which I was a director. At the first reading the cast was bewildered, but before long the rhythm of the dialogue captivated everyone and we found it most effective in action. Studying her work further the sustained technique led me through mists of un-understanding although there are patches which have never cleared. I cannot, for example, understand why *The Making of Americans* had to be so long, but I find much of her writing beautiful, wise and wonderfully funny. One laughs with her rather than at her.

What appeals most to me about Gertrude Stein is her contemporaneousness, her often repeated conviction that the business of art is to live in and express 'the complete actual present', her lifelong effort to do this thing and the pleasure she had in being an artist. 'One of the pleasantest things those of us who write or paint do is to have the daily miracle. It does come.'[2]

I have tried to present an objective picture of the many-sided Gertrude Stein, drawing largely on her autobiographical books to give glimpses of her life in her own words, and also on letters,

[1] Random House, 1946.   [2] *Paris France.*

particularly the correspondence with Carl Van Vechten covering so many years. I have included the conflicting views of some of her contemporaries.

Examples of her unorthodox work are given, showing its nature and development. While not sharing all his views my studies have been greatly stimulated and helped by Donald Sutherland's exposition *Gertrude Stein: A Biography of Her Work*.[1]

While preparing the biography I spent many months in France and in America, examining the Gertrude Stein Collection of books, manuscripts, letters and photographs in the Yale Collection of American Literature, reading the diaries of Gertrude Stein's mother in the Bancroft Library of the University of California at Berkeley, visiting the places where she lived and talking with relatives and other men and women who knew her well at different periods of her life. These conversations and other material are recorded in a journal from which I have quoted extracts.

To all those people who aided my inner and outer journey I give warm thanks. And first must be mentioned Gertrude Stein's lifelong friend Miss Alice Toklas, without whose initial encouragement this work would not have been undertaken.

London. June 1956   E.S.

---

[1] Yale University Press, 1951.

CHAPTER ONE

FROM OLD WORLD TO NEW

'Steins were called Steins in the time of Napoleon before that any name was a name but in the time of Napoleon in any country he went through the name of any one had to be written and so they took the name they gave them and Stein was an easy one.'

Everybody's Autobiography.

'My father's name was Daniel he had a black beard he was not tall not at all tall, he had a black beard his name was Daniel.'

The Mother of Us All.

ALTHOUGH Gertrude Stein in her living and her writing made the present her tense, she did not ignore the past, but believed that to have inside knowledge of ourselves it was necessary to keep alive 'the knowledge of the men and women who as parents and grand-parents came together and mixed up to make us'. As a young woman she wrote about her forebears in *The Making of Americans*,[1] but although this vast book contains fascinating character studies, it is admittedly fiction, so while invaluable for its portraits and its atmosphere, the facts cannot be relied upon. For the beginning of the Stein story therefore we turn to an untitled, undated obituary notice from the Gertrude Stein papers in the University Library at Yale.

Her uncle Meyer Stein was, we learn, born in 1823 in Weikers-grubben, a small Bavarian village. His father, Michael, was a merchant, and when Meyer was eighteen, believing that the new world had better opportunities to offer than the old, he crossed the Atlantic and soon afterwards induced his family to join him in Maryland.

By the time Meyer was twenty-two he had opened a large clothing establishment in Baltimore with his brothers, Samuel,

[1] Written 1906–11. First published 1925.

Daniel, Levi and Solomon. The firm was given the name of Stein Brothers and enjoyed a high reputation in the community. The Civil War was probably an advantage to the business, for many mills closed down through lack of raw material, leaving the market open to products from abroad, and presumably the Stein brothers imported their goods from Europe. In any case they quickly prospered. In 1862, however, the partnership was dissolved—the Steins were always a quarrelsome family—and Meyer and Samuel continued the Baltimore house while Daniel and Solomon moved to Pittsburgh.

One can still see the down-town corner of Wood and Fourth Street in Pittsburgh where the new Stein Brothers traded in 'clothing and cloths', and reconstruct the swiftly growing city at the meet of the three great rivers before commerce quite took over. When the Steins arrived, the horse-drawn cars of the new street railroads were beginning to roll over the cobbled streets, warehouses were springing up along the river banks, and paddle steamers plied between 'Butcher's run', 'Soft Soap run' and the tanneries.

For a few years the directories show Daniel and Solomon at different addresses. Then, when they had made enough money and were beginning to raise families, they crossed the Ohio and built themselves twin houses in Allegheny, now a Northside suburb of Pittsburgh, but in those days a separate town. They chose for the site of their red brick, white-stepped, white-painted homes, Western Avenue, now a shabby fallen street, but which abuts the pleasant park and is described as having originally been the most 'high hat' street in the 'bon ton' section of Allegheny. How well the brothers had already done for themselves! One pictures them, well set-up, rather proud young men in tall hats and smartly cut clothes, a tribute to the firm, respectable and respected citizens enjoying all the amenities of the American middle-class, only a quarter of a century after their parents emerged from their Bavarian village. As a family they took quickly to culture and ideas.

Both brothers were married now. Daniel had brought his bride, Amelia Keyser, from Baltimore, the fact that during the war the Keysers had stood for the South and the Steins for the

North not preventing Daniel and Amelia from marrying before
General Lee's final surrender. The Keysers too were German
Jews, earlier settlers in America than the Steins.

When Daniel was thirty-three—his wife was ten years younger
—their first child was born and called Michael after his grandfather. Other children quickly followed, two of whom died in
infancy, 'or else', Gertrude Stein says in *Everybody's Autobiography*,[1] 'I would not have come nor my brother just two years
older and we never talked of this after we had heard of it that they
never intended to have more than five children it made us feel
funny.'

As it was, however, there were Michael and Simon and Bertha
and Leo, and then on February 3rd 1874, Gertrude was born.
'As I am an ardent californian,' runs a passage in *The Autobiography of Alice B. Toklas*,[2] 'and as she spent her youth there I have
often begged her to be born in California but she has always
remained firmly born in Allegheny, Pennsylvania.'

By this time a second division had occurred in the family and
the period of the twin houses was over. All we know of the quarrel
is that Milly, as Amelia was usually called, and her sister-in-law
Pauline 'who had never gotten along any too well were no
longer on speaking terms'. Why, Gertrude Stein seems never to
have discovered, although she was to become very fond of this
aunt. However, she was always grateful to her mother for refusing to forgive her sister-in-law or even to see her again, for
she surmised that otherwise, when her uncle Solomon moved to
New York, her father would have gone too. And to be brought
up in New York would, she felt, have been a miserable fate. Instead, when the partnership broke up and, in the very year of
Gertrude Stein's birth, Allegheny was devastated by fire and
flood, Daniel took his family over to Austria. He was a man of
ideas, although he seldom carried them through, and an ardent
educationist, 'education was almost the whole of living to
him'. So now he decided that the elder children would benefit
by some European teaching.

Rachel, one of Milly's unmarried sisters, went with them.

[1] Written in 1936. Published 1937.
[2] Written in 1932. First published 1933.

One wonders if she were the favourite or how it was decided which of the Keyser girls should have a trip to Europe in return for her help. Daniel was better off than the Keysers and could offer such inducements. His brother-in-law Ephraim had been helped by his sisters' small savings to study sculpture in Italy; now with Daniel's aid he continued his studies in Germany.

The family went first to Gemünden, then to Vienna, and the sisters' letters home fully describe the development of the children. To add to these are several tiny diaries kept by Amelia Stein, and contemporary photographs fill out the picture.

The Steins took furnished houses and lived well although carefully. They kept a nurse, a tutor, a governess and a full domestic staff, and there were music and dancing lessons and riding and skating and sight-seeing, in fact all the amenities of well-to-do middle-class life in the seventies.

Rachel was sometimes left in charge while Daniel and Milly travelled. 'Mikey' writes to his grandfather in 1875 of Papa and Mama being in Switzerland and 'going on to the Rhine' and 'Papa taking the grape cure'. It seems that Daniel was a faddist, a trait to which the Stein men were given. He used suddenly to decide that no one in the family should eat meat and then as suddenly give up this notion for another. The following year the sculptor brother 'Eph' went to Italy with them, and in their absence Rachel writes home of a change of servants and the arrival of a new governess. Rachel's responsibilities must have been heavy, but presumably she knew German and she was a devoted aunt, particularly fond of the baby, 'the darling little dumpling'. This reminds one how thankful Gertrude Stein always was to have been the youngest child. 'If that does happen', she writes at the beginning of *Wars I Have Seen*,[1] 'it is not lost all the rest of one's life there you are you are privileged, nobody can do anything but take care of you, that is the way I was and that is the way I still am, and anyone who is like that necessarily liked it. I did and do.'

Presently Milly comments to a sister, 'dear Celia you wish to know what the baby speaks well mostly German, and her greatest delight is to play with stones or pebbles', and Rachel records,

[1] Written 1942-4. First published 1945.

'She toddles around all day and repeats everything that is said or done . . . she beats them all', or again, 'The children are all very good, do not worry for Mama or Papa . . . the darling baby is so attached to the nurse girl.' And in the photographs one watches Gertrude growing from a pretty infant into a sturdy sashed and booted toddler with a large head and a grave expression.

Just before Gertrude's second birthday Rachel wrote a letter of extraordinary perspicacity:

> Mikey cannot write this week, he has really very little time; his whole time is occupied with his studies, and the little spare time he has, he devoted to skating; he skates very nicely: he is learning French also, twice a week. Symey hasn't as much desire for learning, he likes comfort and ease too much: he likes to play all the time. Leo will also learn well, I think, he and the baby can sing and repeat some nice little songs and verses. Bertha will be more like Symey as respects learning.

Rachel's prophecy was true. Bertha and Simon remained mentally undeveloped, while Michael was very intelligent and Leo and Gertrude were exceptionally clever.

Living at a loose end in Europe did not suit Daniel Stein for long and presently he returned to America to consider new ways of making money, leaving his family in exile. Milly loved him and found the separation hard; her diaries record her devotion, 'received Telegram from dear Dan that he arrived safely at Sandyhook', 'Answered dear Dan's letter', 'sent children's Photo to Dan', 'Oh God send him a safe return!'

After two years Rachel also returned home. She showed some anxiety at leaving her sister and was glad that Eph was at hand should help be needed. Daniel's brother Levi also paid Milly a visit and she seems to have had a number of acquaintances and to have been in touch with the Hebrew Association. All the same she did not like being left alone in Vienna with the children.

Gertrude Stein touches on her memories of these early years in several of her books and most concretely in *Wars I Have Seen*.

> And so we were in Vienna . . . there was a public garden, a formal garden and in a kind of a way a formal garden

pleases a child's fancy more than a natural garden. It is more like a garden that you would make yourself. And there was music and there was the old emperor who was a natural figure to have in a formal garden and there was his national anthem and then there were the salt caves and then there were birds and butterflies and insects in the woods and there was the catching of them and there was good eating and on my third birthday a taste of Vienna beer. And there were my mother and my brothers on horse-back and there was a Czech tutor, one did not realise how important all these nationalities were going to be to every one then and a Hungarian governess, and there was the first contact with books, picture books but books all the same since pictures in picture books are narrative.

And in *The Autobiography of Alice B. Toklas* she remembers 'that her brothers' tutor once, when she was allowed to sit with her brothers at their lessons, described a tiger's snarl and that that pleased and terrified her'.

Leo Stein, in *Journey Into the Self*,[1] declares that many of his sister's early memories are false or incorrectly dated. The latter is perhaps true, as Gertrude Stein speaks, for instance, of seeing her mother on horseback in Vienna, whereas the diaries tell of Mrs. Stein learning to ride in Paris whither, late in 1878, having dismissed both tutor and governess, she moved her family. There is a picture of her mounted, wearing a shallow top hat with a floating veil in Empress of Austria style, although she had neither the height nor the carriage to do the Imperial habit justice. She also took the children out in a carriage; Mikey was learning to drive, and they played ball in the Bois and went to the Avenue Trocadero to see a military parade, and visited a dentist and Bertha and Gertrude had their pictures taken for their 'camioes'. And every day in the three-inch journal the children's health was noted, and the weather even if it were only a 'sprincle' of rain.

Of this period Gertrude naturally remembered more. She and Bertha boarded for a while at a little school where, their mother

[1] The letters, papers and journals of Leo Stein, posthumously edited by Edmund Fuller. Crown Publishers, New York, 1950.

notes, they both won prizes. There Gertrude speaks of having soup with French bread for breakfast and of trading mutton, which she did not like, for spinach which she did, with the little girl who sat opposite her at dinner. But besides conscious memories many sounds, sights and smells of the city impressed themselves on her young senses, so that when twenty-five years later she came back to make Paris her home it was at once familiar.

Not long after the move to Paris Daniel rejoined them. The picture always brightens when he is there. As he whirls Milly and Mikey off to the opera and ballet, to the Exposition and to see the National Lottery drawn, one has the impression of a man full of nervous energy, anxious that neither he nor his family shall miss anything.

For the end of this sojourn we turn again to *The Autobiography of Alice B. Toklas*, which was of course written not by Miss Toklas but by Miss Stein:

> The family remained in Paris a year and then they came back to America. Gertrude Stein's elder brother charmingly describes the last days when he and his mother went shopping and bought everything that pleased their fancy, seal skin coats and caps and muffs for the whole family from the mother to the small sister Gertrude Stein, gloves dozens of gloves, wonderful hats, riding costumes, and finally ending up with a microscope and a whole set of the famous french history of zoology. Then they sailed for America.

CHAPTER TWO

CALIFORNIAN CORNUCOPIA

'Altogether it was a good way of living for them who had a
passion to be free inside them.'

The Making of Americans.

FOR some months after their return the Steins lived at Milly's old
home, the big Keyser house in Baltimore; but Daniel had already
set his heart on going West. He tried living in Los Angeles and
found that this did not suit him; he then experimented with San
José but did not like it either, and finally in 1880 he moved his
family to Oakland, across the Bay from San Francisco. Henceforward the children 'were really western, all of them, all through
them'.

They spent the first year in an hotel, 'as good a hotel as was then
there existing'. Amelia Stein's diaries give many pictures of those
days: Mike, now fifteen, riding a bicycle, herself taking lessons
in book-keeping at a business college, and Daniel, leaving
clothing far behind him, interested in street railroads, cable
cars, mines and the San Francisco Stock Exchange.

Gertrude's seventh birthday is recorded, 'each of the children
gave her a small preasant', and then they all developed measles.
Sixty years later Gertrude Stein wrote to a friend: 'I remember
my own child's measles and not being able to use my eyes was the
hardship otherwise it was all comfortable.' She loved being
cherished and she was already a reader.

Presently the Steins took what Gertrude called 'the Stratton
place'. In the Oakland records the name of the owner appears as
Templeton and the name Stratton cannot be traced. This was a
small-holding of ten acres on the corner of Twenty-Fifth Street
and Thirteenth Avenue with a rambling timber house on a rise
to rent for fifty dollars a month. One can feel the family's excitement in the mother's journal. They had already bought a piano

for four hundred dollars and acquired some furniture at sales, but now she records the buying of a cow.

The Steins only lived at the Stratton house for a few years— Raymond and Isadora Duncan, incidentally, were their neighbours, and Raymond used to steal the Stein apples—nevertheless this was the place that Gertrude Stein always thought of as her home and lovingly described in *The Making of Americans*. The eucalyptus trees lining the drive specially impressed her as a young child, 'seeming to her so tall and thin and savage', but all her memories are vivid.

In *The Making of Americans* the Steins are the Herslands and Oakland is Gossols.

> It was a very good kind of living the Hersland children had in their beginning, and their freedom in the ten acres where all kinds of things were growing, where they could have all anybody could want of joyous sweating, of rain and wind, of hunting, of cows and dogs and horses, of chopping wood, of making hay, of dreaming, of lying in a hollow all warm with the sun shining while the wind was howling, of knowing all poor queer kinds of people that lived in this part of Gossols where the Herslands were living and where no other rich people were living. And so they grew up with this kind of living, such kind of queer poor, for them, people around them, such uncertain ways of getting education that they had from the father's passion for all kinds of educating, from his strong love of starting and the uncertain things he had inside him.

But although the Stein children had unusual liberty they were 'regular in their living' until their mother grew too ill to manage the household. Certainly Daniel encouraged them to be independent and their playmates were of every race and kind, but the journals still describe the activities of what Gertrude Stein calls in *The Autobiography*[1] 'a very respectable middle class family'.

Although the children felt most at ease with the poorer neighbours, their background included servants and a seamstress and a series of governesses, and they were expected to receive callers

---

[1] Henceforward *The Autobiography of Alice B. Toklas* is referred to, as in Miss Stein's circle, as *The Autobiography*.

and pay visits with their mother, all of which one has to reconcile with the fact that living in California was in itself socially levelling. There was a folk-song that went 'What was your name in the States?' a question never asked, since here under assumed names princes and paupers lived and worked as social equals. So it was natural that Gertrude Stein should be imbued with democracy although her home had all the attributes of a well-to-do household.

Besides being educated at home Gertrude seems to have gone early to school, for in a letter to Robert Bartlett Haas she writes:

> ... my first conscious enthusiastic pleasure was a sunset in East Oakland, the sun setting in a cavern of clouds and my first writing when I was eight years old was a description of it, which pleased the teacher and it was to be carefully copied on to a specially prepared paper ... it was to be xhibited at the Mechanics Pavillon at the annual fair as the xample of our class in the Franklin School, but alas, after several efforts at copying the teacher was discouraged, and it was my composition but another little girl was set to copy it, who(se) handwriting was more certain. I can still see that enormous parchment piece of paper with a sort of red border ...

Gertrude Stein's handwriting did not become more certain with the years, and is a difficulty to those studying her manuscripts and letters. Sometimes she found it difficult to read herself. This way of writing 'x' for 'ex' at the beginning of words was a lifelong habit.

Nor was the children's religious training neglected. Mrs. Stein mentions Mike going with his father to the Temple and the children attending 'Sabath school'. She also occasionally notes a day of Jewish Observance, and Gertrude Stein writes: 'Sometimes their father would be strong in religion and then this would make for the children complications in their daily living.' As an adult she never practised the Jewish religion, but a close friend of hers, himself a Roman Catholic, says that she always had a great respect for it, and considered it an admirably practical religion on account of its concern with life on earth.

Now Mrs. Stein was enjoying new activities such as bottling her own peaches, and the next excitement was the renting of a horse and buggy. She learnt to drive with some trepidation and henceforward frequently drove Daniel to the station when he went to 'Business in the City' by street railroad and ferry. Gertrude Stein remembered with pleasure the free musicians, Portuguese and Italian, playing on the ferry as they crossed the Bay.

These were stirring days in California with full scope for Daniel's enterprising spirit. Like his daughter later he was always beginning. It was just ten years since the construction of the first cable cars which so much helped the development of San Francisco, the city of hills. The Big Four, C. P. Huntington and his colleagues, builders of the Pacific railroads, were at the height of their power and California was following gold boom with wheat boom and throwing up new cities overnight as a vigorous life-seeking population poured in. When, as a student, Gertrude Stein went East again she was to deplore that New Englanders had no struggle in them, and then one remembers how she grew up in the West at a time when struggle was inherent in living.

But against this background the home life of the Steins was gentle and the portraits of her parents in *The Making of Americans* give one some insight into it.

> The little mother was not very important to them. They were good enough children in their daily living but they were never loving to her inside them. They had it too strongly in them to win their own freedom . . .
>
> She was a sweet contented little woman who lived in her husband and her children, who could only know well to do middle class living, who never knew what it was her husband and her children were working out inside them and around them. She had strongly inside her the sense of being mistress of the household, the wife of a wealthy and good man and the mother of nice children.

None the less Gertrude remembered how much they counted on their mother's affection. Nor was Amelia altogether mild, for in spite of her sweetness she had 'a fierce stubborn little temper' which made her husband pay attention to her. Gertrude Stein inherited the temper without the mildness.

Daniel was more complex than his wife and it was to him that the children 'turned in their thinking', although they had to fight him too. There is a description of them being embarrassed as children always are by a parent's eccentricities. It might be that on a walk he would stop and sweep the prospect with his cane, talking aloud to himself, or pick up fruit in a shop and start eating it and giving it to the children. They were uncomfortable and shamed when they went out with him, not realizing that he was liked and trusted. Their perpetual cry was: 'Come on papa all those people are looking.'

He was often morose and irritable, which made things difficult for the children, as did his constantly changing views of how they should be taught, doctored or fed. Gertrude did not really like him, but she admits that he 'was in some ways a splendid kind of person . . . big in the size of him and in his way of thinking'. And she came to have a respect for his 'vital singularity', undoubtedly inherited by her along with the deep hearty laugh which no one who knew her ever forgets.

Such was the relationship of the Stein children to their parents. As for that between themselves, Gertrude was fond of Mike— everyone liked him although he was not easy to please—but he was nine years her senior and went away to college and later abroad, so he did not play a leading rôle in her life until, after their father's death, he became Leo's and her guardian.

Mike was the most musical member of the family, although Leo too played the violin and Gertrude was an adequate pianist. She played Mike's accompaniments and they went as a matter of course to the opera and concerts in San Francisco. As for poor Bertha and Simon:

> My sister four years older simply existed for me because I had to sleep in the same room with her. It is natural not to care about a sister, certainly not when she is four years older and grinds her teeth at night. My sister Bertha did. She was a little simple minded so was my brother Simon that is to say they would have been natural enough if no one had worried about it but Simon was very funny . . . not that it mattered except to my father.[1]

Daniel Stein did not grow resigned to his son's deficiency.

[1] *Everybody's Autobiography.*

There is a pathetic letter from him bidding Simon who was already twenty-two to be prompt and tidy and temperate and educate his mind. 'I hope you will change yet, you are still young, the world is before you.'[1]

It is interesting to note from his letters that Daniel Stein's English was not perfect. Neither was Amelia's.

To Gertrude the most important member of the family was Leo.

> My brother and myself had always been together. . . .
> It is better if you are the youngest girl in the family to have a brother two years older, because that makes everything a pleasure to you, you go everywhere and do everything while he does it all for and with you which is a pleasant way to have everything happen to you.[2]

She writes often and at length about their closeness, and admits, which in view of later events is important, that in their young days Leo was always the leader. Not only was he older and a boy, but he had a domineering disposition and although she was a reader, he was more intellectual. They were equal, however, in their desire for fame, in what field neither of them knew. Simply they wanted *la gloire* and disputed which of them would win it first.

They did everything together. In *Wars I Have Seen* one hears of them camping when they were quite small, walking up the dusty roads into the mountains, dragging a little wagon, shooting jack-rabbits and sleeping closely huddled together. Years after these early expeditions, Gertrude Stein heard 'the legend told of a tiny boy and girl, who had walked twenty miles up the mountain in half a day'. In actual fact on this occasion a farmer had given Leo and Gertrude a lift, but in *Wars I Have Seen* she touches on the incident to colour her brush, then paints as legend everything that a child does or knows or thinks between babyhood and the age of fourteen. In the development of this theme she caught the dreaminess and excitement of young childhood, its joy and sadness in the slow passing of time and 'the struggle not to know that death is there'. She touches often on this subject and says that she, in common with many other small children, sometimes

[1] From an unpublished letter. Yale.   [2] *Everybody's Autobiography.*

wished that she had died before she was old enough to be frightened by the idea of death. When writing of childhood she evokes its extraordinary innocence. 'Later on the legend is not so pure because you mix yourself up with it.'

As an adult Leo believed that his childhood had been unhappy and that its lack of direction had spoiled his life. Although he could be sparkling company he was by nature melancholy and introvert, whereas Gertrude had great vitality, a zest for living, a hot temper and boundless humour. Until 'the dark and dreadful days of adolescence' her memories were radiant.

In *The Making of Americans* she gives this picture of herself as a little girl:

> . . . this one was a very little one then and she was running and she was in the street and it was a muddy one and she had an umbrella that she was dragging and she was crying. 'I will throw the umbrella in the mud,' she was saying, she was very little then, she was just beginning her schooling, 'I will throw the umbrella in the mud,' she said and no one was near her and she was dragging the umbrella and bitterness possessed her, 'I will throw the umbrella in the mud,' she was saying and nobody heard her, the others had run ahead to get home and they had left her, 'I will throw the umbrella in the mud,' and there was desperate anger in her; 'I have throwed the umbrella in the mud,' burst from her, she had thrown the umbrella in the mud and that was the end of it all in her.

Another glimpse of herself in the eighties comes from *Wars I Have Seen*:

> When I was then I liked revolutions I liked to eat I liked to eat I liked to cry not in real life but in books and in real life there was nothing much to cry about but in books oh dear me, it was wonderful there was so much to cry about and then there was evolution. Evolution was all over my childhood . . . with music as a background for emotion and books as a reality and a great deal of fresh air as a necessity, and a great deal of eating as an excitement and as an orgy.

Nor was art neglected in the Steins' normal middle-class approach to culture. Painting was to play a big part in Gertrude Stein's life. Her first memory of a picture was *The Panorama of the*

Battle of Waterloo, seen in San Francisco when she was about eight years old. You stood in the centre of a platform, completely surrounded by the painting, and it was then, she says in *Paris France*,[1] that she 'first realised the difference between a painting and out of doors . . . that out of doors is made up of air and a painting has no air, the air is replaced by a flat surface, and anything in a painting that imitates air is illustration and not art'.

A few years later she was taken to see Millet's 'Man With The Hoe' in an exhibition to which another little girl, Alice Toklas whom she did not know, was also taken. When, fifty years later, the friends saw the picture together, they were surprised to find it so much smaller than in memory. This was the first picture of which Gertrude Stein wanted a reproduction. When she showed the photograph to Mike he commented that it was the hell of a hoe, but Gertrude could see in the painting that French country was 'made of ground, of earth'.

France was to become Gertrude Stein's country and it already touched her Californian days. There were many French families in San Francisco and she played with children who spoke the language. She read Jules Verne and Alfred de Vigny in translation, and saw French plays—Sarah Bernhardt came—and French paintings. Spain and China, she explains, were familiar in San Francisco, 'France was not daily it just came up again and again'. And one of the ways in which it came up was in the smell of her mother's furs and gloves from Paris and the boxes in which they were packed.

Thus Gertrude Stein's early life went vigorously but quietly on. She reminds her reader that in those days there was no war and no radio and nothing more exciting than climbing and watching nature, and nothing more interesting than the white man's burden and Esperanto.

But while the children enjoyed their care-free lives the mother saddened. In 1884 she commented that Dan was constantly unwell and often noted that she herself was tired. Yet she did not spare herself.

Dan in the City the children at school, swept the bed rooms

[1] Written 1939. Published 1940.

and put the store room in order also cleaned some Cloths and at home all day a lovely day all day.

In their simplicity and repetitiveness Amelia's diaries sometimes bring to mind her daughter's writing.

Mike had now gone East to Harvard and Simon was working in one unskilled job after another. In 1885 the Steins moved from the home they loved to a smaller house on Tenth Avenue, one reason for the change being that they wished to be nearer the children's school, and another Mrs. Stein's ill-health. There was also the question of financial insecurity. Daniel had sound ideas about consolidating the railways; but in his own projects although he made money he also sometimes lost it and there were periods of panic. During one of these times Leo and Gertrude spent every cent they could raise buying books as a security in case their father should be ruined.

By the second half of the year, although Milly continued to write 'all well' almost every day, even when the Jersey cow died calving, things were not well at all. She was having electric treatment from a galvanic battery and salt baths, and Bertha 'always goes with me to the Doctor I do not trust to walk alone'. By Christmas day it was Bertha who was preparing the dinner. In 1886 the tiny journal was written in pencil and is less neat than its predecessors; but her loving care for each member of the family continued and she still observed the weather. This is the last of the tiny volumes. In *The Making of Americans* Gertrude Stein writes of the little mother becoming at the end very frail and fretful. Life must indeed have been grim for them all as Mrs. Stein gradually became a complete invalid. In 1888, when Gertrude was fourteen, her mother died.

After this, although Mike had come home and taken a job in San Francisco, the household under Bertha's management grew still more irregular. Meals ceased to be organized; in the end the table was not even laid, each member of the family eating what and when he pleased. Leo and Gertrude if they felt inclined would walk all night or go to the opera and talk all night and sleep away the day. Meanwhile Daniel grew always more eccentric. Gertrude, although she had some regard for him, writes heartlessly enough. Completely unsentimental, she never pretended to feelings, nor did she paint them in false colours.

> After my mother died we went on doing what we had done but naturally our father was more a bother than he had been, that is natural enough. Hitherto we had naturally not had to remember him most of the time and now remembering him had begun.

Daniel was increasingly morose and irritable, and Gertrude Stein comments that fathers in general, whether personal or like dictators national, are depressing. But her attitude surely had to do with his towards her.

> He had impatient feeling in him that she was not the kind of daughter he had wanted to have . . .

This was one reason for adolescent unhappiness. In spite of freedom, of her love for Leo and a passion for reading, Gertrude must often have wished that she were more like other girls. She was already heavy for her small height—in the last journal the mother anxiously noted her weight. Any girl in her teens would be affected by this, and the physical and emotional changes of adolescence troubled her too. She developed early; there are touching little asterisks and initials in Amelia's later diaries marking dates in the month to be remembered.

It has been suggested that the young Gertrude kept a journal herself. If it should come to light more may be learnt of this period in which she was preparing 'to kill the century she was born in'.

Her pursuit of literature, as she tells us in *The Autobiography*, was always vigorous and unselective:

> She read anything that was printed that came her way, and a great deal came her way. In the house were a few stray novels, a few travel books, her mother's well bound gift books Wordsworth Scott and other poets, Bunyan's Pilgrim Progress a set of Shakespeare with notes, Burns, Congressional Records encyclopedias etcetera. She read them all and many times . . . there was also the local free library and later

in San Francisco there were the mercantile and mechanics libraries with their excellent sets of eighteenth century and nineteenth century authors. From her eighth year when she absorbed Shakespeare to her fifteenth year when she read Clarissa Harlow, Fielding, Smollett etcetera and used to worry lest in a few years more she would have read everything and there would be nothing unread to read, she lived continuously with the English language. She read a tremendous amount of history, she often laughs and says she is one of the few people of her generation that has read every line of Carlyle's Frederick The Great and Lecky's Constitutional History of England beside Charles Grandison and Wordsworth's longer poems. In fact she was as she still is always reading.

In this list the Bible is not mentioned but elsewhere Gertrude Stein affirms that at eight years old she read the Old Testament to find out about a future life and was surprised to discover 'there was nothing there. There was a God of course and He spoke but there was nothing about eternity.' She also refers to liking Emerson's poetry, both as an adult and when as a child she learnt it by heart. Certainly she did a great deal of unselective reading, but when seventeen decided with excitement that all knowledge was not her province.

This declaration of precociousness does not imply that Gertrude Stein had done with Shakespeare at this early age. She read him all her life, collecting the plays in odd volumes of the smallest size to carry in her pocket. But although she enjoyed her 'bookish life', and had a passion for the written word, without any notion that it would one day be her métier, this growing avidity for reading matter and the fear that her appetite would exhaust even the great libraries of San Francisco were part of a general adolescent panic.

She separates the age of fifteen from the earlier years and again captures its special flavour, 'fifteen is really medieval and pioneer and nothing is clear and nothing is sure, and nothing is safe and nothing is come and nothing is gone but it all might be'.

Enjoying the 'conquering feeling' of no longer being small, she was at the same time suffering from youthful morbidity. Later, in college essays[1] she describes imagining cruelties worse than anything in *Richard III* or Gessler, and having a fear of madness which reached a climax when she saw Mansfield playing *Jekyll and Hyde* and again when she read *The Cenci*. And she had a darker fear, 'not so much of death as of dissolution'.

So for the first time she was attacked by melancholy and she had a great sense of frustration too. In the same college exercises she gives a description of herself in the corner of a San Francisco library, a dark-skinned, sensuous girl, stirred by Chopin's Funeral March passing in the street. '"Books, books," she muttered, "is there no end to it? Nothing but myself to feed my own eager self, nothing given to me but musty books."'

Her gloom was deepened by the prospect of parting with Leo who was going to Harvard. All their childhood they had been 'two together two' and because of this and their difference from the neighbour children, she had not made close friends. At seventeen her life completely changed.

> Then one morning we could not wake up our father. Leo climbed in by the window and called out to us that he was dead in his bed and he was . . .
> Then our life without a father began a very pleasant one.[2]

A letter from Mike to his uncle Meyer shows him as having more affection than Gertrude for their father, and being prepared to take on the duties of head of the family, although he had no liking for responsibility.

> You can not imagine what a blow the loss of dear Pa is to us all and especially to me, as he was not only a father but a friend . . . He has left a holographic will making Meyer Ehrman, formerly of Balto, and myself executors for California and your son Mike executor for Maryland without bonds and with power to sell any property without an order for court. The will is in course of probate here . . . The children are all of age except Leo and Gertrude to whom I will act as guardian . . .

[1] *The Radcliffe Themes.* Extracts from these from *Gertrude Stein: Form and Intelligibility*, Rosalind S. Miller. Exposition Press, New York, 1949.
[2] *Everybody's Autobiography.*

> As soon as possible we will move to San Francisco where I
> have lived since last March being first assistant superintendent
> of the Omnibus Cable Co. of which corporation Dear Pa
> was vice president . . . The funeral was attended by many
> prominent men of San Francisco and was conducted accord-
> ing to the Jewish rites by Rev. M. S. Levy an(d) old friend
> of Dear Pa's.[1]

Simon too was working for the same company. After failing
in many other jobs he had become a cable car gripman, an occupation he continued for the rest of his working life. He had always
been obese and in the end there was scarcely room for him to stand
at the levers. He was a gentle creature who used to carry candy
both to eat himself and to give to children, and cigars to share
with other men. He died in middle age, according to his sister,
'still fat and fishing'.

Daniel Stein's will shows him as owning four hundred and
eighty acres in the County of Shasta and various shares in cable,
railroad, mining and other companies, but his affairs were not
in order when he died. Mike disliked business, it made him nervous, but he was conscientious, and back to the little house they
had taken on Turk Street in San Francisco he brought his father's
papers and accounts for Leo and Gertrude to go through with
him.

> There were so many debts it was frightening, and then I
> found out that profit and loss is always loss . . . and it was
> discouraging because we always had a habit in the family
> never to owe anybody any money.[2]

But the most important part of the legacy was Daniel Stein's
railroad franchise, and over this Mike made a dramatic coup.
He persuaded Collis P. Huntington, the Central Pacific magnate,
to buy his father's franchise at par. Apparently Huntington could
have acquired this for nothing and also have made use of Stein's
plans for consolidating the railroads, which he had conceived
remarkably early but done nothing to realize. Not only, however,
did the old millionaire pay up, but he was so much impressed by
the young man's acumen that he gave him a post as branch

[1] Yale. Unpublished.   [2] *Everybody's Autobiography.*

manager. Mike disliked the work but had the satisfaction of knowing that he had completely succeeded in what he set out to do. It was already clear to him that not one of his brothers and sisters would find it easy to earn a living; now he had provided each with a small independent income for life.

So Mike and Simon stayed on in San Francisco while, late in 1892, Bertha, Leo and Gertrude went East to make their home in Baltimore with their mother's sister, Fannie Bachrach. Gertrude was now eighteen and never again was she to live in California, but it held her loyalty for ever.

'After all anybody is as their land and air is', she wrote towards the end of her life. 'Anybody is as the sky is low or high, the air heavy or clear and anybody is as there is wind or no wind there. It is that which makes them and the arts they make and the work they do and the way they eat and the way they drink and the way they learn and everything.'[1] Although she lived in France for forty years her land was California.

[1] *What Are Masterpieces.* The Conference Press, Los Angeles, 1940.

CHAPTER THREE

PSYCHOLOGY AND MEDICINE

'A modern sonnet to his mistress' eyebrows.

She was certainly a charming bit of womanhood as she sat carefully imitating rhythms with the electric hammer. The youth gazing at her so earnestly was evidently of one mind. Poor Cupid almost at his last gasp in this home of psychological analysis seeing the tableau plucked up heart and stole a sly peep at the youth's rhapsody. He saw "Noticeable winking of the eye at every beat. A trembling of the lips before the repetition of the rhythm. A contraction of the neck muscles distinctly noticeable."'

The Radcliffe Themes. November 19, 1894.

THERE was pleasure and disturbance for Gertrude Stein in going to live with the Bachrachs. Their ways were strange to her and she had not seen any of these relatives since she was six years old. Once there had been a plan for her and Leo to go to Baltimore, but in the end Mrs. Stein had gone alone, so the young people knew nothing of the east. They seemed in their uncouthness wild westerners to their many little aunts; however, Gertrude took to her mother's family at once, especially to Aunt Fannie, and also liked Uncle Eph, who had become a well-known sculptor. She found their southernness charming and the town with its easy-going Negroes pleasantly dreamy after the sharper west.

Aunt Fannie's daughter, Helen Bachrach, who was seven years old when her cousins came to stay, remembers how popular they were, although they broke all the rules of the well-regulated household. Gertrude, Miss Bachrach says, was the favourite, 'an exceedingly attractive buxom young woman of seventeen, quick-thinking and speaking, original in ideas and manner, with a capacity of humor so deep, kindly and embracing that you found yourself laughing at everything she found extremely amusing, even yourself. Leo made you uncomfortable, you always felt he thought you were ridiculous. . . . Everybody was attracted to Gertrude—men, women and children, our German maids, the negro laundresses, even casual acquaintances she talked to on the long walks we used to take into the country.'

Miss Bachrach also remembers that when she was fourteen a visitor advised her mother not to let her read *Adam Bede*, but that Gertrude persuaded her aunt that no reading could harm a young girl.

As contrast to sleepy Baltimore there was the excitement of New York where they went to the opera and met Uncle Solomon and Aunt Pauline from whom their parents had parted so long ago, and their cousin Fred who at Harvard became one of Leo's closest friends.

In this gentle atmosphere Gertrude became 'more humanised and less adolescent and less lonesome', and presently took her own first step in life, a very important one. Her reading had been wide but her education ragged; she had been to high school for only one year, and felt a need for direction. As the months passed she grew bored with idleness—once childhood was over boredom lurked close behind her interests—and to go to college was the obvious solution, particularly as she could be near Leo. Higher education for women was the topic of the day and Leo was enthusiastic about the Harvard Faculty. One day in 1893, Gertrude, now nineteen, went off to Cambridge and registered at the Harvard Annex, soon to be renamed Radcliffe College after the Englishwoman who endowed it.

There are several stories of how Gertrude Stein came to be accepted as a student. She knew no Latin, which was required for normal entry, but could read German and French and was above the average in knowledge of English literature and general history. Some say that when asked for her qualifications she bluffed about the examinations she had passed, never having sat for one. Others that she simply wrote to the authorities asking to be admitted as a special student so as to be near her brother. In any case her entrance was granted and she went into lodgings in Cambridge which she immediately enjoyed, 'Living in a boarding house was interesting and knowing a whole new lot whom I had never seen before.'

The subjects she took included philosophy, history, English and modern languages. Later mathematics, physics, chemistry and zoology were added. The members of the Faculty strolled across the Harvard Yard, where by custom women did not walk, to the Hall of the Annex and repeated their lectures to the young women whose courses were identical with the men's. Thus came into Gertrude Stein's life the man who was most to influence her way of thinking, William James. His personality enchanted her and, as she tells in *Everybody's Autobiography*, the subjects he taught were after her own heart.

> When I was at Radcliffe I was of course very interested in psychology. I was interested in biology and I was interested in psychology and philosophy and history, that was all natural enough, I came out of the nineteenth century you had to be interested in evolution and biology, I liked thinking so I had to be interested in philosophy and I liked looking at every one and talking and listening so I had to be interested in history and psychology.

William James was now a bright-bearded, exuberant man in the early fifties with neither the appearance nor the manner of a university professor. Largely through the happiness of his marriage he had emerged from the hypochondria and neurosis of earlier life and was now at the height of his pedagogic power. Having for many years held a Chair at Harvard, first in physiology and then in philosophy, of recent years James had turned his attention more to psychology, then considered a branch of philosophy, although James himself stressed its closer affinity to physiology and biology. His *Principles of Psychology* had appeared in 1890 and met with immediate success, and he had recently brought the brilliant young psychologist, Hugo Münsterberg, over from Germany to take charge of the laboratory of experimental psychology at Harvard. He himself was doubtful of the value of this branch of study. 'What is most needed is new ideas', he said. 'For every man who has one of them, one may find a hundred who are willing to drudge patiently at some unimportant experiment.'

George Santayana was another tutor to whom Gertrude Stein acknowledged a debt. The English courses at the Annex did not interest her because she already had 'a pretty close and intimate

feeling about English literature the whole of it', but Santayana's
course in the English philosophers was new reading. There is no
doubt, however, which of her instructors had first place. As she
says in *The Autobiography*:

> William James delighted her. His personality and his way
> of teaching and his way of amusing himself with himself and
> his students all pleased her. Keep your mind open he used to
> say, and when someone objected, but Professor James, this
> that I say is true. Yes, said James, it is abjectly true.

On some days when he felt particularly 'larky' as he called it,
James tried—and seldom failed—to shock both his colleagues and
the students. One can imagine Gertrude Stein's laughter booming
and his blue eyes twinkling back to her brown ones which had
a great sparkle when she was interested or amused. James liked
unusual people and appreciated this rollicking girl, this clever
original pupil, although it was Münsterberg who later called her
his ideal student.

It was owing to the interest of both these men that she was
admitted without qualifications to their seminar in psychology.
She had a knack of getting into things, for she remembered too
enjoying a course on cloud formation without any proper reason
for being there.

Her innate love of liberty, fostered by the physical and psychological freedom of California, responded at once to James's free
nature and she rejoiced in his empiric approach and distrust of
the intellectual method. And not only did he lecture; he tried out
his ideas in discussion at the Philosophy Club of which both Steins
were members and of which Gertrude later became secretary.

The conscious just before it was superseded through the influence of Freud by the unconscious—although never for Gertrude
Stein—was at this time the dear concern of thinking people. She
gave it her attention and some latent awareness in herself was
woken by James's conception of the stream of consciousness.

'Within each personal consciousness, thought is sensibly continuous', James had already written in the *Principles*. 'Consciousness . . . is nothing jointed: it flows.' And so-called interruptions
'no more break the flow of the thought that thinks them than they
break the time and space in which they lie'.

And again:

> When we take a general view of the wonderful stream of
> our consciousness, what strikes us first is the different pace of
> its parts. Like a bird's life, it seems to be an alternation of
> flights and perchings. The rhythm of language expresses this,
> where every thought is expressed in a sentence, and every
> sentence closed by a period.

Gertrude Stein was a thinker and these thoughts of William
James's were engraved upon her mind. In them are the seeds of
the 'continuous present', the 'immediate existing', the 'including
everything', on which later she based her writing. Some students
of her work have also found the mark of Henri Bergson. Certainly
there are echoes of his stream of becoming and mobile reality, but
the flux of living and the ongoing present event were Jamesian
concepts too, and as he talked and wrote about Bergson, whom
Gertrude Stein scarcely mentions, there is little indication of a
direct Bergson influence upon her. James, at the birth of Pragma-
tism, had enough to offer her eagerness, although she did not continue to follow him so passionately as did Leo who wrote later
'James goes directly to my most innards in Phil. as Shakespeare
and Keats do in poetry.' Having nothing of the mystic in her
Gertrude Stein could not follow William James into the twentieth century any more than he, to whom she admitted that she
owed so much, could follow her.

As an exercise in English composition she wrote a glowing
appreciation of him beginning, 'Is life worth living? Yes, a thousand times yes when the world still holds such spirits as Prof.
James', but there is no trace of his influence in these *Radcliffe
Themes*. Nor, although the title of the first one *In The Red Deeps*
came from George Eliot, is there any trace of a favourite author.

These first fragments of writing show Gertrude Stein as young
for her twenty years and now resolving the morbidity which had
made adolescence painful. Largely autobiographical and vehe-
mently introspective, they reveal her rampant nature and analytical mind. The outlook is wider than that of the average student;
there are signs of shrewd observation, compassion, humour and
poetry, but the writing itself is immature. She had no ease of
expression, but exploded into her subject and then felt her way

along with much confusing comment. 'She was as clever as paint', one contemporary observes, 'but we all had to help her with her work. She never wrote good English and grammar meant nothing to her.' The scripts are full of spelling and other errors, but they improve with practice and tuition. Although one does not agree with all the criticisms of Vaughn Moody and her other teachers, Gertrude Stein the writer was not yet born.

She still shows her dark side in subjective studies but the brighter side comes out in descriptions of nature and she makes fun of everything.

> There she stood a little body with a very large head. She was loaded down with books and was evidently very dismal. Suddenly there broke forth a torment, 'I don't want to be superior' she wailed despairingly, 'I am tired to death of standing with my head craned constantly looking upward. I am longing to meet one simple soul that don't want to know everything. One weak happy naive consciousness that thinks higher education is either rot or has never heard of it.'

These exercises give one many snapshots of the college girl. 'I would have liked to have re-written the whole theme but the German opera threw me back in my work', she writes beneath one, and in another, 'What a pleasure in this psychological nineteenth century to live again the simple thoughts and the down-right strokes of the race of Volsung.' Nor was it only the legends that appealed; she used to play the musical themes to her friends before going to the opera, and she also enjoyed symphony concerts in Boston.

There are clues to her reading; *Pembroke* by Mary Wilkins producing 'a feeling of soul sickness'. Her Californian spirit explodes:

> The intolerance of these New Englanders is overwhelming. There is never a curve all the lines are hard and straight. The word sympathy is not in their vocabulary.

And she expresses dissatisfaction with the last part of *Marius the Epicurean*:

> It seemed hardly probable that the student of philosophy

would so completely throw all his systematic thought to the winds and rely on the emotional wave alone.

She only once mentions a painting, a 'Gervelli'[1] at the Art Club, and describes the leader of the procession:

> Its arms wave with a deliciously sensuous movement and through its closed teeth issues a whistling breath that expresses more than the most extatic shout.

There was no time for boredom now. The men and women who knew Gertrude in those days are unanimous that she was splendid company, and Leo too was popular. Talking with her class-mates, those big-hearted, intelligent, witty creatures who are the flower of early higher education for women in America, is like watching an old film. Here are the friends and the beaux and the bicycles. One sees Gertie's shirt-waist never staying with her skirt; one watches her wearing the same old dingy hat despite all protests until someone finds it under her bed and burns it. And how she laughs and how she talks!

She had a magnetic personality. 'She was so stimulating.' 'She poked our eyes open, kept plunging ahead and opening up vistas.' 'A terrific talker but an elegant listener too, although if you asked her a question she did not like she would just look through you and go on with what she was saying.' Argument was, then, Gertrude Stein herself declares, 'as the air I breathe'.

Of course there were theatricals and friends still have memories of a curtain rising to disclose the robust form of Gertie spinning in a swivel chair. They speak of her being very fat, but agree that this did not in the least impair her vitality. 'We were all trackers then and Gertrude was untiring.' Sometimes on Saturday nights a group of students would take the street car to the terminus and walk out into the country. It was considered very bold when a couple of girls did this alone. 'But we said if we have any trouble with a man Gertrude will climb out on the furthest limb of a tree and drop on him.'[2]

These were delightful days with the serious and the frivolous well mixed and enough liberty to satisfy even Gertrude Stein. It was at about this time that she read *The Ballad of Reading Gaol*

[1] Crivelli?   [2] Author's journal.

and was overwhelmed by the thought of Oscar Wilde in prison.

The psychology seminar is described in *Everybody's Autobiography*:

> We were quite a funny lot, Sidis was there who afterwards had the son who passed everything when he was a little boy and then did nothing, McDougall a man afterwards well known who worked on conversion, William James was interested in that in connection with his Varieties of Religious Experience and Thorndyke who was busy with incubating chickens and what they did then and a man named Leon Solomons who came from California and who was an intimate friend of mine . . . Münsterberg had just come from Berlin and was interested in experimental psychology and William James liked thinking and talking and wondering about what any one was doing and we all of us worked with both of them. Sidis was interested in studying sub-conscious reactions but being a Russian he naturally expected us to do things and we did not do them . . . We all of us were somewhat discouraging to all of us . . . Leon Solomons and I were to work together, he was a graduate student taking his doctorate in philosophy, we first were to do something connected with a tuning fork but as neither one of us had a very good ear for music that is for notes that was given up, and then it was suggested that we should do experiments in fatigue, and William James added a planchette, he liked a planchette, we made one out of a piece of wood and strings and then we were to try each other . . .

This project, however, was not fruitful. As she tells us in *The Autobiography*, 'Gertrude Stein never had subconscious reactions, nor was she a successful subject for automatic writing.' She goes on with an anecdote about a student who complained that one of the subjects for his experiments gave absolutely no results:

> . . . as this much lowered the average and made the conclusion of his experiments false he wished to be allowed to cut this record out. Whose record is it, said James. Miss Stein's, said the student. Ah, said James, if Miss Stein gave no response I should say that it was as normal not to give a response as to give one and decidedly the result must not be cut out.

It was then decided that Gertrude Stein should make some experiments herself with students who were not taking psychology. The object was to discover if motor automatism in the normal subject led to action comparable with that of the 'second personality' in hysterical cases. About forty subjects were chosen at random and she tested their reactions to the planchette before and after sitting for examinations, so as to gauge the effects of fatigue. From these experiments came little of value to the department, yet they were of supreme importance to her development. Watching those young men and women using the planchette and listening to them 'hardly vaguely talking', she discovered a passionate interest in human nature, which later she expressed in thousands upon thousands of words.

Gertrude Stein compared the conscious and the automatic (what we would call subconscious) reactions to these experiments with two themes in music alternately dominating. Declare as she did that her eyes were more important than her ears she often used musical parallels, and her co-experimenter, Leon Solomons, observed that her attention was mainly auditory. And she speaks of doing a great deal of listening then, to the conversation for instance of her eleven 'lively little aunts', and taking in not what was being said so much as the way it was being said, the rise and fall, and people's variety of emphasis in repetition. For her this was the rhythm of a personality, and later as a writer, working out the pattern of recurrence in human behaviour, she used rhythm to clarify repetition.

Thus seeds of psychological interest were sown ten years before they matured in writing.

> . . . it was interesting to me to see how I came to feel that I could come sometime to describe every kind there is of men and women and the bottom nature of them and the way it was mixed up with the other natures in them, I kept notes of each one of them and watched the difference between being active and being tired, the way it made some go faster and some go slower and I finally felt and which in The Making of Americans I began to do that one could make diagrams and describe every individual man and woman who ever was or is or will be living . . .[1]
>
> [1] *Everybody's Autobiography.*

In 1896 the *Psychological Review* published *Normal Motor Automatism* by Leon M. Solomons and Gertrude Stein, but she maintained that it was really his report and that she did not think the writing was automatic—'we always knew what we were doing'. She agreed to the article, she explained, as 'after all I was an undergraduate and not a professional and as I am always very docile . . .'.

Afterwards she produced a report of her own: *Cultivated motor automatism; a study of character in its relation to attention*, printed in the *Psychological Review* of May 1898. In this article she classified her best subjects:

> *Type I*. Consisting mostly of girls found naturally in literature courses and men going in for law—nervous, high-strung, imaginative, capacity to be easily roused and intensely interested.
> *Type II*. More varied and results more interesting. In general, the individuals, often blond and pale, distinctly phlegmatic. Highly suggestible, as Type II much nearer the true hysterique.

and she added:

> A large number of my subjects were New Englanders, and the habit of self-repression, the intense self-consciousness, the morbid fear of 'letting oneself go', that is so prominent an element in the New England character, was a constant stumbling block.

This was the beginning of the interest that was to make the stuff of Gertrude Stein's work, but circumstances have encouraged false theories. It is enough for many people who sometimes find her unintelligible to hear that she once had some connection with automatic writing to conclude that this explains her style. In fact, although allowing thought to roam and flow and never forcing its direction, she wrote in full consciousness.

Nevertheless, while insisting on a 'passion for exactitude', fostered by scientific training, she had a bent for diffuseness. Leon Solomons, in a letter, sharply criticized the style of her report:

> The trouble with the article as it stands, is that one has to hunt around too much to find the important points,—it is as

bewildering as a detailed map of a large country on a small scale. What it needs is relief, perspective. You must make perfectly clear to yourself just what you regard as the essentials of the work . . . Don't be afraid of leaving things out. It is the essence of good writing frequently . . . In short don't emulate our friends the Germans, but be a little French.[1]

Thus agreeably the terms passed and the vacations in Baltimore were no less pleasant. One summer Gertrude and Leo went west again to see Mike and meet his fiancée, Sarah Solomons. They were appalled by his engagement, certain that no one could be good enough for Mike. One story is told of the four of them going for a picnic in the course of which Gertrude whipped a volume of Browning out of her pocket and commanded her future sister-in-law to read. Shyly, Sarah complied; Gertrude nodded her head and the girls became friends. Indeed they grew quickly intimate, Sarah taking the rôle of elder sister and concerning herself with Gertrude's emotional development. If no longer gloomy she was stormy, and while describing herself as 'tremendously moral', she was no prude. 'What's the matter with you girls from Smith', she complained to her friends, 'is raw virginity', and she explored emotions with the open-mindedness California bred and William James encouraged. Sarah was frightened as to where this might lead Gertrude and urged a straight and narrow path.

In 1895 Mike and Sarah were married and Leo, having taken his degree, went off as the guest of his Uncle Solomon on a tour round the world with his cousin Fred Stein. During term time now, Gertrude for the first time lived without any relative at hand, and this was the first long separation from Leo. She missed him badly and he did not enjoy the trip, being weighed down by his sense of obligation and 'the foul fiends of dullness'. 'I rather thought I was more completely bore-proof than I have proved to be', he wrote to her from Cairo, and looked forward eagerly to the summer when she would join him in Europe.

Now that they were both of age Mike was no longer their guardian, but he maintained a parental attitude.

[1] Letters to Gertrude Stein, unless otherwise specified, are taken from *The Flowers of Friendship*, edited by Donald Gallup, Alfred A. Knopf, 1953.

San Francisco, Cal.,
June 2, 1896.

Dear Gert.

It is now June 2nd and you had better let me know just when you are going to start and where you are going *to* so I can get your letters of credit for you. Also let me know at once what drafts you want for use before starting. Also see that all your & Leo's bills (room rent etc.) are settled before you go, so as to have everything in ship-shape. . . .

So long

Your aff Bro
Mike

In *Everybody's Autobiography* Gertrude recalls that meeting with Leo:

> . . . we had not seen each other for over a year and I went over to Antwerp and there we were to be together. I remember being very worried as the boat came nearer the shore lest I should not know him when I saw him. After all one never can remember at least I never can remember how anybody anybody really knows looks like . . . Well when I saw my brother it was a surprise to me but I knew quite certainly that it was my brother.

This was the beginning of Gertrude Stein's European experience as an adult. She spent the following summer vacations with Leo in Italy, and one in Spain, walking and sight-seeing, 'and he was always a very sweet a little older brother when we travelled together'.

Leo had become seriously interested in art and she gives him credit for opening her eyes to it and for giving her many books which, left to herself, she would not have found. They were now collecting Japanese prints, familiar from their Californian days. Leo had brought some back from Japan and she followed his taste, developing an eye as good or better than her brother's.

Sometimes college friends went with them on these European holidays which they remember with unmitigated pleasure. For although, to borrow one of her titles, in Gertrude Stein's life frequently 'before the flowers of friendship faded friendship faded', those who knew the Steins well, even when critical, are loyal to their old affection. They say that the devotion of the brother and sister was beautiful and that they were both very generous. Everyone remembers their brilliant talk and Gertrude herself writes: 'We did both love to talk a great deal although I do believe that I listened more or at least if I did not listen more I was silent more.' She seldom refers to her Jewish heritage but in the character of Adele in *Things As They Are*[1] she observes:

> I have the failing of my tribe. I believe in the sacred rites of conversation even when it is a monologue.

Once she and Leo asked Uncle Eph which of them talked most, 'and he looked very carefully first at one and then at the other one and he said well I think you do certainly both do your share'.

An account of Gertrude Stein's Radcliffe days would be incomplete without the story of the unwritten examination paper:

> It was a very lovely spring day, Gertrude Stein had been going to the opera every night and going also to the opera in the afternoon and had been otherwise engrossed and it was the period of the final examinations, and there was the examination in William James' course. She sat down with the examination paper before her and she just could not. Dear Professor James, she wrote at the top of her paper. I am so sorry but really I do not feel a bit like an examination paper in philosophy today, and left.
>
> The next day she had a postal card from William James saying, Dear Miss Stein, I understand perfectly how you feel I often feel like that myself. And underneath it he gave her work the highest mark in his course.

But although William James appreciated Gertrude Stein's brains and excused this unconventionality, she had in the end to take the examinations waived at her entrance. She had never intended taking a degree, but William James encouraged her to continue her education.

> Well, he said, it should be either philosophy or psychology. Now for philosophy you have to have higher mathematics and I don't gather that that has ever interested you. Now for

[1] Written in 1903. Posthumously published in 1951.

psychology you must have a medical education, a medical education opens all doors, as Oliver Wendell Holmes told me and as I tell you.

In this connection it is interesting to remember that the only degree William James himself ever gained by examination was that of doctor of medicine.

To be eligible for a medical school she had to graduate from Radcliffe which entailed passing in Latin. This was a little troublesome, but when she really wanted to learn anything she could, and she arranged for private tutoring from a graduate student. In paying for these lessons came a realization of what it meant to have a private income. She devotes a couple of pages in *The Making of Americans* to this experience, telling it in her peeling-off method, one petal at a time. But in *Everybody's Autobiography* she says more succinctly:

> I had paid her and then one month I had spent all my month's money on going to the opera so I said to her do you mind if I do not pay you as I have not got any money. She said no reflectively and then she said what do you mean when you say you have no money, oh I said I mean I have spent my month's money and I haven't any. Well she said reflectively your father and mother are dead you have your own money haven't you . . . but you see those who earn money . . . when they have not got it they have not got it. I was much impressed and I never forgot it.

Mike had some difficulty in managing the family incomes and preventing Leo and Gertrude from extravagance.

In 1898, a year later than her class, Gertrude Stein graduated *magna cum laude*. In spite of her happiness there, once she had left she took no interest whatsoever in Radcliffe College.

The obvious place to go to continue training as a psychologist was the Johns Hopkins Medical School, for not only was she at home in Baltimore but also Leo had entered the university to take a second degree. The medical school had been added nine years before, endowed by four Baltimore women on condition that women were admitted on the same—not similar but same—terms as men, but the founders could not insist that women students should be welcomed. 'The old battle-axe!' one distinguished retired brain surgeon exclaimed when asked what he thought of his fellow student. 'Miss Stein took the provisions of the Foundation absolutely literally, insisting on seeing and doing things quite unsuitable for a woman, and very embarrassing it was for us.'

Another provision of the foundation was a high standard of scholarship. William Osler is said to have remarked to a colleague, 'It is lucky we get in as professors, we could never get in as students.' Gertrude Stein had now achieved an education, but although she was in an undefined way ambitious, and had discovered an analytical interest in human nature, she was not really bent on a career as a psychologist, but was simply following William James's counsel. Although Mike had been a conscientious guardian and seemed almost of the older generation, he was after all a brother, and William James's interest in her, which she may therefore have exaggerated, met a desire, however unconscious, for parental influence.

One would expect that, having such an admiration for William James, Gertrude Stein would have read his brother Henry's novels at this time, but she did not. She came to have a great admiration for him 'as her forerunner, he being the only nineteenth-century writer who being an American felt the method of the twentieth century. . . . But oddly enough in all of her formative period she did not read him and was not interested in him.' This was, she maintained, because he was too close, too like a parent. She continued to read indiscriminately and joyfully.

Leo and Gertrude now made their first home together. They took a largish house, hung up their Japanese prints and began to entertain relatives and friends, although not in the usual Baltimore style. 'We were born Bohemians', Gertrude wrote of Leo and herself as children, and they had not changed. Contemporaries remember how strange the brother and sister seemed, wild westerners still in spite of six years in the east, who put their feet up on the furniture and did not care how unkempt they looked. One old lady says that indeed they took pains to exaggerate their roughness. And an old gentleman, who married a Stein cousin, gives this description: 'Gertie? She had a face good to look at. She went flopping around the place—other girls wore corsets

then, but I never liked corsets anyway—big and floppy and san-
dalled and not caring a damn.'[1] It is interesting to hear of the
sandals so early; later in Paris they were famous.

It was not in order to call attention to herself or to embarrass
others that Gertrude Stein interpreted the School's regulations so
literally; simply it was in her nature to go straight forward with
what she was doing. The opposition to women was among both
Faculty and students, which was chilling after the *bonhomie* of
Harvard. Nor was it only the men who were critical of her;
fellow students of her own sex speak of her sloppy technique in
the laboratory, of her being always stained up to the elbows in
whatever dye she was using and perpetually in a muddle.

Nevertheless for the first two years things went well. She had
enjoyed biology and chemistry at Radcliffe and started the
medical course with enthusiasm. Before long she was doing research on the brain tracts under Llewellys Barker and writing a
comparative study which, she says in *The Autobiography*, was
later embodied in Dr. Barker's book. There are differences of
opinion as to how big her contribution to this book really was,
but it is clear that Dr. Barker took her work on the brain seriously, although her style of writing troubled him. He asked her
to revise her script 'with special reference to the literary form'.
She enjoyed working with Barker and with the Professor of
Anatomy who directed her studies. 'Doctor Mall believed in
everybody developing their own technique. He also remarked,
nobody teaches anybody anything, at first every student's scalpel
is dull and then later every student's scalpel is sharp, and nobody
has taught anybody anything.' But there was also Dr. Whitridge
Williams, Head of Obstetrics, whom she disliked personally
almost as much as she disliked his subject, and 'the last two years
at the medical school she was bored, frankly openly bored. There
was a good deal of intrigue and struggle among the students, that
she liked, but the practice and theory of medicine did not interest
her at all.'

None the less it was through her practical work and particularly
in midwifery that Gertrude Stein came into close contact with
Negroes in their homes and absorbed the rhythm of their living

[1] Author's journal.

and their feeling and their speaking which she was to use to such effect in *Melanctha Herbert*, the second story in *Three Lives*.[1] The other stories in that volume derive from the German servants whom first she and Leo, and then she and her friend Emma Lootz, employed at this time. The material for her future books was piling up.

The house to which Gertrude moved when after graduating from Johns Hopkins Leo went off again to Europe, stands now just as she describes it in *The Good Anna*:

> It was a funny little house, one of a whole row of all the same kind that made a close pile like a row of dominoes that a child knocks over, for they were built along a street which at this point came down a steep hill. They were funny little houses, two stories high, with red brick fronts and long white steps.

Emma Lootz, later Erving, who shared this house with Gertrude Stein for the rest of her time in Baltimore, died early in 1955. She was a remarkable woman with a wonderfully dry sense of humour, one of the most successful of Gertrude Stein's fellow students, achieving distinction as an orthopaedic surgeon. From her and her friend Miss Mabel Foote Weeks, who first met the Steins through visiting Emma Lootz in Baltimore, comes much first-hand knowledge of Leo and Gertrude in these days. Miss Weeks became a close friend of Leo's and contributed a foreword to his posthumously published *Journey Into the Self*, but her memories of Gertrude too are keen and illuminating. Both these women perceived her quality and adored her company although they only admired a small part of her writing and felt that she was spoilt by self esteem.

'I had the downstairs room', Emma Lootz Erving remembered, 'and Gertrude's living room was the large one over it. In the other house Leo had been the master, in this one Gertrude was. She had more money than I and everything was arranged to her liking.' One remembers how *The Good Anna* opens: 'The tradesmen of Bridgepoint learned to dread the sound of "Miss Mathilda", for with that name the good Anna always conquered.'

[1] Written 1904–5. First published 1909.

Miss Mathilda was of course Miss Gertrude and Anna, who 'led an arduous and troubled life', managed the house for her. 'Our brass rails', Mrs Erving remembered, 'were polished till they glittered.' The Bohemian Gertrude had become house-proud, although the neighbourhood, close to the Medical School, was not refined. Still, according to Mrs. Erving, it was a nice enough street, except for the hens floating down the gutter. 'Once,' she said, 'Gertrude got alarmed about her health. She thought there was something the matter with her blood, so she hired a welter-weight to box with her. The chandelier in my room used to swing and the house echoed with shouts of "Now give me one on the jaw! Now give me one in the kidney!"'[1]

Apart from some depression over work, Gertrude was still the same rollicking girl, remembered at Johns Hopkins as at Rad-cliffe for jolliness and infectious vitality. There was less philosophy and less music now, but there were plenty of other activities. The country excursions continued, all her life she was a walker, and she now began going to the theatre. She had never liked straight theatre as much as opera, it went too fast for her, but she enjoyed the old melodramas given at the Holiday Street Theatre in the same way that she enjoyed reading thrillers.

This reaction to plays brings to mind a remark—Leo's perhaps, with which she agreed—that like George Washington, whose birthday she shared, Gertrude was impulsive and slow minded.

So the years at Johns Hopkins passed and 'it was fairly well known among all her teachers that she was bored'. Let the rest of the story be told in her own words:

> As the graduation examinations drew near some of her professors were getting angry. The big men like Halstead, Osler etcetera knowing her reputation for original scientific work made the medical examinations merely a matter of form and passed her. But there were others who were not so amiable. Gertrude Stein always laughed, and this was difficult. They would ask her questions although as she said to her friends, it was foolish of them to ask her, when there were so many eager and anxious to answer. However they did question her from time to time and as she said, what

[1] Author's journal.

could she do, she did not know the answers and they did not believe that she did not know them, they thought that she did not answer because she did not consider the professors worth answering. It was a difficult situation, as she said it was impossible to apologise and explain to them that she was so bored she could not remember the things that of course the dullest medical student could not forget. One of the professors said that although all the big men were ready to pass her he intended that she should be given a lesson and he refused to give her a pass mark and so she was not able to take her degree. There was great excitement in the medical school. Her very close friend Marion Walker pleaded with her, she said, but Gertrude Gertrude remember the cause of women, and Gertrude Stein said, you don't know what it is to be bored.

An addition to this account comes from a colleague at Johns Hopkins:

Dr. Whitridge Williams, head of Obstetrics, refused her degree and Dr. Franklyn Mall, professor of Anatomy, felt that she should have another chance, so he told her that if she would make a model of an embryo human brain, which he gave her from his own collection, he would see if he could make the medical faculty change their mind.

The embryo was sectioned serially and a reconstruction made of it . . . an intimate friend of mine, Dr. Florence Sabin . . . told me this story.

Dr. Mall brought the model in to her one morning and said that it was beyond him to see what Miss Stein had done. Dr. Sabin, the best woman ever graduated at J. H. Medical and afterwards head of one of the Rockefeller Institute departments, spent hours working over the model and finally decided that Gertrude had bent the spinal cord under the head of the embryo so that every section contained cells of the cerebral cortex and of the cord, so that the reconstruction was fantastic. Dr. Mall listened to the explanation of what Dr. Sabin *thought* had happened and chucked the entire model into the waste basket.[1]

Whatever may have happened she did not make that curious reconstruction as a practical joke. While liking fun and havii g a

[1] Letter from Mrs. Dorothy Reed Mendenhall of North Carolina.

certain child-like simplicity, this would have been out of character. Contemporaries, by the way, if critical, believe that had she wished Gertrude Stein could have succeeded in the field of medicine.

In *The Autobiography* she says herself:

> The professor who had flunked her asked her to come to see him. She did. He said, of course Miss Stein all you have to do is to take a summer course here and in the fall naturally you will take your degree. But not at all, said Gertrude Stein, you have no idea how grateful I am to you. I have so much inertia and so little initiative that very possibly if you had not kept me from taking my degree I would have, well, not taken to the practice of medicine, but at any rate to pathological psychology and you don't know how little I like pathological psychology and how all medicine bores me. The professor was completely taken aback and that was the end of the medical education of Gertrude Stein.
>
> She always says she dislikes the abnormal, it is so obvious. She says the normal is so much more simply complicated and interesting.

In spite of this bravado friends say that she was distressed at failing to get a medical degree. And Mrs. Erving commented: 'Of course she didn't get it. Do you think I'd have got mine if I hadn't worn my best hat? It had roses on it.'

However, Gertrude Stein was now twenty-six and ready for the world, and the twentieth century had come.

CHAPTER FOUR

'Q.E.D.'

'. . . really my chief point is a protest against this tendency of so
many of you to go in for things simply for the sake of an experience. I believe strongly that one should do things either for the
sake of the thing done or because of definite future power which
is the legitimate result of all education. Experience for the paltry
purpose of having it is to me both trivial and immoral.'

Adele in *Things As They Are.*

DURING Gertrude Stein's last years at Johns Hopkins the ties with
America were gradually loosening. She had no thought yet of
making Europe her home, but Leo was living in Florence and her
ardent friendships did not compensate for his absence. In *The
Making of Americans* Martha Hersland, for whom she was proto-
type, marries Phillip Redfern, modelled on Leon Solomons, but
the real Solomons died of an infection contracted in the Harvard
laboratory.

In 1900 Gertrude had what she described as a particularly fruitful holiday with Mabel Weeks and Leo in Italy and France, and
Miss Weeks writing from London, after Gertrude had returned to
Baltimore, showed her dependence upon her lively companion.
'I could get more out of one day in London with you, than all
five weeks by myself. But this verges on sentiment, which you
can't stand I remember.'

In 1901, while Gertrude was still in America, Leo in Florence
was preparing for their future by getting to know Bernard
Berenson, one of the earliest of the famous American expatriates.
He was then thirty-five and had been in Florence since he was
twenty, and although he and the Steins never became close friends,
he and Leo exchanged a good many letters and he had an un-
doubted influence on the young man. Berenson was already an
authority on Italian art, and the Renaissance furniture in his house,
about which Leo wrote to Gertrude, sowed a seed which flowered

in the Steins' home in Paris. Besides encouraging Leo's interest
in painting, Berenson gave the Steins their first social introductions, and it is to him that is attributed the description of Leo:
'He was for ever inventing the umbrella.'

Gertrude joined Leo again in the spring of 1902 and in the
summer they went to England for the first time since childhood.
Having explored the Lake District, they moved at the beginning
of September to London and took rooms at No. 20 Bloomsbury
Square. The first week-end, however, was spent with Berenson at
Fernhurst in Surrey and they found the country so beautiful that
they rented a cottage there for some weeks. Leo was in high
spirits; he sprained his ankle 'turning hand springs for relaxation
. . . on a hillside', and even if in her emotional complexities
Gertrude was not at her gayest, she seems to have been lively.
Berenson had been ill and Leo writes: 'Gertrude has put Berenson
on eggs and milk, under which he is flourishing like a Green Bay
tree', and he also mentions her 'trying to hold up the American
end of a general discussion against Russell, Berenson and a young
journalist . . .'

But after this Gertrude did not enjoy England at all.

> They settled in lodgings in London and were not uncom-
> fortable. They knew a number of people through the
> Berensons, Bertrand Russell, the Zangwills, then there was
> Willard [Josiah Flynt] who wrote Tramping with Tramps,
> and who knew all about London pubs, but Gertrude Stein
> was not very much amused. She began spending all her days
> in the British Museum reading the Elizabethans. She re-
> turned to her early love of Shakespeare and the Elizabethans,
> and became absorbed in Elizabethan prose and particularly
> in the prose of Greene. She had little note-books full of
> phrases that pleased her as they had pleased her when she
> was a child. The rest of the time she wandered about the
> London streets and found them infinitely depressing and
> dismal . . .
>
> She always said that that first visit had made London just
> like Dickens and Dickens had always frightened her. As she
> says anything can frighten her and London when it was like
> Dickens certainly did.

The fear that there would be nothing left to read was over and she bought many books including Trollope, for her the greatest of the Victorians, and eighteenth-century memoirs. She did not care about the appearance of books or their condition, but bought them to read as later she bought pictures to look at, not as a collector, and she lent them freely to her friends, courteously forgetting who had not returned them and filling the gaps with odd volumes picked up at random, preferably small ones which she could carry in her capacious pockets. But she would not touch a book when wearing a glove and was troubled when others did, having discovered as a child that dirty hands damage a book less than a glove.

But in spite of literature and freedom from the boredom of medicine, 'the dismalness of London and the drunken women and children and the gloom and lonesomeness brought back all the melancholy of her adolescence and one day she said she was leaving for America and she left'.

No one has described an American's emotions on regaining his own country more poignantly than she did in her first book written the following year. In the character of Adele in Q.E.D., posthumously published as Things As They Are, she describes her reactions after escaping from the hopeless oppression of the London winter.

> I simply rejoiced in the New York streets, in the long spindling legs of the elevated, in the straight high undecorated houses, in the empty upper air and in the white surface of the snow. It was such a joy to realise that the whole thing was without mystery and without complexity, that it was clean and straight and meagre and hard and white and high . . .

And then Adele goes to Boston.

> She steeped herself in the very essence of clear eyed Americanism. For days she wandered about the Boston streets rejoicing in the passionless intelligence of the faces. She revelled in the American street-car crowd with its ready intercourse, free comments and airy persiflage all without double meanings which created an atmosphere that never suggested for a moment the need to be on guard.

In this frame of mind Gertrude Stein made her last attempt to

settle down in America, joining Mabel Weeks and other friends
in lodgings at The White House in New York. This gracious
colonial building with a garden full of roses and flowering locust
trees running to the river has long vanished from the corner of
100th Street and Riverside Drive. Here the friendships and conversations of student days were resumed, but there was a difference.
These young women were now in their late twenties and all but
Gertrude were absorbed in their professions and their young men.
She was unattached and so a little out of it, but she lived with
vigour, walking, reading and writing letters.

It was during this period that Gertrude Stein made what is
generally taken to be her first purchase of a picture, although in
the guise of Miss Mathilda in *Three Lives*, this taste was indulged
in the earlier Baltimore days. '"And I slave and slave to save the
money and you go out and spend it all on foolishness," the good
Anna would complain when her mistress, a large and careless
woman, would come home with a bit of porcelain, a new etching
and sometimes even an oil painting on her arm.' But the acquisi-
tion of a Schilling landscape was a serious matter since it cost six
hundred dollars.

So in her leisure, brooding and ironic, Gertrude Stein spent
much time ruthlessly analysing herself and her friends, antici-
pating those who a few years later, having read or heard a little
about Freud, turned amateur analysis into anything from a serious
study to a parlour game. The immediate outcome was this short
autobiographical novel, invaluable when one is trying to see the
young Gertrude in the round, to reconcile vitality with inertia,
heartiness with melancholy, and allow for a lack of initiative in a
pioneer spirit, need of direction in a born rebel, resistance to emotion in a rich and warm temperament.

Quod Erat Demonstrandum is dated October 1903. She wrote
it directly she set up house with Leo in Paris and then forgot
it until some thirty years later she chanced upon the manuscript
and showed it to Louis Bromfield. It was posthumously published
in a limited edition, the editor changing the title to a phrase
from the end of the book: *Things As They Are*.[1] It concerns

[1] Author's Note: Certain alterations were made in the text before publication.
The script is reserved in the Yale University Library.

the relationship of three young 'college bred women of the wealthier class', and is, as Edmund Wilson reviewing it said, 'told with complete candor and an astonishing lack of self-consciousness.' He adds:

> When one says that it is told with candor, one does not mean that it has much in common with those case-histories of Havelock Ellis that, published in his 'Studies in the Psychology of Sex' between 1897 and 1910, did a good deal to clear the air. In this document of Gertrude Stein's there is nothing in the least scandalous (unless the subject itself be considered so), and the whole thing is done with a sobriety, even an abstractness of language, that recalls the French classical novels of the type of *Adolphe* and *La Princesse de Clèves*.[1]

This indeed is how one would expect Gertrude Stein to write, for her friends confirm the lack of self-consciousness in discussing human emotions and behaviour, a quality encouraged by medical training and familiarity with the psychological approach. Her candour in describing herself is more surprising, for the fashion and passion for self-revelation belongs to a later period of fiction. This first example of objective subjectivity is a clue to her later books. Herself is the centre of all her work—what she and she only is seeing, hearing, feeling at the moment of writing —but she views herself with detachment.

Mr. Wilson's 'abstractness of language' refers to this detachment, not to any use of words that could fail to be understood. It is a piece of good writing unheralded by the *Radcliffe Themes*. Gertrude Stein seems to have mastered grammar and there is only an occasional idiosyncrasy in punctuation; she had not yet taken against the comma but did not always make it serve her. There is no verbal repetition except that she becomes fond of a word such as 'drearily' and overuses it, but the matter is of its nature repetitive, and one is sometimes tempted to say with one of the characters, 'How you do keep it up!'

All the same the book is extremely readable; its acute and patient analysis of character and situation suggesting that had its

[1] *The Shores of Light*. Edmund Wilson. W. H. Allen & Co. Ltd., London. Farrar, Straus, New York, 1952.

author chosen to continue writing in this vein she could have achieved early recognition as a psychological novelist. There are also pleasant early examples of what a friend calls her 'sensible sayings', such as 'A little knowledge is not a dangerous thing, on the contrary it gives the most cheerful sense of completeness and content', or 'I haven't any objection to apologising, the only thing I object to is being in the wrong'.

Things As They Are being out of print I have quoted freely to show the self-portrait. The book opens with a description of three girls on an ocean steamer, 'They were distinctly American but each one at the same time bore definitely the stamp of one of the older civilisations, incomplete and frustrated in this American version but still always insistent.' There is Helen, 'the American version of the English handsome girl', Sophie, betraying by 'her attitude of awkward discomfort and the tension of her long angular body' her New England origin, and finally Adele who is Gertrude.

> The third member of the group had thrown herself prone on the deck with the freedom of movement and the simple instinct for comfort that suggested a land of laziness and sunshine. She nestled close to the bare boards as if accustomed to make the hard earth soft by loving it. She made just a few wriggling movements to adapt her large curves to the projecting boards of the deck, gave a sigh of satisfaction and murmured 'How good it is in the sun.'

And she proceeds to talk, 'sitting up to the occasion and illustrating her argument by vigorous gestures':

> You have a foolish notion that to be middle-class is to be vulgar, that to cherish the ideals of respectability and decency is to be commonplace and that to be the mother of children is low. You tell me that I am not middle-class and that I can believe in none of these things because I am not vulgar, commonplace and low, but it is just there where you make your mistake. You don't realise the important fact that virtue and vice have it in common that they are vulgar when not passionately given. You think that they carry within them a different power. Yes they do because they have different world-values, but as for their relation to vulgarity, it is as true

of vice as of virtue that you can't sell what should be passionately given without forcing yourself into many acts of vulgarity and the chances are that in endeavoring to escape the
vulgarity of virtue, you will find yourselves engulfed in the
vulgarity of vice. Good gracious! here I am at it again.

As part of the sound middle-class attitude Gertrude Stein gives
Adele, in common with her own family, 'a strong sense of the
sanctity of money obligations'. And the girl also speaks of her
'almost puritanic horror' of the cultivation of physical passion 'in
any of its many disguised forms'. On this Helen observes '"That
is what makes it possible for a face as thoughtful and strongly
built as yours to be almost annoyingly unlined and youthful and
to be almost foolishly happy and content."'
Adele does not however remain content; she is torn between
dread of emotional complexities and fear that she will always
think and never feel. She goes on thinking, considering whether
her feeling for Helen is just another small experience which she
ought to withstand or her chance of learning to care. She acknow-
ledges to herself that even if she did care she would only have a
limited amount to give because her cousin (who is Leo) has first
claim. She tries to understand the implications of such a relationship with another woman and has a sudden Alice-in-Wonder-
land reaction: '"Why" she said in a tone of intense interest, "it's
like a bit of mathematics. Suddenly it does itself and you begin to
see."'
Always honest, she argues it out with herself and her friends
and page by page the self-portrait grows. 'Heavens what an ego-
tist I am!' Or:

> 'I know that I always take an everlasting time to arrive any-
> where really and that the rapidity of my superficial observa-
> tion keeps it from being realised.'

And again:

> 'And then you really want things badly enough to go out
> and get them and that seems to me very strange. I want
> things too but only in order to understand them and I never
> go and get them. I am a hopeless coward, I hate to risk hurt-
> ing myself or anybody else.'

Adele really does mind hurting other people; she is shocked and penitent when she discovers how much pain she has caused by using Helen as a subject for psychological experiment. She has humour too. '"I always did thank God I wasn't born a woman!"' she exclaims as her friends are exchanging prolonged and insincere courtesies, and when she has to listen to unwanted confidences prefaced by the inevitable, '"of course I wouldn't say such things to anyone but you,"' retorts '"isn't there anything else that you would like to tell me just because I am I. If so don't let me get in your way."'

Thus, through the pages of *Things As They Are* one watches Gertrude Stein developing from a raw girl to a mature young woman, and realizes that she had to break away from what she called 'the general American sisterhood'. A passage in *Paris France* about the Radcliffe days comes to mind:

> I was on a train and sitting next to me was a Frenchman. I recognised him as a visiting lecturer and I spoke to him. We talked about American college women. Very wonderful he said and very interesting but and he looked at me earnestly, really not one of them, now you must admit that, not one of them could feel with Alfred de Musset that le seul bien qui me reste au monde c'est d'avoir quelque fois pleuré. I was young then but I knew what he meant that they would not feel like that.

In the summer of 1903 she rejoined Leo, intending the usual holiday in North Africa and Spain. She found the pleasure of her brother's company undiminished—he was still more important to her than anybody else—and when autumn came she went back to live with him, thus settling in France for the rest of her life. 'America is my country and Paris is my home town and it is as it has come to be.'

CHAPTER FIVE

PARIS AND PICTURES

'Paris, France is exciting and peaceful.'
Paris France.

LEO had taken a little two-storey *pavillon* with a large atelier next to it in the courtyard of 27 rue de Fleurus, a street of tall houses in the 'just a hundred year old quarter' behind the Luxembourg gardens. There, although the surroundings and the interiors have changed a little, this rendezvous of the creators of the twentieth century still stands.

Leo had begun to paint, but this he did elsewhere. The rue de Fleurus studio, on the walls of which hung the Japanese prints, was the Steins' main living-room and in it Gertrude at once wrote *Quod Erat Demonstrandum*, while their excellent servant, Hélène, kept house. To judge from a letter of October 1903 from Emma Lootz Erving, now married and living in Boston, Gertrude greatly enjoyed writing this short novel and intended to continue with portraits of other friends.

> Thanks for a letter from gay Paree. I'm glad literatoor is entrancing, and I am willing to hand over any reasonable amount if you will do me nicely in a story. I must see the job before I pay, though. I have to be a real interesting heroine . . .

Gertrude was immediately at home in Paris; childhood smells, sights and sounds mingling with sharp new impressions. 'Paris was where the twentieth century was.' This was her element and she had come here to find it, as she later told in her book *Paris France*. America was the oldest country in the world, having begun the twentieth century with new conceptions in the sixties, but she was no longer able to be creative in it; England, having gloriously created the nineteenth century, was consciously refusing the twentieth, feeling that it might be one too many for her, and France alone, although not very consciously, had accepted and was living it.

France where life was tradition and human nature, Gertrude Stein said, where scientific methods were used but not expected to change anything, where governments unless they taxed you too much or got you defeated were unimportant, but fashions, 'the real thing in abstraction', mattered, where foreigners remained foreigners, 'if you are a writer you have privileges, if you are a painter you have privileges and it is pleasant'. All these and more Gertrude Stein gives as reasons why 'Paris was the place that suited those of us who were to create the twentieth-century art and literature, naturally enough'.

Picture galleries were familiar to the Steins; they had done their sightseeing thoroughly, and Gertrude liked to sit and meditate before a great master or even, in those days of liberty, to lie down on one of the red plush benches and doze off, waking to new appreciation. Now Gertrude enjoyed the Louvre with a catholic taste which included the gold frames and the view from the windows. She always liked looking out of windows, and most of all when the walls behind her were covered with pictures.

Leo was not by nature contemporary, but had been hurled into awareness of modern painting by hearing in Florence of Cézanne and then seeing some of his work owned by Charles Loeser. He was eager for his sister to share this exciting experience. America had begun to import the Impressionists, but not yet those whom a few years later Roger Fry would dub post-Impressionist. The Steins therefore—Mike and Sarah too were living in Paris with their small son Allan, and Sarah too liked pictures—had a great leap to make. They landed in the mid-stream of contemporary art and their enterprise started an important chapter of its history, for their buying set a new fashion for American collectors.

Ambroise Vollard was then the only Paris picture dealer stocking Cézanne. Encouraged by Pissarro, he had been collecting Cézanne for years and in 1895 had given him a one-man show in the rue Lafitte. 'Curieuse la maison Vollard, tout se passait dans les caves.'[1] To these cellars Leo now took Gertrude.

Anyone interested in this magical decade in Paris must have

[1] *Picasso et Ses Amis.* Fernande Olivier. Éditions Stock, Paris, 1933, p. 101. Republished 1955.

read *The Autobiography* with its witty and controversial account of current pursuits and personalities, and any biography of Gertrude Stein must draw from it. After a vivid description of Vollard and his shop, she writes:

> They told Monsieur Vollard they wanted to see some Cézanne landscapes . . . After a quite long wait he came down again and had in his hand a tiny picture of an apple with most of the canvas unpainted. They all looked at this thoroughly, then they said, yes but you see what we wanted to see was a landscape. . . . this time (he) came back with a painting of a back, it was a beautiful painting there is no doubt about that but the brother and sister were not yet up to a full appreciation of Cézanne nudes and so they returned to the attack . . . This time after even a longer wait he came back with a very large canvas and a very little fragment of a landscape painted on it. Yes, that was it, they said, a landscape but what they wanted was a smaller canvas but one all covered . . . By this time the early winter evening of Paris was closing in and just at this moment a very aged charwoman came down the same back stairs, mumbled, bon soir monsieur et madame, and quietly went out of the door, after a moment another old charwoman came down the same stairs, murmured, bon soir messieurs et mesdames and went quietly out of the door. Gertrude Stein began to laugh and said to her brother, it is all nonsense, there is no Cézanne. Vollard goes upstairs and tells these old women what to paint and he does not understand us and they do not understand him and they paint something and he brings it down and it is a Cézanne. They both began to laugh uncontrollably. Then they recovered . . . They said what they wanted was one of those marvellously yellow sunny Aix landscapes of which Loeser had several examples. . . . this time he came back with a wonderful small green landscape. It was lovely it covered all the canvas, it did not cost much and they bought it. Later on Vollard explained to every one that he had been visited by two crazy americans and they laughed and he had been much annoyed but gradually he found out that when they laughed most they usually bought something so of course he waited for them to laugh.

Vollard, for his part, in *Souvenirs d'un Marchand de Tableaux*, describes Leo Stein at the rue de Fleurus lounging in an arm-chair with his feet on the top bookshelf, declaring this good for the digestion. And Mademoiselle Gertrude, he says, with a corduroy dress, sandals and a bland expression, looked like a housewife whose horizon was no wider than her relations with the trades-men. 'But when her eyes meet yours you realise at once that there is something in Mlle Stein that is not just *bourgeoise*. Her lively gaze soon reveals the observer whom nothing escapes. But how can one be on one's guard . . . when one hears her laughter, "un rire railleur, comme si elle se moquait d'elle-même?"'

Chez Vollard they were soon allowed to rummage through the stacks of canvases for themselves, and they visited other art dealers too. There was Durand-Ruel and Sagot, the ex-clown, and Mademoiselle Weill, who besides pictures sold books and bric-à-brac, and the ex-café owner and photographer Druet. 'Also on the rue Lafitte was the confectioner Fouquet where one could console oneself with delicious honey cakes and nut candies and once in a while instead of a picture buy oneself strawberry jam in a glass bowl.'

This was the beginning of the Stein collection, to make room for which the Japanese prints gradually came down from the atelier walls. The transition was a more natural one than the Steins themselves realized for, as Sir Herbert Read points out in *Art Now*, imported Japanese prints had an enormous influence on the Post-Impressionist movement in France. The Steins' eyes were ready for painting that did not seek to copy nature.

They began by buying very small pictures: a Daumier, a Manet, two Renoirs and, having by then grown used to his nudes, two small Cézanne groups, one of which was 'The Bathers'. They frequently bought in twos because one of them usually liked one more than the other did.' They also had a Toulouse-Lautrec and a Manguin, and with these hung a Greco 'so much longer and so much and Anthony and so much', and a Florentine Madonna. Then one day they saw some Gauguins, 'they were rather awful but they finally liked them'. Gertrude preferred his sunflowers and Leo his figures, so they bought one of each.

Although none of these pictures cost more than a few hundred

francs, before the winter was over they decided to call a halt. As
a final burst they determined to get a big Cézanne and succeeded
with some difficulty in convincing Mike that this last outlay was
necessary. This time it was to be a portrait which, as few big
Cézanne portraits had so far been sold, delighted Vollard. Leo and
Gertrude spent happy days choosing their painting and refresh-
ing themselves at Fouquet's; finally they narrowed the choice to
one of a man and one of a woman, and as this time they could not
afford two pictures settled on the portrait of Madame Cézanne.
When they came to fetch it, according to Monsieur Vollard they
handed over their money as if paying the ransom of some precious personage. Then they took it home in a cab and, to quote
The Autobiography:

> It was an important purchase because in looking and look-
> ing at this picture Gertrude Stein wrote *Three Lives*.

Later she said that the Cézanne portrait had not at once seemed
'natural', but this did not alarm her. Having an incipient desire to
write with new sensibility, she was ready for the new movement
in painting. She was now giving words much attention, and after
finishing *Q.E.D.* began as an exercise to translate Flaubert's
Trois Contes. In general French literature did not interest her; what
little she read was in translation—Zola, for instance, whose
realism she admired although less than that of the Russians. For
Gertrude Stein French was a speaking language and English the
writing one; she liked to hear French spoken all round her,
leaving her alone with English. So this translation is surprising,
except that Leo had been reading Flaubert, and Gertrude was still
his disciple.

Before she had gone far she found that she wanted to write
again herself. The heroine of *Un Cœur Simple* recalled one of
her own servants and she was eager to portray some such strong
simple character. So, with Flaubert in the forefront of her mind
and William James at the back of it, Cézanne before her eyes and
Baltimore in memory, she began to write *Three Lives*.

Any literary influence came less from Flaubert than from other
reading. One remembers that she admired the prose of Robert
Greene, Defoe and Trollope, and there are American qualities

too in her work, Poe defiance, Walt Whitman robustness, Mark
Twain humour-sadness and a Californian freshness. But the surprise of *Three Lives* is its originality. Evolution was 'all over'
Gertrude Stein's childhood, and philosophy and science were all
over her youth. Now, as she entered her thirties, symbolism was
about her, but this she did not know. She was learning to look at
contemporary painting, but she was not reading contemporary
literature and was unaware of the revolt against nineteenth-
century materialism that had taken place in letters. *Three Lives*
can be called realist but it is a realism made from the inside, and
not this time from the inside of herself.

Observing the subjects for experiment in the Harvard psychological laboratory, Gertrude Stein had learnt to read their 'bottom
nature' through the different rhythms of movement and speech;
now she began to use this knowledge in her fiction. And in thus
living her characters, almost it seems breathing for them, she
became one of the first stream-of-consciousness novelists, inevitably to be listed, although she saw no connection, with such
writers as Proust, James Joyce, Virginia Woolf and Dorothy
Richardson.

On the canvas in front of her Cézanne had painted with passionate simplicity his 'real' vision of a woman; Gertrude Stein was
not less concerned with the truth of her creation.

Flaubert's Félicité and her good Anna have certain similarities.
Both are young unfortunates who drift fortunately into service
and have sharp tongues and tender hearts, a great capacity for
devotion and a strong sense of the proprieties, particularly as
regards knowing their own places, who stint themselves to save
their employers' money and give open-handedly to the needy,
however undeserving. And Anna has her adored dogs to match
Félicité's parrot, even if her devotion does not go to the fantastic
length of the latter's. The characters of the dogs are so lifelike
that even on paper they tire one.

So, through skilful, inexact repetition of simple words and
phrases one sees and hears the good Anna scolding and cherishing her various employers of whom the star is the author herself.
It is a remarkably patient study to emerge as a result of the stimu-
lus of the Cézanne portrait, and surprisingly American to have

been written in that first exciting year when Paris might have claimed all her attention. One is at once reminded of Sherwood Anderson, but he, two years her junior, although deeply influenced by her work, had not yet begun writing.

One also immediately thinks of music, although Gertrude Stein observed that music was an art for the adolescent and that she used nothing but her eyes for writing. Music was in the literary air that Gertrude Stein was unconsciously breathing. Composers having become with Wagner too literary, writers were now getting their own back by trying to produce the effect of music with words. And although Gertrude Stein discounted her ears, there are many proofs of the influence of sound upon her. Grounded in music, she phrased musically—indeed she once said that writing should be written like music, but also that 'melody should always be a by-product'. Her early work cannot but bring counterpoint to mind.

She had in fact a phenomenally retentive ear so that she was able to reproduce the tense jerky speech of German Anna and the deep softly flowing voices of the Negroes. It took her several months to finish the first story. She wrote little at a time, composing in pencil on scraps of paper and then copying the script in ink, sometimes more than once over, into French children's exercise books. Mike noticed that she never destroyed any piece of paper on which she had written; indeed she was a great hoarder of anything anybody wrote. At the beginning of the first little copy-book of squared paper is written: *The Life and Death of the Good Anna*, by Jane Sands, the pseudonym she then intended to use. By the time she began the next story much had happened.

The purchase of the big Cézanne, far from being the end of picture collecting, was only the beginning. In the autumn of 1905, the year after Matisse's one-man show at Vollard's, which Leo saw, the Salon d'Automne was held at the Petit Palais, 'a step in official recognition of the outlaws of the independent salon'. This greatly excited Leo, Gertrude and Sarah and, because of them, Mike. A number of Cézannes and one huge Douanier Rousseau 'Jungle' were shown, and encouraged by Sarah, Leo and Gertrude bought Matisse's brilliantly daring 'La Femme au

Chapeau'.[1] This, as Alfred Barr puts it in *Matisse, His Art and His Public*, 'was roaring the loudest in the *cage centrale* of the Autumn Salon'. And the public was roaring too, with fury and with laughter, as people tried to scratch the paint off the canvas.

This behaviour angered Gertrude Stein. In spite of finding its colour and anatomy strange, she said this first *fauve* picture seemed perfectly natural to her.

Meanwhile, seeing clearly that a revolution had taken place in painting, and with new pictures beginning to cover the walls round her, she went on sitting at her fine Italian renaissance table working at her stories. The loose-jointed bodies of Negroes fill the canvas of *Melanctha*, their voices streaming in long loose dialogue or breaking into 'the free abandoned laughter that gives the warm broad glow to negro sunshine', their hearts melting in sweetness or closed in stubborn suffering. There is a skilful duet of a slow Negro voice with a girl's quicker one, but Gertrude Stein never let the dialect intrude. Her characters are individuals, not Negro types such as former writers had portrayed. The story moves like a melancholy fugue and if one's attention wanders it is soon brought back by some passage of particular beauty.

> It was summer now and the coloured people came out into the sunshine, full blown with the flowers. And they shone in the streets and in the fields with their warm joy, and they glistened in their black heat, and they flung themselves free in their wide abandonment of shouting laughter.

The Gentle Lena, written second, is a slight pathetic tale of another German servant girl. In subject and treatment *Three Lives* is impressively ahead of its time.

Gertrude Stein was now thirty, perceptive, humorous, original and compassionate. She would never again be purposeless or bored; in Paris, the city of métier, she had found her own. Nevertheless she wrote to Mabel Weeks:

> I am afraid that I can never write the great American novel. I don't know how to sell on a margin or to do anything with shorts and longs, so I have to content myself with niggers and

[1] 'La Femme au Chapeau' was eventually taken to America by the Michael Steins and now hangs in a private collection in San Francisco.

servant girls and the foreign population generally. Leo he said there wasn't no art in Lovett's[1] book and then he was bad and wouldn't tell me that there was in mine so I went to bed very miserable but I don't care there ain't any Tchaikovsky Pathetique or Omar Kayam or Wagner or Whistler or White Man's Burden or green burlap in mine at least not in the present ones. Dey is very simple and very vulgar and I don't think they will interest the great American public.

And again:

My book is finished now and the worst thing will be to get it published . . . it will certainly make your hair curl with the complications and tintinabulations of its style, but I'm very fond of it. I think it a noble combination of Swift and Matisse . . . just starting on a new one . . . it does not seem to matter much to me whether it gets published or not. [2]

In time, however, publication was to matter a great deal and the wound of Leo's lack of appreciation never healed. Nor, although still profiting by his knowledge of art, did she like Leo's painting. The first rift between them had come.

Through the purchase of *La Femme au Chapeau* the Steins and the Matisses became friends and presently Sarah went as a student to the atelier where Matisse taught. What Gertrude Stein wrote a quarter of a century later about his work and his life roused much resentment, but at present everyone was on excellent terms, and Matisse remained devoted to Sarah all her life. And if Gertrude did describe Madame Matisse in *The Autobiography* as having 'a firm large loosely hung mouth like a horse', she also expressed her admiration of her, and she was after all only taking the same liberty that her fellow artists took when painting a portrait. Besides, it was part of Montmartre and Left Bank living to pull each other to pieces and gloat over *les histoires*, although some of Gertrude Stein's more wounding remarks were made, those who knew her well suggest, by sheer *inconscience*. *The Autobiography* was written for a joke and at speed in 1931. One has to sift and sort and supplement the writer's memories of this

[1] Robert Morse Lovett.
[2] Letters from Gertrude Stein in this book are all unpublished and come from the Stein Collection in the Yale Library and/or private owners.

truly rose period. Of the art of the time she gives a more serious account in the later admirable book *Picasso*.[1]

The year 1905–6 was eventful. The Steins were constantly at Matisse's top floor studio-apartment with the view of Notre Dame across the river which he liked to paint particularly in winter. He was now at work on 'Le Bonheur de Vivre,' making small and large studies and using 'his distorted drawing as a dissonance is used in music or as vinegar or lemons are used in cooking'. This picture too, because Matisse had not room to hang it, came to the rue de Fleurus. The Michael Steins had not much wall space either and only bought smaller canvases, but the important purchases of this time were decided upon by the four Steins together. Daniel-Henry Kahnweiler, the enterprising young man who was to become Picasso's dealer, met the Steins through Matisse in 1907. He says that they were always better at buying pictures as a group than individually, and that Leo and Gertrude could not have been more different in their approach to painting, she concrete and he abstract. 'Her taste and her choice were entirely personal and came from her heart rather than her head. The painters whose work she bought always became her friends.'[2] But it is important to remember that she did buy their pictures before she met them.

People had begun visiting the rue de Fleurus now to see the pictures, and the atelier grew quickly famous. Painters and sculptors came, collectors and critics, connoisseurs and amateurs of art, musicians and writers, tourists and society. 'Matisse brought people, everybody brought somebody, and they came at any time and it began to be a nuisance, and it was in this way that Saturday evenings began.'

In the middle of this life which had become so full that Gertrude Stein only found undisturbed hours for writing in the middle of the night, one of the twentieth century's most fruitful meetings occurred—that of Pablo Picasso and Gertrude Stein.

[1] *Picasso*. Written 1938. First published in French, Librairie Floury, 1938. Batsford, 1938. Charles Scribner's Sons, 1939.
[2] Author's journal.

CHAPTER SIX

PICASSO AND PORTRAITS

'How it came about they do not know. Picasso had never had anybody pose for him since he was sixteen years old, he was then twentyfour and Gertrude Stein had never thought of having her portrait painted, and they do not either of them know how it came about. Anyway it did and she posed to him for this portrait ninety times and a great deal happened during that time.'

The Autobiography of Alice B. Toklas.

PICASSO had then been living in Paris for five years, and in him Gertrude Stein, who was now thirty-two, for the first time met a vitality to match her own.

Leo saw his paintings first at Sagot's, with those of another forgotten young Spaniard, and took his sister to see them. Here was the now famous *Young Girl with a Basket of Flowers.*

Gertrude Stein did not like the picture, she found something rather appalling in the drawing of the legs and feet, something that repelled and shocked her.

She did not want it in the house but Leo did and they quarrelled and Sagot suggested that the girl should be guillotined. Finally Gertrude agreed to the purchase for a very small sum, and the first Picasso came to the rue de Fleurus. It still hangs with much else of his work in Gertrude Stein's last home in Paris. Then Monsieur H. P. Roché, whom she called 'a general introducer', took Leo to see Picasso, and at about the same time he saw Gertrude at Sagot's and asked who she was because he wanted to paint her.

In his book *Appreciation* Leo compares the neat home and person of Matisse, the last man one would expect to be called *fauve*, with Picasso's wild disorder, and describes the latter as 'more real than most people without doing anything about it'. In *The Autobiography*, quoting a friend, Gertrude calls him 'a good-looking bootblack', and gives this account of the first time he and his friend, the beautiful Fernande Bellevallée, later Olivier, came to dinner at the rue de Fleurus.

> He was thin dark, alive with big pools of eyes and a violent but not a rough way. He was sitting next to Gertrude Stein at dinner and she took up a piece of bread. This, said Picasso, snatching it back with violence, this piece of bread is mine. She laughed and he looked sheepish. That was the beginning of their intimacy.

After dinner Leo got out his portfolios of Japanese prints and Picasso 'solemnly and obediently' looked at them and listened to the descriptions.

> He said under his breath to Gertrude Stein, he is very nice, your brother, but like all Americans . . . he shows you japanese prints. Moi j'aime pas ça no I don't care for it. As I say Gertrude Stein and Pablo Picasso immediately understood each other.

Elsewhere in the book she describes him as having been 'illuminated as if he wore a halo', and as having 'the isolation and movement of the head of a bull-fighter at the head of their procession'.

Fernande Olivier, writing *Picasso et Ses Amis* at about the same time as *The Autobiography* was written, describes Leo Stein with his tall, thin awkward body, bald head, gold-rimmed spectacles and long reddish beard as looking like a professor and conforming to a type of American German Jew. Gertrude, she says, was short, stout, massive, with a beautiful strong head, noble features, intelligent clairvoyant *spirituels* eyes, and *l'esprit net, lucide*. Picasso was strongly attracted both by her physique and by her personality.

Like many other people connected with the painters of this time Fernande Olivier refers to the Steins as rich, a term to which they certainly would not have agreed, but compared with the hand-to-mouth existence of most of the artists it is accurate enough.

Everyone remembers the brother and sister at this period wearing brown corduroy suits and sandals 'à la Raymond Duncan'. The Duncans were neighbours and the Steins took a hand in their affairs when, after what Gertrude calls their Omar Khayyam stage and Italian renaissance stage, they went Greek, and Raymond acquired a Greek girl, although more Turkish than Greek, and before long a baby. It was Sarah who persuaded Raymond to marry Penelope against the wishes of Isadora, who did not believe in marriage. Gertrude preferred Raymond to his sister, finding in him true American quality, but she was interested in Isadora's dancing, 'a Californian cornucopia'.

The Steins' sandals were now famous—Gertrude wore hers which had 'toes like the prow of a gondola'[1] with thick woollen stockings. Marie Laurencin remembered the brother and sister being turned out of the Café de la Paix because of them—'how bête we French can be!'—and Kahnweiler quotes from memory a couplet of Apollinaire's:

> Leurs pieds sont chaussés de sandales bachiques,
> Ils lèvent vers le ciel des yeux scientifiques.

Now began the sittings for one of the twentieth century's most famous portraits which Gertrude Stein bequeathed to the Metropolitan Museum in New York. And with them grew the close friendship of painter and writer. Picasso needed people with ideas, she says, but not the ideas of painters, and so chose writers for his friends. Max Jacob, Guillaume Apollinaire and André Salmon were all deeply concerned in their own art with the development of Picasso's, as was he with theirs.

One reason for the quick sympathy between him and Gertrude Stein was her love of Spain. He has remained Spanish just as she was for ever American, and she loved not only Spain's landscape and architecture but its human character. And as her work is 'essentially, and in the great sense comic',[2] and the comic does not exist without its counterpart, it was natural that she should understand Picasso's tragic Spanish nature.

The blue period, which she relates to his return to uncolourful Spain after the first Toulouse-Lautrec phase, although he had in fact begun to paint blue before that visit, had ended, and Picasso was now in the waning of the rose. His Montmartre studio, in a

[1] Robert McAlmon.
[2] *Gertrude Stein: A Biography of her Work.* Donald Sutherland.

ramshackle building on the rue Ravignan resembling a Seine laundry boat and so affectionately known as *Le Bateau Lavoir*, was full of enormous canvases. There, among dogs and confusion, Gertrude posed in a large broken arm-chair while Picasso sat on a little kitchen chair in front of a big easel and, despite many interruptions, painted. She sat, as was her habit, in the way Spanish women sit of an evening outside their houses, on a low chair, leaning forward, her hands dropped upon her lap. The hands in the portrait are true to life. As a friend says, 'they dropped like flowers'.

The account of the first sitting goes on:

> Fernande was as always, very large, very beautiful and very gracious. She offered to read La Fontaine aloud to amuse Gertrude Stein. [Fernande also had a very beautiful voice.] She took her pose, Picasso sat very tight on his chair and very close to his canvas and on a very small palette which was of a uniform brown grey colour, mixed some more brown grey and the painting began.[1]

Towards the end of that first afternoon Mike, Sarah, Leo and a friend came to see how the portrait was going. All of them were excited by the beauty of the sketch and the friend begged that it should be left as it was.   'But Picasso said, non,' and the sitting went on.

After posing, Gertrude Stein would walk home across Paris, meditating and making sentences, the beginning of a life-long habit of walking about the city. She was still writing *Melanctha* when the portrait was begun and she wove into the story things she noticed as she walked. She constantly used in her text an immediate incident or emotion; it was part of the method of recording the stream of consciousness and creating a continuous present. Yet not one spark of Paris disturbs the soporific atmosphere of Baltimore. Open as she was to the influence of Cézanne and now of Picasso, the concentration on her own line of thought was absolute. During those walks she did not think about her conversations with Picasso, which were, she said, about ordinary things, she made sentences—before long the enormous sentences from

[1] *The Autobiography.*

which *The Making of Americans* is built. But how remarkable that dialogue in two kinds of bad French must have been, and Gertrude's deep laughter, which the writer Mabel Dodge said was like a beefsteak, mingling with Picasso's high Spanish whinney.

After William James and Cézanne, Picasso undoubtedly had the greatest influence upon her work, but there was this exciting difference: the others had been masters; Picasso was a contemporary, younger than herself, and she could watch him working. Now he was, as she puts it, emptying himself of the gentle poetry of France and the circus—and they met here too in liking to express the sweetness and sadness of certain kinds of human living. The Jules Laforgue quotation on the title page of *Three Lives*, '*Donc je suis un malheureux et ce n'est ni ma faute ni celle de la vie*', might equally apply to Picasso's harlequins. Not that the circus itself was a source of sadness; it was an enchantment to the whole circle; they went to the Médrano almost every week and delighted in their intimacy with the clowns.

As he worked at the portrait, Picasso's palette became less rose. Both of them valued tenderness but refused sentimentality; it was the beginning of his struggle to express the nature of people and objects as he, not as others, saw them and not to express anything that he did not see. At the same time Gertrude Stein was working towards her particular way of expressing human nature, and painter and writer were agreed that the present, nothing but the present, was the artist's concern. It was not for them to paint what had been painted or write what was written. Their business was to create the now and each of them was full of inspiration. 'One of the pleasantest things those of us who write or paint do is to have the daily miracle. It does come.'[1] They accepted each other's work without question, and the world was for them as for some philosophers an 'ongoing present event'.

Then one day winter was over and Picasso painted out Gertrude Stein's head. He said he could no longer see her when he looked, so he stopped painting, leaving the portrait headless. Monsieur H. P. Roché remembers the first head well and regrets that it was not photographed. 'Then we would have had two Picassos and two Gertrude Steins.'

[1] *Paris France.*

In this same year Picasso made the sensitive gouache of the red-bearded melancholy Leo and a delicate one of the Michael Steins' son Allan, now in the Cone Collection at the Baltimore Museum of Art.

Dr. Claribel and Miss Etta Cone, who formed the collection, were Baltimore sisters of whom both Matisse and Picasso made portraits. Gertrude Stein speaks of them as connections, but there was in fact no kinship; they were simply old friends. Dr. Claribel was engaged in medical research and both she and Etta were amateurs of the arts who constantly visited Europe and became collectors not only of contemporary painting, drawing and sculpture, but also of furniture, rugs, jewellery, lace and ceramics of any period. Gertrude Stein also was a great collector of miscellaneous objects, particularly of the minuscule in silver.

At last *Three Lives* was finished and Sarah was much moved by it which 'pleased Gertrude Stein immensely', she did not believe any one could read anything she wrote and be interested'. Now it was a matter of getting the manuscript typed; the author tried to copy it on the portable which she seldom used, but the attempt made her nervous, and presently Etta Cone came to the rescue and typed faithfully away without reading a word until she was given permission. Nor was this her only service.

> Etta Cone found the Picassos appalling but romantic. She was taken there by Gertrude Stein whenever the Picasso finances got beyond everybody and was made to buy a hundred francs' worth of drawings.

And the Cones bought still more from Matisse whose work formed the nucleus of their collection.

Picasso, who called the sisters the Miss Etta Cones, welcomed them not only as clients, but because they gave him the comic sections of their American newspaper the Baltimore *Sunday Sun*. The Steins too kept him and Fernande supplied with comics for a long time, and when they separated which of them should have these treasures became a problem. 'There were strange groups of Americans then, Picasso unaccustomed to the virginal quality of these young men and women used to say of them ils sont pas des hommes, ils sont pas de femmes, ils ont des américains.'

When *Three Lives* was typed Gertrude Stein showed it to
H. P. Roché who was much impressed, and then with some mis-
givings sent it to her friend Hutchins Hapgood, a writer living
near Florence. His response was complimentary, particularly about
Melanctha, but he criticized the many repetitions and the 'pain-
staking but often clumsy phraseology', and warned her of difficulty with publishers, partly because of the stories' length, partly
'because to get their real quality, patience and culture are demanded of the reader'. At his suggestion the script, then called
Three Histories, was sent to the New York publisher, Pitts
Duffield.

In that spring of 1906 had come other historic meetings.

> And the Matisses were back and they had to meet the Picas-
> sos and to be enthusiastic about each other, but not to like
> each other very well. And in their wake, Derain met Picasso
> and with him came Braque.
>
> It may seem very strange to everyone nowadays that
> before this time Matisse had never heard of Picasso and
> Picasso had never met Matisse. But at that time every little
> crowd lived its own life and knew practically nothing of
> any other crowd. Matisse on the Quai Saint-Michel and in
> the indépendant did not know anything of Picasso and
> Montmartre and Sagot.

But the Steins knew them all and everybody met at the rue de
Fleurus. Matisse was now thirty-six and Derain was the youngest
of the group; in this year too, at the age of sixty-seven, Paul
Cézanne died.

On April 18th, 1906, San Francisco was devastated by earthquake and fire, and the Michael Steins returned at once to look
after their property, taking with them a number of small Matisse
canvases. These paintings play a direct part in Gertrude Stein's
story, for seeing them in San Francisco increased Miss Alice
Toklas's determination to go to Paris. She had not heard of
Gertrude and Leo then and thought that Mike was an only child.

Summer found the Picassos in Spain—Gertrude Stein en-
chantingly describes a French woman's preparations for a journey
—and Leo and Gertrude at the Casa Ricci in Fiesole where they
were now to spend many summers. Here, while taking daily

walks in the blazing heat—she adored the sun and said that it rested her eyes and head to look straight up into it—and devouring books from the English lending library and seeing the Berensons and many other interesting people, she began to write *The Making of Americans*. In preparation she had done much diagramming, as she called it, of characters and had made copious notes which are said to be of great interest and to contain many references to Picasso and analyses of his character.[1] It was, by the way, to Leo that Picasso addressed his little Spanish-French notes, enclosing once a wonderful sketch, but he always sent messages to Gertrude.

To Fiesole came Gertrude Stein's first letter from a publisher— Pitts Duffield declining *Three Histories*. 'The book is too unconventional, for one thing, and if I may say so, too literary.' It was passed on to Miss Holly, a New York literary agent.

Gertrude arrived back in Paris under the spell of her book and now was often caught working by the dawn, although she tried to go to bed before the birds became too lively. And the early morning beating of rugs in the courtyard, including her own, became one of her most 'poignant irritations'.

The summer break had not broken the thread of inspiration. Artists' Paris was electric with endeavour. Derain and Braque had 'gone Montmartre', and Gertrude Stein describes Picasso as 'the little bull-fighter followed by his four enormous grenadiers', the other two being Guillaume Apollinaire and André Salmon. Max Jacob, staunch admirer of Picasso's, was always there too, and the fascinating Marie Laurencin was very much in the picture, for she and Braque had been art students together and Apollinaire was her friend. In the meetings of this group were sown the dragon's teeth soon to flower into what Max Jacob called 'the heroic age of cubism'. Marie Laurencin, however, in spite of the starkness of the movement growing up round her, continued to paint what Apollinaire called her 'feminine arabesques'. She recorded these days in the absurd and delightful *Group of Artists* painted in 1908, in which Apollinaire sits largely in the centre with a tiny volume in his tiny hands, flanked by Fernande and

[1] Author's Note: This material is reserved for later publication at the request of Miss Stein's literary executor.

Marie holding flowers, while a Greek-nosed Picasso with a splendid ringed eye sits in the foreground with a dog like a lamb.

As soon as Picasso was back in Paris he painted in the head of Gertrude Stein before seeing her and presented her with the portrait. The face is mask-like, in keeping with the style he was now developing, but here are Gertrude Stein's attentive eyes and the finely modelled mouth which was a little Greek. Nobody liked the picture except the painter and the painted and there are many anecdotes about it, including that of Picasso's answer, when somebody said Gertrude Stein did not look like the painting, 'Never mind, she will.' Shortly afterwards Vallotton painted a realistic portrait of her which also hung for some years at the rue de Fleurus,[1] but although she was often painted, carved and modelled, the Picasso remained to her the truest portrait.

Now came a new development in twentieth-century art through the influence of African sculpture. Until then, Gertrude Stein points out, this had been the concern not of artists but of curio hunters; now it bit deep into the consciousness of those painters and sculptors aiming, as Apollinaire said, 'not at an art of imitation, but at an art of conception'.

Some artist must have been the first to be fired by Negro art, but accounts vary—Matisse, some say, or Maillol or Derain. In any case African sculpture became for Picasso and his friends the chief attraction of the Trocadero and a burning topic of discussion.

Gertrude Stein did not like these African carvings—in fact she did not care for sculpture at all. She said that as an American she preferred primitive things to be more savage. But in the book *Picasso* she makes this point:

> The Arabs created both civilisation and culture for the negroes and therefore African art which was naïve and exotic for Matisse was for Picasso, a Spaniard, a thing that was natural, direct and civilised.
>
> So then it was natural that this reinforced his vision and helped him to realise it and the result was the studies which brought him to create the picture of Les Demoiselles d'Avignon.

The portrait of Gertrude Stein, painted before the African in-

[1] Cone Collection. Baltimore Musuem of Art.

fluence, was already moving in the direction of these narrow, long-featured heads which she did like and of which she and Leo bought a number.

Cubism had now been born, although it was not named until the autumn of 1908, by Louis Vauxelles who had invented the term Fauves for the earlier *avant-garde* artists. Matisse told Vauxelles that Braque had sent some paintings to the Salon d'Automne 'avec des petits cubes'. He drew an example, and so mockingly the name was given, although Picasso, supported by his friends André Salmon, Max Jacob and Guillaume Apollinaire, the reshapers of the poetry of France, is often considered Cubism's true creator. In the *Testimony against Gertrude Stein*, published by *transition* in 1935, Braque accused her of misunderstanding the movement and seeing it 'simply in terms of personalities', and of not recognizing 'the real struggle we were engaged in'. This was scarcely fair. Certainly she was interested in the personalities of all these twentieth-century creators, but she too was struggling and had a deep respect for the artist's labour. The soft and the tamely beautiful repelled her and she held by what she quotes Picasso as saying, that he who creates is forced by the intensity of the struggle to produce a certain ugliness, out of which his followers can more easily make a thing of beauty. Gertrude Stein identified herself with the painters' 'struggle to express in a picture the things seen without association but simply as things seen', for this was how she was endeavouring to use words. To free them from all associations of memory and emotion and from the tyranny of time, thus allowing them pure immediate meaning. She was not alone in this adventure, but as she did not like reading French and few of the writers in Paris read English, she had little professional contact with them. True, she observes that they were all young and all had something to give one another, but she did not talk writing with the writers as she talked painting with the painters. This is to be regretted, for she and Apollinaire were both aspiring to '*mots en liberté*', both discarding punctuation as a crutch that weakened understanding, both enjoying puns and onomatopoeia. And the whole group of writers, in common with Gertrude Stein, was influenced by the determination of the artists to achieve '*la peinture pure*'. Max Jacob, by the way, painted in water-colour and Apollinaire liked to draw; Gertrude Stein alone had no desire to express herself other than in words.

It has been suggested that Apollinaire was influenced by Gertrude Stein's writing, but although he found both her and Leo stimulating and, liking foreigners, enjoyed the rue de Fleurus, the only influence he acknowledged was Picasso's. Gertrude Stein came to like Max Jacob's poetry, but she never mentions the influence of a living writer on her work. Nor can one compare it with that of these poets; although often poetic she was at this time essentially a novelist; moreover they were using a rich imagery and a large vocabulary, both things which she refused. However, there they all were, breathing the same twentieth-century air in their common concern with the conflict between tradition and revolution and between order and adventure. '*Pardonnez-moi mon ignorance*', Apollinaire was soon to write in *Alcools*, '*pardonnez-moi de ne plus connâitre l'ancien jeu de vers.*'

The fact that she did not talk about writing with these poets whom she often saw adds to one's sense of her being, as far as her work was concerned, quite extraordinarily aloof. Even when wars shook earth and skies, even when her race was persecuted and when she was herself in danger, her inner world was unshaken. She did not seek inspiration or experience, but pursued her writing life privately and inexorably and nothing diverted her attention from its importance.

Cubism, however, captured her imagination and one sees it in the texture of her writing and the continuity of conception. Her first portraits are wonderfully built up of balanced cubes of quiet-coloured words, recalling such paintings as Picasso's portrait of Kahnweiler. But Gertrude Stein's first portrait of Picasso preceded this; true to the Stein blood which had sought the new world she was a pioneer; *Ulysses* was not yet written, nor was *A la Recherche du Temps Perdu*. Analyst, inner chronicler, Cubist writer she stood alone, and in one respect she differed from the visual artists with whom she was in such accord. Although not yet consciously afraid, the Cubist painters foretold the coming age of machine dictatorship and of shrinking flesh which was to find full expression in the iron spikes and metal cages of the mid-century sculptors. When in the thirties Gertrude Stein for the first time flew, she saw on the earth 'all the lines of cubism made at a time when not any painter had ever gone up in an airplane'. These artists were prophets, but the pioneer Gertrude Stein was not a prophet. True, the poet David Gascoyne places her early in the gradual emergence of a socially self-conscious democracy,[1] but Gertrude Stein was not herself consciously concerned with any future development. The present was her period.

[1] Unpublished notes.

CHAPTER SEVEN

THE MAKING OF AMERICANS

'It is a wonderful thing as I was saying and as I am now repeating, it is a wonderful thing how much a thing needs to be in one as a desire in them how much courage any one must have in them to be doing anything if they are a first one.'

The Making of Americans.

THERE then she sat making her enormous sentences, a democrat of language, using simple everyday words with a reformer's urge to emancipate them from the fetters of tradition, association, rhetoric, grammar and syntax. She knew them intimately, carried them about with her to caress and meditate upon, 'every word I am ever using in writing has for me very existing being', and each time she found herself using a new one she was disturbed, as when a stranger joins a circle of old friends.

This passion for words was balanced now by her interest in human character, but it could transcend everything. Then words became coins not to be spent in mere meaning, jewels not set for ordinary wear, and she defeated her democratic intention. And she sometimes hypnotized herself, for she had, as she said, a great deal of inertia and did sometimes 'stay on with her own methods' because of the pleasure they gave her. How unlike Picasso who, according to her, 'once remarked I do not care who it is that has or does influence me as long as it is not myself'.[1] What an extraordinary mixture Gertrude Stein was of vitality fired by the creative struggle, rebelliousness upsetting the comfortable order of things, and an inertia making her unwilling to move from where she was or to change what she was doing.

The Making of Americans, The History of a Family in Progress[2]

[1] *What Are Masterpieces.*

[2] Published as *The Making of Americans Being a History of a Family's Progress.* Contact Editions, Paris, 1925.

is a stupendous achievement, packed with riches. The matter and
method of presenting it are new and important, but the reader is
usually defeated by sheer quantity of words. The huge manuscript is written in pencil in notebooks and on small pads of
paper, half sheets used horizontally or vertically and foolscap
roughly torn in half. As her handwriting had grown larger and
more straggling there are very few lines to the page; she seldom
used an abbreviation and made few corrections.

Working from charts and diagrams begun at Radcliffe, she
started a history 'of every one who ever can or is or was or will be
living', in 'a space of time that is always filled with moving',
a conception she considered typically American. One thinks of the
cinema, and although Gertrude Stein had not then seen a film, in
Lectures in America[1] thirty years later she observed, 'any one is of
one's period and this our period was undoubtedly the period of
the cinema and series production'.

She was aware that she had set herself a tremendous task, but
she felt it a charge since she had a key to the 'bottom nature' of
men and women. 'When I was working with William James',
she explained later, 'I completely learned one thing, that science
is continuously busy with the complete description of something,
with ultimately the complete description of anything with ultimately the complete description of everything.'

So, courageously, she went to it, manipulating language to
express the discovery that 'every one always is repeating the whole
of them'. There could, she saw, be false repeating, when people
went on copying their own or somebody else's kind of repeating
because they were too indolent 'to really live inside them their
repeating', but true repeating, which by the way she always
found in children, truly expressed a person's 'being existing'.
Repetition could irritate even her who loved it, 'loving repeating
is one way of being', and it could take a very long time to achieve
complete understanding of a character in this way, 'to feel the
whole of anyone from the beginning to the ending', but when this
happened the long labour was rewarded. For this was her aim, as
she explained in her lecture *The Gradual Making of the Making of*

[1] Random House, 1935.

Americans,[1] to 'put down' 'a whole human being felt at one and the same time'.

By now Leo had discovered Freud—psycho-analysis was to play a large part in his future—but Gertrude did not read Freud and was her own analyst, giving us her discoveries as she went. 'I am writing everything as I am learning everything.'

> More and more I would like to make it clear to some one how I see men and women, how I see kinds in men and women. I know a good deal of it now though I am always puzzling, beginning again and again and again, feeling it all is fabrication and always I am knowing that really I see a very certain thing in my way of seeing kinds in men and women, that I am really understanding the meaning of the being in them.
>
> I know a great deal then and I tell it now when I am still puzzling.

She was continually discovering more things that had to be said about people and rebeginning was part of the fugal method, many sentences opening 'To begin then again', or 'As I was saying'. Building with persistent repetition and wonderfully sustained present participles she analyses a large number of men and women 'being living', based on her relatives, governesses, acquaintances —her characters stem from observation not invention—and records her discoveries. She found, for instance, that 'loving is a thing a great many are doing', and unhelped by Freud, years before D. H. Lawrence, wrote in a new way about sex.

Quoting from *The Making of Americans* is unsatisfactory as each passage reflects the last and loses depth without it, but as an example of her findings:

> Some men have it in them in their loving to be attacking, some have it in them to let things sink into them, some let themselves wallow in their feeling and get strength in them from the wallowing they have in loving, some in loving are melting strength passes out of them, some in their loving are worn out with the nervous desire in them, some have it as a dissipation in them, some have it as they have eating and sleeping, some have it as they have resting, some have it

[1] *Lectures in America.*

as a dissipation of them, some have it as a clean attacking, some have it as a simple beginning feeling in them, some have it as the ending always of them, some of them are always old men in their loving.

She perceived that people were not generally pleased with others' ways of loving, but it was part of her own 'loving being' to like loving. 'Slowly it has come to be in me that any way of being a loving one is interesting and not unpleasant to me.'
Her awareness of states of anxiety was equally advanced:

> There is then a whole to living, mostly everybody has for this an anxious feeling, some have not any such anxious feeling to the whole of them, many have the anxious feeling in every minute of their living, every minute is a whole to them in an anxious feeling which each minute ends [in] them . . .
>
> Anxious feeling can be in some as always an ending to them, it can be in some as always a beginning in them of living, there are some who have it in them as their own way of living.

David Gascoyne finds in this passage and generally in Gertrude Stein's 'analytical description of human beings existing and of their being beings' an anticipation of Heidegger's analyses and of existentialist phenomenology.[1] This would surely have surprised and amused her, for after William James and briefly Whitehead she took little interest in contemporary philosophy. But in her twentieth-century awareness she thought contemporarily and thus reflected Heidegger's concern with being and existing. His *Sein und Zeit* was published at about the same time as *The Making of Americans*, but Gertrude Stein's book was written fifteen years earlier. As psycho-philosopher and as novelist how startlingly ahead of her time she was. And although, as she was well aware, repetition in itself was not new, mystics and poets having always recognized its power, her way of using it to build up character and make fugal variations was original.

Loving, quarrelling, eating, sleeping, washing, listening, smelling, breathing, making money and having religion— interminably the ways of being and doing are explored and analysed. She divides people into dependent independants and independent

[1] Unpublished notes.

dependants, 'the first have resisting as the fighting power in them, the second have attacking as their natural way of fighting,' and each have their own kind of sensitiveness, their own strength and weakness, stupidity and passion, contentment and melancholy.

She also uses herself as a subject:

> I have it in me in being that I am resisting in being, I am fairly slow in action and in feeling, if I am not slow in acting and in feeling and in listening I am not certain that I myself am doing that acting listening feeling, I would be thinking something was happening, it would be over and I would not be realising that I myself was listening, feeling, acting . . .

She conceives millions of each type of human being that she describes, and description is for her explanation. All the characters are American, 'the old people in a new world, the new people made out of the old . . . for that is what really is and what I really know'. It was part of her strength, her sincerity and singleness of mind, to keep to what she really knew and one of the problems was to find a way of making what she knew come out as she knew it and 'not as remembering'. 'I was faced by the trouble that I had acquired all this knowledge gradually but when I had it I had it completely at one time.' She was bent on expressing the sense of immediacy.

One of the most beautiful passages in the book is a description of a humble European family leaving its native village to journey to the unknown New World. It is an imaginary picture of the emigrant Steins; rebel though she was Gertrude Stein, true to her race, had a strong sense of the importance of her forebears. She believed that to know ourselves we must always have in us 'a lively sense' of the men and women who made us what we are. And although she was so American she was fully aware—this is already expressed in *Things As They Are*—of an insistent heritage from an older civilization.

In *The Making of Americans* the name David Hersland is given to a man of each generation, representing Gertrude Stein's grandfather and father, and Martha is the grandmother whom she admired and was said to resemble but never knew. After their father's death his portrait of her was given to Gertrude by Mike. She must have listened carefully to any stories of her forebears told when she was young, and she had an unusually retentive memory. Both sides of the family are described in remarkable detail. The book nevertheless is fiction and the author took what liberties she wished, making herself, for example, the eldest of three children instead of the youngest of five, and the Stein grandfather a butcher for which there is no evidence. But the character drawings seem authentic:

> David Hersland's mother was that good foreign woman who was strong to bear many children and always after was very strong to lead them. The old woman was a great mountain. Her back even in her older age was straight, flat and firmly supporting. She had it in her to uphold around her, her man, her family, and everybody else whom she saw needed directing . . .
>
> She led her family out of the old world into the new one and there they learned through her and by themselves, almost every one of them, how to make for themselves each one a sufficient fortune . . .
>
> The father was not a man ever to do any such leading. He was a butcher by trade. He was a very gentle creature in his nature. He loved to sit and think and he loved to be important in religion. He was a small man, well enough made, with a nice face, blue eyes, and a little lightish colored beard. He loved his eating and the quiet life, he loved his Martha and his children, and mostly he liked all the world.
>
> It would never come to him to think of a new world. He never wanted to lose anything he ever had had around him. He did not want to go to a new world. He would go, —yes to be sure it would be very nice there . . . Yes, alright perhaps, maybe she was right, there was no reason, the neighbors had all gotten so rich going to America, there was no reason they shouldn't go and get rich there . . .

So Martha sold the business and David liked this for it made him feel important, but he did not like it when he saw another man in his shop and found that he no longer had any place of his own. And when at last they were all on the road, with the littlest children on top of their belongings in a wagon and the rest of the family walking, he slipped away.

The mother went back patiently to find him. He was sitting

at the first turning, looking at the village below him, at all the things he was leaving, and he simply could not endure it in him . . .

He sighed and she came to him. 'Don't you want to be going David,' she said to him. 'If you don't really want to be going you've just got to say David what you want to be doing. I'll never be a woman to make you do anything you are not really wanting . . .'

'Of course Martha you know I do what I got to do for you and the children . . . Yes I come now Martha . . . I go on with you now I got another look to see I don't forget it.' . . .

All, the wagon and the driver and the horses and the children, had waited for them to come up to it. Now they went on again, slowly and creaking, as is the way always when a whole family do it.

Slowly and creaking, yet like the book rolling indomitably on. One feels this grandmother's persistence and courage in Gertrude Stein as she followed her chosen, lonely trail. Yet she was often discouraged:

> I am all unhappy in this writing. I know very much of the meaning of the being in men and women. I know it and feel it and I am always learning more of it and now I am telling it and I am nervous and driving and unhappy in it.

She comforts herself by adding, 'sometimes I will be all happy in it', then again comes a weary, 'sometimes I am almost despairing'. And, although she believed that she had 'very much wisdom', without which conviction she could not have carried on the herculean labour, she admitted the fallibility of her judgment.

> I have been very glad to have been wrong. It is sometimes a very hard thing to win myself to having been wrong about something. I do a great deal of suffering.

Besides the painful struggling in the thinking and the writing there was other cause for distress. Leo had no faith in her work and while her belief in its importance was unshaken, doubt of having readers grew. The agent had not found a publisher for *Three Lives*, nor in spite of much effort had Mabel Weeks. Finally, through a friend of hers, the script was sent to the Grafton Press, a firm specializing in private printing, and publication was at last arranged. It was not unusual or discreditable then for an author to publish his own book, but it was a pointer, and quite early in *The Making of Americans* Gertrude Stein writes:

> Bear it in your mind my reader, but truly I never feel it that there ever can be for me any such a creature, no it is this scribbled and dirty and lined paper that is really to be to me always my receiver.

And later:

> I am writing for myself and strangers. This is the only way that I can do it. Everybody is a real one to me, everybody is like someone else too to me. No one of them that I know can want to know it and so I write for myself and strangers. . . . I want readers so strangers must do it.

'Disillusionment in living', she discovers, 'is the finding out nobody agrees with you not those that are and were fighting with you', and she reflects how much desire and how much courage any one must have to do something new.

Her social life in the rue de Fleurus, where the walls were now crammed with paintings from floor to ceiling, was full and fascinating, but in her work she was alone when Miss Alice Toklas arrived in Paris.

CHAPTER EIGHT

CHANGING RELATIONSHIPS

> 'I was impressed by the coral brooch she wore and by her
> voice. I may say that only three times in my life have I met a
> genius and each time a bell within me rang and I was not mis-
> taken, and I may say in each case it was before there was any
> general recognition of the quality of genius in them. The three
> geniuses of whom I wish to speak are Gertrude Stein, Pablo
> Picasso and Alfred Whitehead.'
>
> *The Autobiography of Alice B. Toklas.*

SUCH was the impact on Alice Toklas at her first meeting with
Gertrude Stein. She also found in the writer 'a certain physical
beauty, great power and an enormous sense of life, of what life
was, the thing that was alive'. And although only two years
younger than Gertrude Stein, who was now thirty-three, she felt
her to be vastly older in experience.

Except for an early visit to Europe her own life had been spent
in California. The Toklases were of Polish Jewish extraction and
Alice, as *The Autobiography* relates,

> . . . led in my childhood and youth the gently bred existence
> of my class and kind . . . I led a pleasant life, I had many
> friends, much amusement many interests, my life was rea-
> sonably full and I enjoyed it but I was not very ardent in it.

Her education had included much music—once she meant to be
a pianist but interest waned—and wide reading in French and in
English. As a girl she had an unusual share of domestic responsibility, after the death of her grandmother and mother keeping house
for the two widowers in San Francisco and looking after a younger
brother. But whenever possible she went into the country where
riding was her great pleasure.

By 1906, when the earthquake brought the Michael Steins back
to California, Alice Toklas was living alone with her father and

brother. She had had no thought of change, but the desire to re-visit Europe was strengthened by the Steins' descriptions of life in Paris and the excitement of seeing their Matisse paintings. A legacy from her grandfather made it possible for her to cross the Atlantic in 1907 with her friend Harriet Levy.[1]

On the day of their arrival they called on the Michael Steins, who had returned earlier to Paris, and met Gertrude whom Harriet Levy already knew. The friends took an apartment in the nearby rue Notre Dame des Champs, visited exhibitions and went to the Saturday evenings at the rue de Fleurus. Soon Alice Toklas began calling on other days too and going for long walks with Gertrude Stein. She also found Leo charming and kind, and appreciation was mutual.

Before long she was helping to correct the proofs of *Three Lives*. The Grafton Press had called attention to some slips in grammar which they attributed to the typing, but Gertrude Stein insisted that the work should stand exactly as written. When the proofs were finished Alice Toklas began the formidable task of typing *The Making of Americans* and was henceforth the writer's faithful amanuensis.

When asked what her first reaction to Gertrude Stein's writing had been she said: 'When I first saw Picasso's painting I was breathless. Then I was convinced.' And with Gertrude Stein's work too, 'being convinced followed very quickly on being breathless'.

Miss Toklas had done no typing until she started on *The Making of Americans*.

> I taught myself. The typewriter had a rhythm, made a music of its own I don't mean the script I mean the type-writer. In those complicated sentences I rarely left anything out. And I got up a tremendous speed. Of course my love of Henry James was a good preparation for the long sentences. I remember being given Balzac to read when I was quite young and so much preferring Henry James.[2]

[1] Author and dramatic critic. Her autobiographical book 920 *O'Farrell Street*, Doubleday and Company, Inc., New York, 1947, contains a description of the youthful Alice Toklas who lived next door.

[2] Author's journal.

Nevertheless when *The Making of Americans* was eventually printed Gertrude Stein apologized for the script, explaining that typing had then 'been with them in its infancy.'

It is not difficult to imagine what Alice Toklas's whole-hearted appreciation meant to Gertrude Stein at this time. As she went on working, doubting if she would have readers but never doubting the necessity of writing, I am reminded of an artist's title for her abstract canvases: '*Lettres sans réponses.*'[1]

When summer came Harriet Levy and Alice Toklas took the Casa Ricci at Fiesole, while the Steins shared a larger villa in Florence, and everyone constantly met. Alice Toklas was bringing Gertrude Stein a much needed sense of security, for she and Leo were drifting steadily apart. Besides finding her writing senseless, he was coming to detest everything that Picasso was painting.

In considering the relation of the Steins to contemporary art one has to remember that Leo was the first of the circle to see Cézanne, that he discovered Picasso and that he forced his views upon others. People frequenting the rue de Fleurus in those early days remember him standing in front of the canvases, his glasses shining and his beard wagging, as he denounced the conventions enervating the arts and demanded tension. He fought the apathy and mockery of their visitors and his fervour speeded the day of recognition for Matisse and Picasso. Gertrude did not hold forth about the pictures; she led people to them and left them to look for themselves, and talker as she was, while Leo lectured she was silent. Yet, after a very few years, he ceased to follow the trail he had blazed. He could not advance; in the end even Cézanne meant little to him. But Gertrude went on because of her passionate understanding of the twentieth century, 'it is a time when everything cracks, where everything is destroyed, everything isolates itself, it is a more splendid thing than a period where everything follows itself'.[2]

She exemplified her definition, 'a creator is contemporary, he understands what is contemporary when the contemporaries do not yet know';[3] Leo, although more intellectual, was not creative and once she ceased to be his disciple she found his academic dis-

[1] Karskaya. Paris.   [2] *Picasso.*   [3] Ibid.

sertations tedious—he had ideas on every subject including cooking. And he found his sister's dogmatism, not always logically supported, foolish; moreover his affection for her was further distracted by falling in love.

Nina Auzias, when a friend first brought her to the rue de Fleurus, was still pursuing, as Leo put it, a varied career. She had sung in the street; she was an artists' model and had led the Bohemian life. Although it was years before they married she and Leo quickly became friends. To her he was brilliant and attractive, 'a handsome Egyptian statue', while he, painfully introverted and the victim of what he called crippling neurosis, found in her a fascinating psychological study. He needed this new element in his life as much as Gertrude Stein needed the new one in hers. To add to his natural melancholy, although still under forty he was growing very deaf, which did not however stop him from continuing to share with Gertrude, if little else, a taste for hilarity. There are glimpses in *The Autobiography* of him still being wonderfully funny, as when for instance he gave a lively rendering of Isadora Duncan's dying dance.

Naturally Gertrude did not approve of her brother's new friendship. Apart from disturbing old emotions, it offended her middle-class principles and family feeling, but after her first meeting with her future sister-in-law Nina Auzias wrote:

> His sister, Miss Gertrude Stein, a wonderful strong person, came to my side and amiably opened a great folder full of sketches. Her magnificent voice, like heavy velvet, came to me, but senseless I knew not what she was saying. And for two hours Leo talked . . . But I could do nothing except look at him.[1]

In spite of this attachment Leo did not leave the rue de Fleurus for several years after Alice Toklas joined the household. Asked how this occurred she said:

> I am a person acted upon not a person who acts, I was at Fiesole that summer with Leo and Gertrude, and Harriet Levy suddenly wired she was going back to America with the Mike Steins. So Gertrude said, you don't want to go

[1] Extract from the journal of Nina Stein (Auzias) in *Journey Into the Self*.

back to the apartment alone, do you, and I said no, and so it was.[1]

But even if acted upon, Alice Toklas was an independent character. Independence is a Californian quality, 'you win it early and have it for the rest of your life', and neither she nor Gertrude Stein understood the fuss made about it in other parts of the world. Independently she chose her rôle, that of cherishing Gertrude Stein who so much liked to be cherished and making the best possible conditions for the work in which she so steadfastly believed. From this time onward there are innumerable photographs of Gertrude Stein with, behind her handsome Roman Emperor's head, the delicate aquiline profile of her friend. 'They' henceforward meant not Leo and Gertrude but Gertrude and Alice. A new 'two together two' had begun which would never be broken.

It has been assumed that the coming of Alice Toklas caused the departure of Leo, but writing to Mabel Weeks when the final break came in 1913, he made the position clear.

> One of the greatest changes that has become decisive in recent times is the fairly definite 'disaggregation' of Gertrude and myself. The presence of Alice was a godsend, as it enabled the thing to happen without any explosion.

In the same letter he says, 'when I read anything, I can understand it if it has anything for me, if not "*je m'en fous*",' and expresses the view that Picasso, 'one of the greatest illustrators ever born', and Gertrude, to whom he attributes 'a certain power', were on the wrong track.

> Both he and Gertrude are using their intellects, which they ain't got, to do what would need the finest critical tact, which they ain't got neither, and they are in my belief turning out the most Godalmighty rubbish that is to be found.

It may be that while sincerely holding these views Leo was embittered by his discovery that his own gifts were only critical. In any case there was no more to be said.

[1] Author's journal.

CHAPTER NINE

CUBISM AND WRITING

'If a thing can be done why do it.'
'Any copy is a bad copy.'
Gertrude Stein.

IN that same autumn of 1909, when Alice Toklas joined the Stein ménage, Picasso brought back from Spain three pale gold landscapes, two of which still hang in Gertrude Stein's apartment, the third being in Moscow. These she referred to as 'the beginning of classic and classified cubism', and she said that they exactly expressed the opposition in Spain between nature and man. Italian and French architecture followed the line of the landscape, but Spanish architecture cut its lines, the round opposed to the cube, the landscape and the houses in disagreement. She found it natural that a Spaniard should express this opposition in the painting of the twentieth century, the century where nothing was in agreement.

When Gertrude Stein was next in Spain she found Cubism everywhere, and soon afterwards had one of the Picasso paintings reproduced opposite a photograph of the same hill village to show how close his vision was to the original. Braque was equally involved in Cubism, and for a while neither painter cared if his canvases were mistaken for the other's. In the struggle of escaping from centuries of naturalistic representation they were both inspired with open-mindedness, and the enterprising young picture dealer, Daniel-Henry Kahnweiler, was there to share the great adventure. It was a time of brilliant endeavour, vitality and gaiety.

At the rue de Fleurus in those last years before the 1914 war, 'it was like a kaleidoscope slowly turning'. Gertrude Stein flings the pieces into *The Autobiography* to make brilliant pictures of Picasso and Fernande, their parting, rejoining and parting again for ever, of Eva who succeeded Fernande, of Sabartes, friend of

Picasso's earliest youth. One sees the thin, wild Marie Laurencin
going over whatever pictures she could reach inch by inch with
her lorgnette because she is so short-sighted. One watches the
big florid Guillaume Apollinaire and the small colourless douanier
Rousseau and notices that Braque is often mentioned but never
described. One sees Roché and Rönnebeck, the Delaunays and the
Raynals, the sisters Cone—Dr. Claribel read Gertrude Stein aloud
with great effect—Mildred Aldrich, Henry McBride and Mabel
Dodge. Epstein, in Paris for the placing of his Oscar Wilde tomb-
stone, brings his young wife; Bernard Berenson still on occasion
puts in an appearance; Lady Cunard comes with the young Nancy,
and Lady Ottoline Morrell is there, 'looking like a marvellous
feminine version of Disraeli'. The Clive Bells arrive and Roger
Fry, collecting pictures for the post-Impressionist exhibition at
the Grafton Gallery; Augustus John, Henry Lamb, Wyndham
Lewis, Duncan Grant, scores of interesting visitors came as the
months rolled by, but however scintillating the atmosphere and
however strong the cross-currents, Gertrude Stein's own stream
was undisturbed and nightly the exercise books were filled.

The Making of Americans was not finished until 1911. Meanwhile
she began A Long Gay Book, intended to be longer still, and Many
Many Women. On the fly-leaf of its first notebook is written:
'How women are lived and what they are. Alice, Nellie, Marion,
Bird, Helene, Mabel Dodge, Emma, Harriet Levy, Germaine,
Fernande, Marie Matisse, Olga', names of friends and cousins and
the housekeeper. In the third notebook she adds Mabel Weeks
and a long list of aunts. It is instructive to study her manuscripts.
From the handwriting and the placing of the lines on the page
one gets something of the day's mood and from the text and
the odd notes much of her process of thought. On the purple
fly-leaf of an exercise book marked Two is written large 'Leo
and Sally', and round this lightly: 'Complete sound and then
a bit of what they did and how. Then do Alice and me and
what we did and how, use the introduction for Alice about . . .'
Two, however, whatever its intention, became a book in an
abstract way about herself and Leo.[1]

---

[1] Two (Gertrude Stein and Her Brother) and Other Early Portraits. Written
1908–12. Published 1951.

Or again: 'Serge is what we do not like.' 'Keep away and visit every Saturday . . . It is not open to stay. There is a way to go away.' 'Dearest, when you wake up call. The new volume begins this way.' The script, sometimes only a few lines crossways to the page—in all her mass of writing she seldom used abbreviations—seems to flow with current life—air, food, pictures, people, whatever was then moving the mind of the writer.

She abandoned these further long books in favour of short portraits, and the first of these, *Ada*, had as subject Alice Toklas. *The Autobiography* tells how one Sunday evening when, because Hélène was out, Alice had prepared a special American dish for supper, Gertrude Stein came in from the atelier very much excited. She would not sit down and insisted on Alice reading what she had written in spite of the food cooling. 'I began it and I thought she was making fun of me and I protested, she says I protest now about my autobiography. Finally I read it all and was terribly pleased with it.' *Ada*[1] is indeed an amusing, tender piece of work. *Miss Furr and Miss Skeene*[2] is another charming early one.

Portraits of practically everyone Gertrude Stein knew followed. Among the first were *Matisse* and *Picasso* which Alfred Stieglitz enterprisingly published in August 1912 in a special number of his American magazine *Camera Work*. Gertrude Stein asked him to be careful about the punctuation, 'it is very necessary as I have put in all of it that I want and any that is introduced will make everything wrong.' With the text were fourteen reproductions of Matisse and Picasso paintings and sculpture, but Stieglitz emphasized that the articles themselves, not the painters or their work, were the *raison d'être* of the special issue.

Carl Van Vechten, in a note in *Selected Writings of Gertrude Stein*,[3] says that Stieglitz told him that he accepted the portraits principally because he did not immediately understand them. As a matter of fact, although they confuse some readers with their repetitions and double present participles the meaning of the words is perfectly clear, as it is in every line of *The Making of Americans*. Perhaps this writing seemed more obscure in 1912

---

[1] *Geography and Plays*. The Four Seas Company, Boston, 1922.
[2] Ibid.   [3] New York, Random House, 1946.

than it does today just as much visual art which mystified then is to us lucid. In these early portraits, still without having seen a film, 'I was doing what the cinema was doing, I was making a continuous statement of what that person was until I had not many things but one thing.[1] As a point of interest Moholy Nagy observes, although not of this work, that 'her writing very often reads like a shooting script for a motion picture, including sound effects'.[2]

In spite of her theory that she wrote only with her eyes, *Picasso* and *Matisse* gain by being read aloud, and most of all in the author's fine voice.[3] Then the subtle entry of their fugal voices and their changing inflections can be fully appreciated. There can be no better approach to a fuller understanding of her serious work.

The portrait of Picasso begins:

> One whom some were certainly following was one who was completely charming. One whom some were certainly following was one who was charming. One whom some were following was one who was completely charming. One whom some were following was one who was certainly completely charming.
>
> Some were certainly following and were certain that the one they were then following was one working and was one bringing out of himself then something. Some were certainly following and were certain that the one they were then following was one bringing out of himself then something that was coming to be a heavy thing, a solid thing and a complete thing.
>
> One whom some were certainly following was one working and certainly was one bringing something out of himself then and was one who had been all his living had been one having something coming out of him.
>
> Something had been coming out of him, certainly it had been coming out of him and it had meaning, a charming meaning, a solid meaning, a struggling meaning, a clear meaning.

[1] *Lectures in America.* New York, Random House, 1935.
[1] *Vision in Motion.* Paul Theobald. Chicago, 1947.
[3] *Gertrude Stein read by Gertrude Stein.* Dorian Records. Long Playing, DR-331-1 and 2.

One whom some were certainly following and some were
certainly following him, one whom some were certainly
following was one certainly working . . .

Gertrude Stein calls this method of repetition 'insistence'.
With each subtly different repetition the emphasis is changed.
'It is exactly like a frog hopping,' she said, 'he cannot ever hop
exactly the same distance or the same way of hopping at every
hop', her version of William James's description of the stream of
consciousness, 'like a bird's life, it seems to be an alternation of
flights and perchings'.

She sent a copy of this issue of *Camera Work* to Bernard Berenson who responded:

My cordial thanks for the pamphlet full of extraordinarily
fine reproductions of Matisse's & Picasso's. In a moment of
perfect peace when I feel my best I shall try again to see
whether I can puzzle out the intention of some of Picasso's
designs.

As for your own prose I find it vastly more obscure still.
It beats me hollow, & makes me dizzy to boot. So do some
of the Picasso's by the way. But I'll try again.

Meanwhile there were flutters of interest from America and
Mabel Dodge reported that in Venice Gertrude Stein was considered something between a prophet and a bombshell. She adored
the attention and was in general happy in this new phase of work.
'How terribly exciting each one of these were,' she wrote of these
phases, 'first there was the doing of them, the intense feeling that
they made sense, then the doubt and then each time over again
the intense feeling that they did make sense.'[1]

Often she used to say to people, 'just be simple, it's all there to
read', yet she did sometimes have her doubts.

Meanwhile, at the end of 1909, the privately printed *Three
Lives* had come out in New York, and been greeted in a couple
of dozen reviews with a good deal of interest and only mild
disparagement. The reviewers' commonest phrase was 'an extraordinary piece of realism', and they looked hopefully to her
future work.

[1] *A Message from Gertrude Stein. Selected Writings of Gertrude Stein.* Carl
Van Vechten.

She had naturally sent a copy of it to William James, and on 25th May, 1910, only three months before he died, received a letter from him from Bad-Nauheim. The Steins appear to have been quite out of touch with him for he says, 'I passed a week at Paris 10 days ago, and thought of you and your brother a good deal. I should have sought a meeting had I known your address.' And, after a mention of his poor health, he adds:

> I have had a bad conscience about 'Three Lives.' You know (?) how hard it is for me to read novels. Well, I read 30 or 40 pages, and said 'this is a fine new kind of realism— Gertrude Stein is great! I will go at it carefully when just the right mood comes.' But apparently the right mood never came. I thought I had put the book in my trunk, to finish over here, but I don't find it on unpacking. I promise you that it shall be read *some* time. You see what a swine I am to have pearls cast before him! As a rule reading fiction is as hard to me as trying to hit a target by hurling feathers at it. I need *resistance*, to cerebrate!

The pieces of *The Making of Americans* that Gertrude Stein was showing her friends as they came off the typewriter roused much enthusiasm. The American authoress Mabel Dodge wrote from Florence:

> To me it is one of the most remarkable things I have ever read. There are things hammered out of consciousness into black & white that have never been expressed before—so far as I know. States of being put into words the 'noumenon' captured—as few have done it. To name a thing is practically to create it & this is what your work is—real creation. It is almost frightening to come up against reality in language in this way. I always get—as I told you—the shivers when I read your things. And your palette is such a simple one— the primary colours in word painting & you express every shade known and unknown with them. It is as new & strange & big as the post-impressionists in their way &, I am per- fectly convinced, it is the forerunner of a whole epoch of new form & expression. It is very morally constructive for I feel it will alter reality as we have known it, & help us get at Truth instead of away from it as 'literature' so sadly often does.

One cannot read you and still go on cherishing the consistent illusions one has built up about oneself and others.

This letter expresses extraordinarily well Gertrude Stein's aim, parallel with that of the post-Impressionist painters, to reassess primary factors.

In that same summer of 1911 she went to tea with Mabel Dodge at the Villa Curonia, and her hostess wrote: '*Why* are there not more *real* people like you in the world? Or are there and one doesn't attract them? Miss Fletcher[1] and I both felt as though we had been drinking champagne all the afternoon . . .' Gertrude Stein's presence was dynamic.

She was still trying to find an English publisher for *Three Lives*. Grant Richards refused it on the grounds that short stories with an American setting would have no appeal to English readers, but expressed interest in anything else she could offer him. Her star was slowly rising.

In the summer of 1912 she and Miss Toklas went to Spain again, Gertrude Stein wearing her brown corduroy jacket and skirt and one of the small straw caps crocheted for her by a woman in Fiesole, carrying a cane, and Alice Toklas in what she called her Spanish disguise, a black silk coat, black gloves and a black hat. 'The only pleasure I allowed myself were lovely artificial flowers on my hat', which the Spanish women thoroughly appreciated.

They went first to Avila, where Miss Toklas would gladly have stayed for the rest of her life—but Gertrude Stein never had any doubt about Paris being the place to live in. On the advice of their friend the English painter, Harry Gibb, they visted Cuenca and delighted in it, but were so conspicuous there that it became embarrassing. Sometimes in Spain, particularly later when she wore her hair short. Gertrude Stein was taken for a member of a religious order. Indeed she was once mistaken for some bishop expected in a village, and when she went for a walk and sat down under a tree to rest, the population followed and queued to kiss her ring.

In Madrid they went often to a music hall to see La Argentina, whom the journalists had just discovered, and also to bullfights,

[1] Constance Fletcher, the American playwright, who became a friend of Gertrude Stein's.

Gertrude Stein telling Alice Toklas when to look and when not, until she found she could look all the time. Finally they visited Granada, which Gertrude Stein had always liked, and here came a new impulse.

> We enjoyed Granada, we met many amusing people english and spanish and it was there and at that time that Gertrude Stein's style gradually changed. She says hitherto she had been interested only in the insides of people, their character and what went on inside them, it was during that summer that she first felt a desire to express the rhythm of the visible world.
>
> It was a long, tormenting process, she looked, listened and described. She always was, she always is, tormented by the problem of the external and the internal. One of the things that always worries her about painting is the difficulty that the artist feels and which sends him to painting still lifes, that after all the human being essentially is not paintable . . .
>
> These were the days in which she wrote Susie Asado[1] and Preciosilla[2] and Gypsies in Spain. She experimented with everything in trying to describe. She tried a bit inventing words but she soon gave that up. The english language was her medium and with the english language the task was to be achieved, the problem solved. The use of fabricated words offended her, it was an escape into imitative emotionalism.
>
> No, she stayed with her task, although after the return to Paris she described objects, she described rooms and objects, which joined with her first experiments done in Spain, made the volume Tender Buttons.[3]

This passage shows one reason why Gertrude Stein denied any similarity between her work and that of James Joyce. She was not concerned with the disintegration or reconstruction of words; she liked and used them as they were.

While they were in Spain Mabel Dodge was having an uproarious house party in Florence with a couple of ghosts as highly successful uninvited guests. She wrote Gertrude an hilarious

[1] In *Geography and Plays*.

[2] *Composition as Explanation*. The Hogarth Press, London, 1926. Doubleday, Doran & Company, Inc. New York, 1928. And in *What Are Masterpieces*.

[3] Claire Marie, New York, 1914. *transition* No. 14. 1928.

account, wishing she were there to share the fun, and in the autumn the friends went to stay at the Villa Curonia. Here among the many visitors they met André Gide, but he and Gertrude Stein were not interested in one another. In her book *European Experiences* Mabel Dodge wittily and wickedly describes this visit, in the course of which Gertrude wrote the *Portrait of Mabel Dodge at the Villa Curonia*.[1] Nobody pretended that this was not difficult to understand, particularly if one had no clues to the subject matter, for she now often abandoned sense as it is commonly understood.

The portrait begins lucidly enough:

> The days are wonderful and the nights are wonderful and the life is pleasant.

And then wanders into such elusive passages as:

> Blankets are warmer in the summer and the winter is not lonely. This does not assure the forgetting of the intention when there has been and there is every way to send some. There does not happen to be a dislike for water. This is not heartening.

Or:

> There was not that velvet spread when there was a pleasant head. The color was paler. The moving regulating is not a distinction. The place is there.

Much of the portrait is suggestive and it is a pleasant pastime to build from it pictures of the house party and its hostess, to catch glimpses of events and hear echoes of conversations, but there is no sustained logic to help meaning.

Mabel Dodge tells how Gertrude wrote at night after everyone else was asleep, leaving the pages for Alice to type first thing in the morning. 'Then she and Gertrude would always be so surprised and delighted at what she had written for it had been done so unconsciously she'd have no idea of what she'd said the night before!' And although Gertrude Stein always asserted that her writing was in no way automatic, she did also tell her friends that she wrote down whatever came into her head and stopped when the flow ceased.

[1] Published 1912.

Mabel Weeks, H. P. Roché and others of her friends who had followed her development so far with interest and hope were 'naturally cast down', to use Miss Weeks's phrase, by their inability to understand this new phase and by feeling that Gertrude Stein was misusing her gifts. Mabel Dodge, however, was enchanted with her portrait, had it printed, bound in assorted Florentine wall-papers and circulated among her friends. 'I must snatch a lucid moment', she wrote to Gertrude, 'when "argument is clear" [a quotation from it] to tell you that I consider the "Portrait" to be a master-piece of success from my (& your) point of view *as* a portrait of *me as* I am to others.' Later she added: 'Some days I don't understand it, but some days I don't understand things in myself, past or about to come!' This portrait was a source of endless fun and Gertrude Stein loved fun. When Mabel Dodge returned to America she gave a number of the gay little volumes to people she thought might boost the author. It was in this way that Carl Van Vechten, who became one of Gertrude Stein's dearest friends and staunchest champions, first saw her work. He met her in Paris the following year.

Back at the rue de Fleurus she resolved her Spanish inspiration in *Objects Food Rooms*, the series of short often parodied pieces which make up the volume *Tender Buttons*, so called because of her predilection for buttons. The change of method from her earlier work she attributed to having changed herself from feeling that everything was simply alike to feeling that everything was simply different. In *The Making of Americans* she had been concerned with classification and types; now she was concerned with the unique and came closer to those painters for whom a thing exists only as at the moment of vision. And she was using shock tactics to obtain fresh unprepared-for experience.

A BLUE COAT

A blue coat is guided guided away, guided and guided away, that is the particular color that is used for that length and not any width not even more than a shadow.

RED ROSES

A cool red rose and a pink cut pink, a collapse and a sold hole, a little less hot.

WATER RAINING

Water astonishing and difficult altogether makes a meadow
and a stroke.

CELERY

Celery tastes tastes where in curled lashes and little bits and
mostly in remains.
A green acre is so selfish and so pure and so enlivened.

In these short pieces Gertrude Stein used a poetic economy of
expression, although she admitted that in working out a new conception she was inarticulate at first. All her life she declared a
passion for exactitude, and she tells us that she now imposed upon
herself a strict discipline, never using a word that was not an
exact word. One sees the struggle in handwriting wilder than
ever, but she had her reward, for she felt that in this period she
achieved 'an extraordinary melody of words', and there was 'a
melody of excitement in knowing that I had done this thing'.

Since the days of the old melodrama in Baltimore and the opera
in New York she had not been interested in the theatre. But dance
—Isadora Duncan, Nijinsky and La Argentina—and the bull-
ring brought her mind back to it. She began thinking about the
plays she had read in childhood, the many characters, the poetry
and the scenery which always was, and she was sure always should
be, woods and streets and windows.

So suddenly she began to write plays. These are even more unlike other plays than her novels are unlike other fiction. She does
not keep a single rule so it is very hard to follow the game, but
she gives us a few clues. Coming home one night from a dinner
party she reflected on the number of stories that were always told
in the newspapers and in private life. She made up her mind to
write 'what everybody did not always know or always tell. By
everybody I do of course include myself . . . The idea in What
Happened, A Play was without telling what happened, to make a
play the essence of what happened.'

She also tells us that for her there was a connection between
war and dance and between plays and landscape, 'a landscape is
such a natural arrangement for a battlefield or a play that one
must write plays'. Later she observed that plays, like dance and

war, are 'the thing anybody can see by looking'. Seeing was believing. Picasso's cubist décor for *Parade* was accepted, she said, because 'when a work is put on the stage of course everyone has to look at it and . . . since they are forced to look at it, of course, they must accept it, there is nothing else to do'.

Her first play begins:

WHAT HAPPENED[1]
A Five Act Play

Act I

(One.)
Loud and no cataract. Not any nuisance is depressing.
(Five.)
A single sum four and five together and one, not any sun a clear signal and an exchange.

Silence is in blessing and chasing and coincidences being ripe. A simple melancholy clearly precious and on the surface and surrounded and mixed strangely. A vegetable window and clearly most clearly an exchange in parts and complete.

A tiger a rapt and surrounded overcoat securely arranged with spots old enough to be thought useful and witty quite witty in a secret and in a blinding flurry.

While accepting the fact that Gertrude Stein did seriously intend such plays to be staged, it is also worth remembering that she adored playing the fool. 'If it can be done why do it', was one of her favourite sayings.

The idea of writing plays went quite to her head and presently she concluded that anything that was not a story could be a play. She made them out of advertisements or anything else that took her fancy and we get absurdities like this:

COUNTING HER DRESSES
A Play
PART I
Act I
When they did not see me.
I saw them again.
I did not like it.

[1] In *Geography and Plays*.

Act II
I count her dresses again.

Act III
Can you draw a dress.

Act IV
In a minute.

continuing for forty-one parts mostly of one-line acts.

Besides such plays she was still writing portraits and stories and pieces about places and races. Indeed, although no longer at work on an enormous book, between 1912 and 1914 her output was prodigious. Like Picasso, now using ripolin paints and making constructions in paper and in tin, she was overflowing with new ideas which made writing an adventure.

The other side of her life too was happy, for behind the changing social kaleidoscope was the unchanging devotion she had always needed. Yet something was missing from those earliest days of which both she and Picasso thought with nostalgia. She says that although this was not an unhappy time for him, after the Montmartre days one never heard his high whinnying Spanish giggle. And the only members of the old circle whom he saw regularly were Guillaume Apollinaire and herself.

Of her friend Mildred Aldrich she uses the phrase, 'she too was not unhappy but rather sad', which seems to give the colour of that time. Youth was over and with it had gone not the zest for living but some of the young century's exuberance. Gertrude Stein was now thirty-nine and the old life was on the wane.

CHAPTER TEN

WAR INTERLUDE

'I am also fond of saying that a war or fighting is like a dance
because it is all going forward and back, and that is what everybody likes they like that forward and back movement, that is the
reason that revolutions and Utopias are discouraging they are up
and down and not forward and back.'

Everybody's Autobiography.

In January 1913 Gertrude Stein received a letter which pleased
her very much.

17, Church Row, Hampstead

Dear Miss Stein

I have just read *Three Lives*. At first I was repelled by your
extraordinary style, I was busy with a book of my own and I
put yours away. It is only in the last week I have read it—
I read it with a deepening pleasure and admiration. I'm very
grateful indeed to you for sending it to me and I shall watch
for your name again very curiously and eagerly.

Very sincerely yrs

H. G. Wells

That same month, largely through the insistence of Myra
Edgerly, an artist from California 'who had miniatured everybody
and the royal family', the friends paid a short visit to England.
The main purpose was that Gertrude Stein should make personal
contact with John Lane, and she was indeed delighted to have her
first conversation with a publisher.

They enjoyed themselves so much that she forgot her early
dismal memories of London, but she did not like the country-
house visits as much as Miss Toklas who revelled in the gracious-
ness of the living and the beauty of the gardens and the interiors.
Her only complaint was that one had to wait so long for one's
breakfast coffee and make conversation while waiting, which did

not trouble Gertrude Stein who stayed in bed, although she was bothered by 'the never ceasing sound of the human voice speaking in english'.

Early in February she wrote from the Knightsbridge Hotel to Mabel Dodge:

> John Lane is an awfully funny man. He waits round and he asks a question and you think he has got you and then you find he hasn't. Roger Fry is going to try to help him land me . . . but the most unexpected interested person is Logan Pearsall Smith. He went quite off his head about your portrait and is reading it to everybody. Never goes anywhere without it and wants to do an article on it for the English Review. Among other things he read it to Zangwill and Zangwill was moved. He said 'And I always thought she was such a healthy minded young woman, what a terrible blow it must be for her poor dear brother.' And it seems he meant it. Then when L. would persist in reading it and re-reading it Z. got angry and said to Logan 'How can you waste your time reading and rereading a thing like that and all these years you've refused to read Kipling.' And the wonderful part of it was that Z. was not fooling.
>
> We have been seeing all kinds of people and last night we had an evening with Paul and Muriel [Draper]. We were there for dinner. [Robert de la] Condamine and the younger Rothenstein were there and Condamine and I got along beautifully . . .
>
> Roger Fry is being awfully good about my work. It seems that he read 3 Lives long ago and was much impressed with it and so he is doing his best to get me published. His being a Quaker gives him more penetration in his sweetness than is usual with his type, it does not make him more interesting but it makes him purer.

It was generous of Roger Fry to be so helpful, for he was at this time busy organizing the Omega Workshops.

In a later letter to Mabel Dodge Gertrude Stein speaks of hearing *Elektra*.

> I enjoyed it completely. It made a deeper impression on me than anything since Tristan in my youth. He has done what Wagner tried to do and couldn't he has made real

conversation and he does it by intervals and relations directly without machinery. After all we are all modern.

Altogether the visit was a success, and if spirits were damped by Austin Harrison, editor of the *English Review*, writing, 'Dear Madam, I really cannot publish these curious Studies', they were raised by the interest of the *Oxford Fortnightly* and there was a general sense of encouragement. And Mabel Dodge reported from New York, 'You are just on the eve of *bursting*! Everybody wherever I go—and others who go where I don't say the same thing—is talking of Gertrude Stein!'

Presently Donald Evans wrote to ask if his small firm Claire Marie might publish the plays of which he had heard from Mabel Dodge. He offered a distinguished format, much publicity and the most civilized public in America. She would not let him have the plays however, because she wanted them produced first, and gave him *Tender Buttons* instead.

On the return to Paris the final break was made with Leo. He was generous over the division of their now valuable collection of pictures. All the Renoirs, all the Matisses except 'La Femme au Chapeau' and most of the smaller Cézannes he took to his house near Florence.

Gertrude kept the rest, including the Picassos, but presently sold some of these to Kahnweiler and bought new ones. 'La Fillette sur la Boule' and several other Picassos originally in the Stein collection were subsequently bought from Kahnweiler by Russian collectors and are now in Moscow.

Leo's letter about the separation ends: 'I hope that we will all live happily ever after and maintain our respective and due proportions while sucking gleefully our respective oranges.' At the end of his life he repudiated the widespread belief that there had been a 'feud' between him and Gertrude.[1] Be this as it may, the brother and sister never met again and in later letters Leo was aloof and cynical about her. For her part Gertrude preferred not to hear him talked of; she was bitter now about his early domination and later lack of understanding. All her youth she had bowed to his judgment, but when years after the separation she saw a

[1] Leo Stein died in 1947, a year after Gertrude Stein.

familiar, but for the moment unrecognized, face in the street she wrote a poem with the line: 'She bowed to her brother. Accidentally. When she saw him.'

At the time Leo left, Gertrude and Alice Toklas also intended moving from the rue de Fleurus. They had chosen an apartment overlooking the gardens of the Palais Royal, but finding that they could not have the new premises altered to their requirements, they decided to stay on in the old ones and improve them by building a little covered way so that one did not have to go out of doors to reach the atelier.

Mabel Dodge arrived back from America with a *collection de jeunes gens assortis*, among whom was the young writer Carl Van Vechten. Gertrude Stein's first note to him is characteristic:

May 31, 1913

My dear Van Vechten,
    Will you dine with us tomorrow Saturday evening at 7:30. Let me know immediately.

Yours sincerely,

He accepted formally though not so brusquely and a lasting friendship was begun.

This was an exciting season. Now came the first performances of Stravinsky's ballet *Le Sacre du Printemps* which set Paris in an uproar. Gertrude Stein, who went to the second performance, said there was so much commotion in the theatre that she did not hear a single note of the music. However, she enjoyed the dancing, 'Nijinsky did not dance in the Sacre du Printemps but he created the dance for those who did.'

The whole year, 1913–14, was one of rising excitement fanned by approaching doom, although 'Americans living in Europe before the war never really believed that there was going to be a war.' But war was in the very air and Gertrude Stein now began to find the press interesting. She still did not read French newspapers but she added the English *Daily Mail* to her American *Herald*.

She liked to read about the suffragettes and she liked to read about Lord Roberts' campaign for compulsory military service in England. Lord Roberts had been a favourite hero of

hers early in her life. His Forty-One Years in India was a
book she often read . . . She read the Daily Mail, although, as
she said, she was not interested in Ireland.

She was not interested in women's suffrage either, but only in
the character of the suffragettes. She considered Emily Davison,
the woman who threw herself in front of the King's horse at the
Derby, a heroine, and at the end of her life she wrote an opera
about Susan B. Anthony, the American champion of women's
rights. Although she herself had insisted on equal rights in her
education she cared little for the cause. Responsive as she was to
human nature she was aloof from the topics of the day.

In June 1914 her new book was published in New York and
the *Chicago Tribune* commented:

> *Tender Buttons* is the most recent product of Miss Gertrude
> Stein, the literary cubist. Miss Stein, an affluent American
> resident in Paris, has been for years the high Priestess of the
> New Artists, the Cubists and Futurists. Her own gyrations
> with words have been printed before, but Privately. *Tender
> Buttons* is the first volume to be vouchsafed the Public.
> It is a nightmare journey in unknown and uncharted seas.
> Miss Stein's followers believe she has added a new dimension
> to literature. Scoffers call her writings a mad jumble of words,
> and some of them suspect that she is having a sardonic joke
> at the expense of those who profess to believe in her.
> . . . It is not clear whether 'Tender' of the title means a
> row boat, a fuel car attached to a locomotive or is an
> expression of human emotion . . .

This is typical of the reviews the book received, which disappointed the author for although she allowed herself to be out-
rageously funny she wanted her work taken seriously.

On 5 July the friends set off for England again, expecting this
to be as short a visit as the last. On the first Sunday they went
to a party at John Lane's house, in the course of which, although
the conversation was chiefly about war, Lane told Gertrude Stein
that his wife and his readers were enthusiastic about *Three Lives*
and asked her to come to his office to sign a contract.

A visit to Cambridge followed. They met many new people,
including A. E. Housman and the Alfred Whiteheads—Dr.

Whitehead being the third genius of Alice Toklas's trio—and returned to London in the highest of spirits.

There they occupied themselves with ordering a large and sumptuously upholstered couch and armchairs to replace some of the Italian furniture Leo had removed. 'This took a great deal of time. We had to measure ourselves into the chairs and into the couch and to choose chintz that would go with the pictures, all of which we successfully achieved.' A more extraordinary achievement was the arrival of this bulky furniture at the rue de Fleurus after the outbreak of war. The only difficulty was how to install it, for they had closed up the door to the studio and it was too big to go into the *pavillon*, but with much French commotion this was at last achieved.

Having dined in London with the Whiteheads—Dr. Whitehead had now moved from Cambridge to London University—at the end of July Gertrude Stein and Alice Toklas were invited to their country house at Lockridge. 'As one of my friends said to me later, they asked you to spend the week end and you stayed six weeks. We did.'

How they were caught there by the war is vividly described in *The Autobiography*. They were determined to get back to Paris as soon as possible, but Mrs. Whitehead insisted on their remaining meanwhile at Lockridge. She had French blood and strong French sympathies and what with this and her son's departure for the front she was profoundly troubled. But this did not prevent her from immediately organizing help for the Belgians.

Gertrude and Alice went to London to get their trunks and to see about money. The former's letter of credit on a French bank was useless, but Alice managed to cash the small remainder of a Californian draft, while Gertrude cabled for funds to her cousin Julian Stein in Baltimore.

Back at Lockridge Alice Toklas helped Mrs. Whitehead, while Gertrude Stein and Dr. Whitehead went for long walks.

> Gertrude Stein used to come back and tell me [Alice Toklas] about these walks and the country still the same as in the days of Chaucer, with the green paths of the early britons that could still be seen in long stretches, and the triple rainbows of that strange summer.

In the course of these conversations she conceived a great admiration for Whitehead, the most profound thinker she had met since William James, and not only for his mind but for his nature. Referring to his appreciation of Bertrand Russell and their collaboration in *Principia Mathematica* she wrote: 'Doctor Whitehead, the gentlest and most simply generous of human beings never claimed anything for himself.'

Gertrude Stein believed that Whitehead influenced her writing and he, although not seeing how, was satisfied that if she said so it must be true. In any case, it is not difficult to see how she would have been stimulated by him, alert as he was to what he called 'the delicate inner truth of art', and concerned, like Gertrude Stein and the visual artists of the time, with the relation of appearance to reality. His opinions, although she did not agree with all of them—he, for instance, holding that truth in art without beauty must sink to triviality, and she that beauty was often an obstacle to truth—were on the whole an intellectual confirmation of much that she intuitively felt. To talk philosophy and history with such a man was sheer delight.

Bertrand Russell was one of the people who often 'turned up' at the Whiteheads'. He came on the day that their son left for the front, making it hard for them, old friends though they were, to bear his pacifism. Gertrude Stein describes how in order to divert their minds from the war she introduced the subject of education and 'fussed' Mr. Russell with her views. He had been deploring the American neglect of Greek and she declared that Greek was essentially an island culture and therefore useful to England, while America needed the culture of a continent, to which the answer was Latin.

> She grew very eloquent on the disembodied abstract quality of the american character and cited examples, mingling automobiles with Emerson, and all proving that they did not need greek, in a way that fussed Russell more and more and kept everybody occupied until everybody went to bed.

Lytton Strachey, living nearby, was another visitor.

> He was a thin sallow man with a silky beard and a faint high voice. We had met him the year before when we had been

invited to meet George Moore at the house of Miss Ethel Sands. Gertrude Stein and George Moore, who looked very like a prosperous Mellins Food baby, had not been interested in each other . . .

She recalls Lytton Strachey's inability to ask for an interview with someone Mrs. Whitehead thought might help to rescue his sister from Germany. 'Not', replied Lytton Strachey faintly, 'if I have never met him.' This showed, indeed, more than ordinary shyness, but Gertrude and Alice were often struck by this English trait which they found attractive. Americans, they held, were never shy.

Another story of these Lockridge days tells how 'Mrs. Bishop', the wife of Dr. Whitehead's bishop brother, solemnly suggested to Gertrude Stein that as she was a neutral and an important person in Paris she should 'suggest to the french government that they give us Pondichéry'. Gertrude Stein replied politely that her importance such as it was was not among politicians, and after lunch said to Alice Toklas under her breath, 'where the hell is Pondichéry'.

It would, however, be misleading if such anecdotes were to suggest that at this tense moment Gertrude Stein was frivolous.

> The germans were getting nearer and nearer Paris and the last day Gertrude Stein could not leave her room, she sat and mourned. She loved Paris, she thought neither of manuscripts [Dr. Whitehead was worried about hers] nor of pictures, she thought only of Paris and she was desolate. I [Alice Toklas] came up to her room, I called out, it is alright Paris is saved, the germans are in retreat. She turned away and said, don't tell me these things. But it's true, I said, it is true. And then we wept together.

Her views on Germany, as she thought back to them while writing The Autobiography in 1931, are particularly interesting in view of her own German heritage.

> Gertrude Stein used to get furious when the english all talked about german organisation. She used to insist that the germans had no organisation, they had method but no organisation. Don't you understand the difference, she used to say angrily, any two americans, any twenty americans,

any millions of americans can organise themselves to do something but germans cannot organise themselves to do anything, they can formulate a method and this method can be put upon them but that isn't organisation. The germans, she used to insist, are not modern, they are a backward people who have made a method of what we conceive as organisation, can't you see. They cannot therefore possibly win this war because they are not modern.

Then another thing that used to annoy us dreadfully was the english statement that the germans in America would turn America against the allies. Don't be silly, Gertrude Stein used to say to any and all of them, if you do not realise that the fundamental sympathy in America is with France and England and could never be with a mediaeval country like Germany, you cannot understand America. We are republican, she used to say with energy, profoundly intensely and completely a republic and a republic can have everything in common with France and a great deal in common with England but whatever its form of government nothing in common with Germany.

Presently funds arrived from Gertrude Stein's cousin and Alice Toklas's father, and the American Embassy provided temporary passports. By the fifteenth of October Thomas Cook advised that they could travel and they left London with Mrs. Whitehead. Tragic though these days were one is almost nostalgic for a war in which a mother, albeit with papers from the War Office and Lord Kitchener, could follow her son abroad so as to take him the overcoat and revolver he had left behind. Nor did the other women have any difficulty in visiting their friend Mildred Aldrich[1] who had chosen this summer to move for quietness to a house on the Marne and had already had battles fought all round her.

In the autumn of 1914:

There were not many people in Paris just then and we liked it and we wandered around Paris and it was so nice to be there, wonderfully nice.

But then came a dreary winter with darkened lights and

[1] Author of *A Hilltop on the Marne*.

Zeppelin alarms and even Paris was gloomy. On December the third Gertrude Stein wrote to Carl Van Vechten, 'I suppose hell is lively and the war isn't that', and added, 'everybody who intends to be back is back by now. This doesn't refer to Germans.' She told him that all the Paris artists were having a bad time and would have a harder one and that she herself needed to earn some money. 'After all I've got ten years work and I want to dispose of some of it.' She had already written to Mabel Weeks, whose efforts to further her work were unceasing. 'I know I am doing more important things than any of my contemporaries and waiting for publication gets on my nerves.'

According to *The Autobiography*:

> Picasso and Eva were living these days on the rue Schoelcher in a rather sumptuous studio apartment that looked over the cemetery. It was not very gay. The only excitement were the letters from Guillaume Apollinaire who was falling off horses in the endeavour to become an artilleryman. The only other intimates at that time were a russian whom they called G. Apostrophe and his sister the baronne. They bought all the Rousseaus that were in Rousseau's atelier when he died . . . Picasso learnt the Russian alphabet from them and began putting it into some of his pictures.

Indeed it was not gay for Picasso with Eva's health failing and his friends dispersed—Braque and Derain had been called up and Apollinaire, not being a French subject, had volunteered for service, but Gertrude Stein had the distraction of a friendship with another Spaniard, the painter Juan Gris,[1] then in his late twenties.

She had liked Gris's work at once and had bought two of his paintings from Kahnweiler shortly before the war. Then, Kahnweiler being a German subject, his gallery was taken over by the authorities while he sought refuge in Switzerland. This was a disaster for the artist, but although Gertrude Stein sent him some money, he would not sell her other pictures in spite of his sore straits, out of loyalty to his dealer. This caused a temporary breach between them, but Juan Gris nevertheless became after Picasso her dearest friend.

[1] See *Juan Gris: His Life and Work* by, Daniel-Henry Kahnweiler (Lund Humphries).

For a while he lived in one of the old studios in the rue Ravignan, and Gertrude Stein's visits to Montmartre began again. She says 'Juan was in those days a tormented and not particularly sympathetic character. He was very melancholy and effusive and as always clear sighted and intellectual.' She often declared that she did not like intellectuals, but in *The Autobiography* she wrote:

> Juan Gris also conceived exactitude but in him exactitude had a mystical basis. As a mystic it was necessary for him to be exact. In Gertrude Stein the necessity was intellectual, a pure passion for exactitude. It is because of this that her work has often been compared to that of mathematicians and by a certain french critic to the work of Bach.
>
> Picasso by nature the most endowed had less clarity of intellectual purpose. He was in his creative activity dominated by spanish ritual, later by negro ritual . . . and later by russian ritual . . .

Picasso was not pleased with her enthusiasm for Juan Gris. How could he have been? A young painter, a Spaniard, living in the rue Ravignan, when he himself had such nostalgia for the old Montmartre days that he hated to hear them talked of. He never liked being reminded of the past; besides he thought that Gertrude Stein was overrating the younger man's work.

During this winter too she first heard the music of Erik Satie. Later, through Virgil Thomson, she came to know him, and he was also a close friend of Marie Laurencin's. From the beginning she liked his work. While continuing to say that her ears meant nothing to her and that she had no use for music, she was always belying the statement. Birdsong, waves, the sound of traffic, a dog's lapping, all contributed at one time or another to her writing, and her ear was as quick as her eye for the painters to recognize in Satie a fellow pioneer, one who had broken from Wagnerladen nineteenth-century tradition, who refused to imitate and was seeking lost purity in a simple form.

In February 1915 a letter to Van Vechten reported:

> I am writing sentimental novels and I like doing them, three at a time. They are very good I think only just begun.

This month she sold 'La Femme au Chapeau' to the Michael

Steins for five hundred dollars in order to have more cash in hand. They spent the war in the South of France, but Leo returned to America. In March Gertrude wrote:

> We are rather full up with war and expect to stay some weeks in Palma where they haven't got it. The zeppelins didn't make much noise and what there was rather barrel like and soft but the alarm does.

They had been to Majorca and liked it and they had there a good friend in William Cook, an American painter with a French wife who could be relied upon to help them with all arrangements. They took a little house in Palma, sent for the Bretonne servant who had succeeded Hélène at the rue de Fleurus, and settled down contentedly with a plentiful supply of books from Mudie's Library. Gertrude read Queen Victoria's letters aloud to Alice and went on writing and walking. And they ate extremely well. In May Carl Van Vechten was briefly in prison over a matter of alimony for his first wife and Gertrude wrote:

> Do get out soon. We are peacefully on our island. Cigarettes are excellent and contraband. The natives piratical but round faced.

In August she said:

> We have just been to Valencia for a week and saw all that there is to see of bull fights. Gallo, Gallito, and Belmonte . . . it's the only thing that can make you forget the war that is it's the only thing that made me forget the war.[1]

They returned to Palma and with a few Americans and other foreigners lived on there contentedly enough. The islanders continually discussed how many millions of pesetas the war was costing; a German governess hung out her flag every time there was a German victory, and the allies and their friends did the same on the rare occasions when their side won. The waiter at the hotel looked forward to Spain coming in with the allies; the Bretonne maid wore a tricolour on her hat and Gertrude Stein knitted for

[1] Further correspondence between Gertrude Stein and Carl Van Vechten marked 'C.V.V.' at foot of page.

the soldiers, progressing from slow to quick and from quick to being able to read and knit at the same time.

At the end of the year came one of Picasso's rare letters, telling her that Eva was desperately ill and that he was spending half his time in the Métro journeying to and from the nursing home. All the same he had done a painting of a harlequin that was said to be one of his best, and he ended the letter: 'Enfin ma vie est bien remplie et come toutjours je ne me arrete pas' [sic]. A month later he wrote:

8 janvier 1916

Ma chère Gertrude,
    Ma pauvre Eva est morte . . . une grande douleur pour moi . . . elle a été tout jours si bonne pour moi.
    Moi aussi je serais bien content de vous voir depuis si longtemps que nous sommes separes. Je aurais été bien content de parler à une amie comme vous [sic].
                                                        Picasso.[1]

Throughout this spring Gertrude Stein was working at her plays. 'Conversations are easy but backgrounds are difficult',[2] but on the whole she was pleased with her results. 'I have been working very prettily. I have done several plays and some funny things quite a number of funny things.'[3] A fortnight later she added:

Alas about every three months I get sad. I make so much absorbing literature with such attractive titles and even if I could be as popular as Jenny Lind where oh where is the man to publish me in series. Perhaps some day you will meet him. He can do me as simply and cheaply as he likes but I would so like to be done. Alas.[4]

But now the mood of the islanders had changed. 'We were all desperately unhappy. I had been so confident and now I had an awful feeling that the war had gotten out of my hands.' In *The Autobiography* is this description of a German ship which had been caught by the war in the port of Palma.

It looked very rusty and neglected and it was just under our windows. All of a sudden as the attack on Verdun com-

[1] Yale Collection, unpublished.   [2] C.V.V.   [3] Ibid.   [4] Ibid.

menced they began painting the Fangturm. Imagine our feelings. We were all pretty unhappy and this was despair. We told the french consul and he told us and it was awful.

Day by day the news was worse and one whole side of the Fangturm was painted and then they stopped painting. They knew it before we did. Verdun was not going to be taken.

After this Gertrude Stein, Alice Toklas and William Cook were determined to get into the war, and Cook and Gertrude did nothing but talk about automobilies. They reached Paris without difficulty, where Cook, having learnt to drive and being penniless, became a taxi driver. Then on dark nights outside the Paris fortifications he taught Gertrude Stein to drive the old two-cylinder Renault taxi.

Gertrude Stein now asked her New York relatives to collect funds to send over a Ford motor-van for her to drive for the American Fund for French Wounded. Meanwhile 'it was a changed Paris . . . and everybody was cheerful'.

Picasso moved out to Montrouge and once more brought many people to the rue de Fleurus including Satie, whom they all enjoyed, not least because he was a gourmet. And then:

> One day Picasso came in and with him and leaning on his shoulder was a slim elegant youth. It is Jean, announced Pablo, Jean Cocteau and we are leaving for Italy.
>
> Picasso had been excited at the prospect of doing the scenery for a russian ballet,[1] the music to be by Satie, the drama by Jean Cocteau. Everybody was at the war, life in Parnasse was not very gay, Montrouge with even a faithful servant was not very lively, he too needed a change. He was very lively at the prospect of going to Rome. We all said goodbye and we all went our various ways.

In this same winter of 1916–17 they met Mary Borden and her English husband, Captain Turner. 'She was very enthusiastic about the work of Gertrude Stein . . . and Gertrude Stein was immensely interested in her and in Chicago.' The friends found it, moreover, pleasant to visit the house near the Bois from which Mary Borden travelled to and from the hospital she was running

[1] *Parade* for Diaghilev.

at the Front, for it was heated and coal was scarce. On occasion, the police themselves helped to get fuel for the rue de Fleurus.

The Ford arrived early in 1917, but its truck body had still to be built. 'We waited a great deal', and meanwhile Gertrude Stein wrote little war poems. But at last it was ready and they christened it 'Auntie' after Gertrude's Aunt Pauline, 'who always behaved admirably in emergencies and behaved fairly well most times if she was properly flattered'. On the first drive they stalled between two street-cars and everyone got out and pushed them off the track. On the second, 'Auntie' stopped dead in the Champs-Elysées and Gertrude Stein cranked and the crowd cranked until they discovered that there was no petrol. These small setbacks did not prevent the friends from reporting immediately for duty with the A.F.F.W., Gertrude Stein to be the driver and Alice Toklas to do everything else.

They were sent off to distribute hospital supplies in the Per-pignan region. It was an adventurous journey through the snows with Gertrude an inexperienced but forceful driver who once started in any direction, right or wrong, had to go on because she could not reverse. In fact she never learnt to do this well. 'She goes forward admirably, she does not go backwards success-fully.' Perhaps this observation applies not only to her driving but to her character. Certainly she never did retract.

Naturally, there were many vicissitudes on the way, but there was always a soldier or some other man to change the tyre or repair the car. 'This faculty of Gertrude Stein of having every-body do anything for her puzzled the other drivers of the organi-zation', but she explained that it was because she was not efficient, she was good-humoured and democratic and knew what she wanted done. 'The important thing, she insists, is that you must have deep down as the deepest thing in you a sense of equality. Then anybody will do anything for you.'

Driving night and day down the lonely roads they gave lifts to any soldier they saw and in this way made 'military godsons'. They found out all about the families of these French soldiers and afterwards kept in touch, regularly sending them parcels and answering their letters at length. There has been some derision over Gertrude Stein's affection for the G.I.'s at the close of the

Gertrude Stein's parents

Stein Collection, Yale University Library

The Stein children in Vienna with governess and tutor

Stein Collection, Yale University Library

Gertrude Stein at the age of four

Stein Collection, Yale University Library

Gertrude Stein at the age
of nineteen

*Stein Collection, Yale University
Library*

The studio at 27
rue de Fleurus,
1910

*Stein Collection, Yale
University Library*

'The Bathers' by Cézanne, 1895

Cone Collection, Baltimore Museum of Art

'Group of Artists' by Marie Laurencin, 1908

Cone Collection, Baltimore Museum of Art

'La Femme au Chapeau' by Matisse, 1905

Mrs. Walter Haas

Portrait of Leo Stein by Picasso, 1906

Cone Collection, Baltimore Museum of Art

Portrait of Kahnweiler by Picasso,
1910

Galerie Louise Leiris

Once an angry man

~~There is~~ ... ~~that~~ tell

of a ~~man who~~ ... ...

~~an~~ dragged his ~~old~~ father along

the ground through his own orchard

"Stop!" cried ~~out~~ the groaning old

man at last, ~~stop~~ I did not

drag my father beyond this

tree."

It is a ~~very~~ **hard work** ~~to~~ living down

the tempers we are born with. We

~~all~~ begin well, for in our youth there

is nothing we are more intolerant of

Beginning of script of The Making of Americans

Stein Collection, Yale University Library

Picasso, 1924, by Man Ray

Man Ray, Paris

Head by Picasso, 1907

Galerie Louise Leiris

Gertrude Stein during the First
World War

Stein Collection, Yale University Library

Gertrude Stein during the Second
World War

Stein Collection, Yale University Library

Gertrude Stein in 1930 by Man Ray

Man Ray, Paris

'Basket' by Man Ray

Man Ray, Paris

Gertrude Stein by Picabia, 1933

Stein Collection, Yale University Library

Gertrude Stein by Jo Davidson, 1923

Stein Collection, Yale University Library

Gertrude Stein in 1928 by George Platt Lynes

George Platt Lynes

Gertrude Stein and Alice Toklas at the Palais Idéal of the Facteur
Cheval at Hautrives, Provence, 1939

Cecil Beaton

27 rue de Fleurus

Photo Leirens

'The House Across the Valley' (Bilignin) by Francis Rose

Sir Francis Rose, Bart

Gertrude Stein at Lucey Church

Gertrude Stein and Alice Toklas in America

ertrude Stein with Picasso at Bilignin

Gertrude Stein at rue Christine shortly before her death

Cecil Beaton

Second World War; but that feeling was not new. She liked these French godsons of the first war and the men in the hospitals to whom she and Alice Toklas personally presented the American 'comfort-bags', but when the Americans arrived she loved the doughboys best of all. And the soldiers, in spite of Miss Stein's appearance being very odd, specially to the eyes of a Frenchman, loved her. Nobody at this time, neither soldiers nor authorities, even when these were American, knew that she was a writer. Mrs. Methol, whose mother ran a hospital near Nîmes which 'Auntie' often visited, says that all that they then knew of Gertrude Stein's peace-time life was that she liked food and pictures. She was interested in the house because it had been built for the Quakers by Elizabeth Fry, and both staff and patients found her the most kindly and cheering visitor. It was only when Mrs. Methol afterwards spoke of Gertrude Stein to her cousin Joseph Hone in Dublin that she discovered that she was a well-known writer.

Tender Buttons had indeed, even if only through being ridiculed, made the author better known, and a few small things were being published. The short-lived magazine *Rogue* took a piece called *Aux Galeries Lafayette* which brought her a welcome cheque—it was satisfying to earn money, however little—and Carl Van Vechten wrote that he was much in demand for reading it aloud. In June 1917 *Vanity Fair* printed *Have they attacked Mary. He giggled. (A Political Caricature)*, which has nothing political about it and is a *genre* portrait of several people, including the art critic Henry McBride. Now instead of two-line 'acts' she had one or two-line 'pages', mocking the hide-bound and the pompous, but surely laughing too at her own long-windedness, and inviting the reader to laugh with her.

PAGE XXII.

Believe me in everything.

PAGE XXIII.

I can go.
Don't remind the English.

PAGE XXIV.

You mean of everything.

PAGE XXV.

It is wonderful the way I am not interested.

And so on.

In December *Life* published her 'little poems', *Relief Work in France*, printed all in capitals. The first goes:

ADVANCE

In coming to a village we ask them can they come to see us, we mean near enough to talk: and then we ask them how do we go there.

This is not fanciful.

And the last one:

AGAIN

When the camellias are finished, the roses begin.
Are the French people healthy?
I think them healthy.
And as to their institutions, there is no doubt that they like a park.
And forests?
In the sense in which you mean, yes.
That is a question I meant to ask.
It is answered.

This was the present trend. She now had little time for writing, but like Picasso she never really stopped.

Leo broke silence only to send his sister without comment an extract from one of their Aunt Rachel's letters from Vienna, 'Our little Gertie is a little Schnatterer.' But she had news of him from a New York connection:

Leo . . . is psycho-analysing and being psycho-analysed, philosophizing and perambulating; also, he is writing things that are being published. And, of course, everything he writes justifies itself through the detachedness and clarity of its view-point. . . . (I am reminded here that the clarity is only perceptible to the elect.)

Truly this brother and sister were the other ends of the same stick.

By the time of the return journey to Paris in blazing heat, America had come into the war and at Nevers the women were thrilled to meet 'the first piece of the american army', the first 'americans just americans, the kind that would not naturally ever have come to Europe'. Gertrude Stein talked to the men and she talked to the French girls about them and henceforward maintained that to get to know Americans 'the war was so much better than just going to America'. She was particularly interested in the differences in the men from different states and contemplated writing about this.

They were only in Paris for a short time before being sent to Nîmes where American troops soon arrived. Gertrude Stein enjoyed her compatriots so much that at this point in *The Autobiography* she says that she would like to tell nothing but doughboy stories, and she beautifully observes the differences between the Americans and the French working side by side on the railroads; the Americans working too concentratedly to stand the long French hours. 'There was a great deal of friendly rivalry. The American boys did not see the use of putting so much finish on work that was to be shot up so soon again, the french said they could not complete work without finish. But both lots thoroughly liked each other.'

The A.F.F.W. delegates were now extremely busy—the hardest part of the job for Gertrude was having to get up early which had never been her habit. Also she did not like making practical use of her medical training, but when a French doctor requested her to attend the sickbed of an American soldier or even his operation, she considered it her duty to comply.

We are fortunate to have a first-hand description of Miss Stein and Miss Toklas at this time from W. G. Rogers, their first Nîmes doughboy, who years later became a close friend. Mr. Rogers, author and arts editor of the Associated Press, was nicknamed by the ladies 'The Kiddie', as which he appears in text and photograph in *Everybody's Autobiography*. In his book *When This You See Remember Me, Gertrude Stein in Person*[1] he tells us that, abandoning campus for camp at the end of his junior year in college, he volunteered for service. On furlough in the fall of 1917 he decided to see something of Roman Provence, and booked the cheapest room in the best hotel at Nîmes.

Early in the evening he followed a pair of oddly dressed

[1] Rinehart and Company Inc., New York, 1948.

women from lobby into dining room and thus for the first
time laid surprised and amused eyes on Miss Stein and Miss
Toklas.

Though both were short, one had twice the girth of the
other. The sturdy and stocky Miss Stein walked with a slow,
deliberate tread, as if walking were more than a means of
locomotion. Miss Toklas, slight, wiry and nervous, moved
with a quicker step. Viewed from the rear, it was tramp
tramp tramp against a canter, ponderous half notes overlaid
with lively eighths . . .

Compared to this couple, the overalled farmerettes at
whom the folks back home were gawping were incon-
spicuous. Miss Toklas wore a sort of uniform, a skirt and
long cloak over it, belted, with baggy unbuttoned, official-
looking pockets like those sported by British officers. Both
had helmet-shaped hats, Miss Toklas' over hair clipped short
and Miss Stein's over hair which was still long. Miss Stein
dressed even more outlandishly, with sandals buckled on over
the ankles, a full skirt, knitted vest and shirt-waist with sleeves
gathered at the wrists—in the uniforms of Greek Evzones, at
least from the hips up, there was something of the same
bizarre fashion . . .

With Miss Toklas the mode, if the word may apply to
something so unrelated to modish, was military; in Miss
Stein's case it was homely with no elegance at all, and still
somehow regal.

Rogers admits that for a young, self-conscious New Englander
the appearance of these two women, then in their early forties,
was formidable, but he quickly came to appreciate Miss Toklas's
dark attractiveness and sparkle and to find Miss Stein's face distinguished and beautiful, reminding him 'of eighteen-inch sculpture which mysteriously produces an eighteen-foot effect'. And
of course he liked her laughter which 'would sometimes rumble
like thunder'. How often that laughter has been described!

They invited him to tea and he found that they were the most
fascinating conversationalists, delving into the field of ideas with
flashes of gossip and scandal. They made him tell them everything about himself, and Miss Toklas explained that they lived
in Paris and that Miss Stein wrote. This was the only time her
work was mentioned.

The Kiddie now went out every day with his new friends in 'Auntie', but conditions were firmly decreed by Miss Toklas. He must fix the car if anything went wrong; they must be back by nightfall as Miss Stein did not like driving in the dark; he must sit on the floor with his feet on the running-board so that there would be every inch as much room for Miss Stein as if he were not there.

> I sat on a pillow, half out the open door, my knees up under my chin, and I crowded Miss Toklas but not Miss Stein. Miss Toklas has devoted practically all her adult life to the prevention of any crowding of Gertrude Stein. Alone by themselves, Miss Toklas was 'Pussy' and Miss Stein 'Lovey' and a deep attachment united them for almost half a century. Miss Toklas determinedly put Miss Stein on a higher level and stayed carefully, even religiously, off it; she deferred, played second fiddle, knew her place.[1]

So they sightsaw, and 'every minute of the furlough was an education for this lucky doughboy', to whom Gertrude Stein gave the impression 'that nothing in the world mattered to her so much as showing me the marvels and beauties of the region'.

His leave over, Rogers returned to the front and after the exchange of a few letters intercourse ceased. He did not see these strange fascinating friends again for very many years.

Early in 1918 came a letter from Picasso 'announcing his marriage to a jeune fille'—Olga Khokhlova, whom he had met in Rome while designing *Parade*. As 'a wedding present' he sent Gertrude Stein a little painting and a photograph of a portrait of his wife. Soon afterwards she and Alice saw Braque and his wife in Avignon—he had been invalided out of the army with a severe head wound—and in the course of much welcome gossip about their friends heard 'that Apollinaire too had married a real young lady'.[2]

'Time went on, we were very busy and then came the Armistice. We were the first to bring the news to many villages.' They were at once ordered to Alsace and on the mud-bogged roads, crowded with French armies on the move, had their only acci-

---

[1] *When This You See Remember Me*, pp. 13–14.
[2] See p. 196 *Testimony against Gertrude Stein*.

dent, the car being hit by a horse-drawn army kitchen. However, with American and French help they were soon on their way again and reached the battlefields which Gertrude Stein found, in the words of a French nurse, 'un pays passionant'.

> Another thing that interested us enormously was how different the camouflage of the french looked from the camouflage of the germans, and then once we came across some very very neat camouflage and it was american. The idea was the same but as after all it was different nationalities who did it the difference was inevitable. The colour schemes were different, the designs were different, the way of placing them was different, it made plain the whole theory of art and its inevitability.

From Strasbourg they went on to Mulhouse where they stayed until May 1919, distributing blankets and clothing to families returning to their ruined homes.

> There was a legend that the quantity of babies' booties sent to us came from the gifts sent to Mrs. Wilson who was supposed at that time to be about to produce a little Wilson. There were a great many babies' booties but not too many for Alsace.

At last they went home 'by way of Metz, Verdun and Mildred Aldrich'.

They had been with the Whiteheads at Lockridge when war was declared and now Mrs. Whitehead had come to Paris with the Peace Commission and they watched the victory procession from her hotel overlooking the Arc de Triomphe.

> Gertrude Stein remembered that when as a child she used to swing on the chains that were around the Arc de Triomphe her governess had told her that no one must walk underneath since the german armies had marched under it after 1870. And now everybody except the germans were passing through.
>
> All the nations marched differently, some slowly, some quickly, the french carrying their flags the best of all . . .
>
> However it all finally came to an end. We wandered up and we wandered down the Champs Elysées and the war was over and the piles of captured cannon that had made two pyramids were being taken away and peace was upon us.

CHAPTER ELEVEN

THE FIRST DISCIPLES

'Picasso used to say during the war will it not be awful when
Braque and Derain and all the rest of them put their wooden
legs up on the chair and tell about the fighting, but it never did
enter his head that their generation would completely not think
about those happenings and that if they did he would not be
there to listen as they were certainly not to see each other often.'

Everybody's Autobiography.

THE war was over, but 'the old crowd' had disappeared. Matisse
was living in Nice, Braque and Picasso had gone their separate
ways, and Guillaume Apollinaire was dead.

Of the breach between Picasso and Braque, which was in fact
slight, Gertrude Stein tells this anecdote. Braque happened to be
at the rue de Fleurus when Man Ray brought over one of his
photographs of Picasso. It was handed round and 'when it came
to Braque he looked at it and said I ought to know who that
gentleman is, je dois connaître ce monsieur'.

Then there was Juan Gris who, although Kahnweiler soon came
back, opened his gallery and helped him again, was 'ill and discouraged', and difficult to get on with. Moreover Gertrude
Stein and Picasso, now living with his wife in the rue de la
Boétie, quarrelled, although neither of them knew why. 'They
always talked with the tenderest friendship about each other to
anyone who had known them both but they did not see each
other.'

This was one of the periods which Gertrude Stein later cele-
brated with a piece entitled *A History of having for a long time not
continued to be friends*, but Leo did now make a move towards re-
conciliation. Having spent the war in America, partly on a farm
of Mabel Dodge's, he returned to Italy late in 1919, and wrote
from Settignano:

Dear Gertrude,

I sent you a note from New York before I left as I found
that the antagonism that had grown up some years ago had
gotten dissipated and that I felt quite amiable, rather more so
even than I used to feel before that strain developed. It's
rather curious, the change that has come over me in the last
month or so. You know all those digestive troubles, and most
of the others that I had I eventually found to be merely
neurotic symptoms, and all the time in America I was trying
to cure the neurosis. But they're damned hard things to
cure . . . Then, indirectly . . . I got on a tack that has led to
better states. This has finally led to an easing up and simpli-
fying of most of my contacts with things and people and
brought about a condition where it was possible to write to
you. The fact that I was coming to Europe had nothing to
do with it, as I was thinking of writing anyway. 'The family
romance' as it is called is almost always central in the case of
a neurosis, just as you used to get indigestion when we had a
dispute. So I could tell pretty well how I was getting on by
the degree of possibility I felt of writing as I am doing
now . . .[1]

He spoke of his past life as having been 'a kind of mild insanity'
and told his sister that his first attempts to be psycho-analysed had
failed. Otherwise, he assured her, his time in America would have
been successful, as there was a demand both for his writing and
his lecturing. But he never could be sure of himself in either capacity, and his deafness now made teaching impossible. He concluded the letter by saying that he was going to Algiers, but
did not mention that this was where Nina Auzias was living. He
sent his regards to Alice, but did not express any affection for his
sister or ask after herself or her work. In the spring of 1921 he and
Nina were married and set up house in Settignano.

So, although cousins and acquaintances now came flocking
from America and new people from everywhere filled the rue de
Fleurus, to see the pictures and enjoy the hospitality, nothing was
the same as before the war.

It was a changed Paris . . . We saw a tremendous number
of people but none of them as far as I can remember that we

[1] *Journey Into the Self.*

had ever known before. Paris was crowded. As Clive Bell remarked, they say that an awful lot of people were killed in the war but it seems to me that an extraordinary large number of grown men and women have suddenly been born.

The tragic death of Apollinaire at the age of thirty-eight had much to do with the break-up of the old circle, for he had, as Gertrude Stein says, 'a quality of holding people together', and his exuberance endeared him to his friends. After a head wound in 1916 his skull was twice trepanned and the deadly influenza of 1918 struck him down. He was passionately patriotic about the country of his adoption, which makes doubly ironic the story Gertrude Stein and others tell of him—that he thought, as he lay dying in Paris while the armistice was signed, that the shouts in the street of 'à bas Guillaume!' were meant for him.

Apollinaire had understood the Cubist movement better than any of its other exponents and had written of the painters with sympathy and conviction. Now pure Cubism was passing; indeed the whole heroic age, which Max Jacob claimed for Cubism but which had begun with Impressionism, was over. 'Pity made Picasso harsher', Apollinaire had written, although he was not to live to see how completely his words were proved, but at this moment Picasso was not harsh. *Parade* had, Gertrude Stein says, freed him, and the war by making people understand that things did change had forced them to accept him. He was painting more realistically again, portraits soon to be followed by his large nude women.

In general there was a lull in visual art after the shock of the war, a solstice in which Mondriaan returned to Paris, also liberated from Cubism but into the realm of abstraction, and the Surrealists began to incarnate their uneasy dreams. Gertrude Stein had no use for the Surrealists; she saw them at once as falsifiers of what had gone before, 'taking the matter for the manner as is the way of the vulgarisers. . . . The surréalistes are the vulgarisation of Picabia as Delaunay and his followers and the futurists were the vulgarisation of Picasso.' Picabia, although he tired her by talking too much—she often found the human voice fatiguing—was becoming one of her favourite painters.

Piet Mondriaan was born two years before Gertrude Stein in that decade which saw the birth of so many twentieth-century creators, among them Stravinsky, Schoenberg, Diaghilev, James Joyce and Jung. Gertrude Stein was not interested in Mondriaan, but as Pavel Tchelichew observed: 'Like Mondriaan she was assisting at a becoming, at the birth of a form.'[1]

Indeed, however different their expression of them, Mondriaan and Gertrude Stein evolved similar convictions as they worked to free painting and writing from associational emotion. Mondriaan declared that not only the visual arts but verbal art had become impure through writers using paraphrase and other indirect forms of expression instead of the word itself. And he believed that it would take longer for writing than for painting to liberate itself from its old limiting form.

Gertrude Stein, who had been writing steadily since she got back to Paris, was because of her idiosyncrasy and her aloofness from other writers still alone in her work. For that matter there never could be many at one time on such a path. As she says in *Picasso*, 'another vision than that of all the world is very rare'. None the less she was writing in an age of explorers who were sharpening their sensibilities to achieve the new experience in art that they had come to believe possible.

Mondriaan was making new paintings of horizontal and vertical lines with rectangles of the primary colours, Stravinsky, the Picasso of music, was waging the revolution begun by Erik Satie. Nor can one leave out Schoenberg or the American composer Charles Ives, both born in the same year as Gertrude Stein. When Ives was asked why he did not write music people might like he simply answered: 'I can't do it. *I hear something else*', and further remarked that 'initial coherence today may be dullness tomorrow'.

Thus the visual and musical explorers were creating their own time, while the field of writing, where Gertrude Stein had never been as alone as she believed, was now crowded with stream-of-consciousness novelists, Proust and James Joyce, Virginia Woolf, Dorothy Richardson, Sherwood Anderson and the rebel poets T. S. Eliot, Ezra Pound and E. E. Cummings. Gertrude Stein greatly admired Cummings's autobiographical novel *The Enor-*

[1] Author's journal.

mous Room, when it appeared in 1922, but of these writers Sherwood Anderson alone acknowledged her influence and became her friend.

E. M. Forster considers that Gertrude Stein inevitably failed in her attempt to abolish time in fiction and 'to express in it the life by values only', but he acclaims this as 'a noble motive' and adds: 'There is nothing to ridicule in such an experiment as hers. It is much more important to play about like this than to re-write the *Waverley Novels*.'[1]

Although Gertrude Stein had quickly resumed her writing habits conditions were no longer so easy.

> We had spent a great deal of our money during the war and we were economising, servants were difficult to get if not impossible, prices were high. We settled down for the moment with a femme de ménage for only a few hours a day. I [Alice Toklas] used to say Gertrude Stein was the chauffeur and I was the cook. We used to go over early in the morning to the public markets and get in our provisions. It was a confused world.

Even the car was a different one. 'Auntie', worn out with war service, had been replaced by 'Godiva,' a runabout Ford, so-called because she came to them naked and was gradually fitted out with necessary gadgets. And Gertrude Stein no longer wrote only at night, 'but anywhere, in between visits, in the automobile while she was waiting in the street . . . while posing'. For although she did not like sculpture, she did like sitting for sculptors, and in 1921 posed for Lipchitz who made a life-size bronze of her head.[2] He had just finished a bust of Jean Cocteau, and through him she met Jean Cocteau again and was delighted to find that he had quoted from *The Portrait of Mabel Dodge* in his *Potomak*. He was the first French writer to mention her work. And presently she sat again in her most characteristic pose, leaning forward with hands dropped on widespread knees, for Jo Davidson, the American sculptor. She looked extraordinarily young considering that she was nearly fifty.

[1] *Aspects of the Novel*, 1927.
[2] Cone Collection, Baltimore Museum of Art. Musée de l'Art Moderne, Paris, Yale Gallery of Fine Arts.

Much was written at this time, plays, portraits and short pieces, and she did a great deal of listening.

> She was much influenced by the sound of the streets and the movement of the automobiles. She also liked then to set a sentence for herself as a sort of tuning fork and metrenome and then write to that time and tune.

Mildred Aldrich who was 'enthusiastic about *Three Lives*, deeply impressed but slightly troubled by *The Making of Americans*, quite upset by *Tender Buttons*, but always loyal and convinced that if Gertrude Stein did it it had something in it that was worth while', now urged her to send some short scripts to *The Atlantic Monthly*. Miss Aldrich herself had had a great success with *The Hilltop on the Marne* and 'had spent royally all she earned royally'; and she wanted to see her friend's gifts recognized. It used to anger her that Gertrude Stein's name was not in the American *Who's Who*, and she 'always felt and said that it would be a blue ribbon if the Atlantic Monthly consented, which of course it never did'. At least not yet, even when Gertrude Stein wrote persuasive letters to the editor, Ellery Sedgwick, whose name she misread as Ellen and whom she consequently addressed as *Miss*.

However, in September 1920 John Lane at last published *Three Lives* and she received a number of letters of appreciation, among others from Israel Zangwill and Frank Swinnerton. But reviewing the book in *The Athenaeum* on October 15th under the title *Some New Thing* Katherine Mansfield wrote:

> Miss Gertrude Stein has discovered a new way of writing stories. It is just to keep on writing them . . . *Good Anna* is soothing, German life told in a German way . . . but let the reader go warily, warily with *Melanctha*. We confess we read a good page or two before we realised what was happening. Then the dreadful fact dawned. We discovered ourselves reading in *syncopated time*. Gradually we heard in the distance and then coming uncomfortably near, the sound of banjos, drums, bones, cymbals and voices. The page began to rock. To our horror we found ourselves silently singing 'Was it true what Melanctha said that night to him' etc. Those who have heard the Syncopated Orchestra sing 'It's

me—it's me—it's me' or 'I got a robe' will understand what
we mean. *Melanctha* is negro music with all its maddening
monotony done into prose; it is writing in real ragtime.
Heaven forbid Miss Stein should become a fashion.

In America, however, there were signs that she *was* becoming a
fashion, for she already had imitators. And Henry McBride urged
her to print a volume of her latest pieces at her own expense.
'You see you are handicapped by writing in a language that is
behind the arts. *There is a public for you but no publisher. . . .*'

An important Left Bank event in 1919 had been the opening of
Sylvia Beach's bookshop and lending library 'Shakespeare and
Company'. Gertrude Stein, as voracious a reader as ever, at once
subscribed and the two American women became friends. Like
so many others this friendship cooled, but Miss Beach if critical
still speaks warmly of Gertrude Stein and the enormous pleasure
she had from her company, and on her walls, filled with the books
she successfully hid during the Occupation, hangs a photograph
of Gertrude Stein sitting while Jo Davidson 'sculptured' her.
He was also one of the people who did a great deal of propa-
ganda for her writing. 'Shakespeare and Company' quickly
became a famous cosmopolitan meeting-place for writers and
artists, and the people whom she met through Sylvia Beach en-
riched Gertrude Stein's circle.

'Would you let me bring around Mr. Sherwood Anderson
of *Poor White* and *Winesburg, Ohio* . . . ?' Miss Beach wrote in the
summer of 1921. 'He is so anxious to know you for he says you
have influenced him ever so much and that you stand as such a
great master of words.' And Gertrude Stein, who seldom shows
her heart in *The Autobiography*, writes tenderly of his visit. She
confesses that she was feeling a little bitter with middle-age upon
her and so many unpublished manuscripts and no hope of serious
recognition, and here came this compatriot, two years her
junior and successful in spite of his subtle inconclusive way of
writing, who told her how important her work had been in his
development, 'and what was even rarer he told it in print immediately after'.

When Sherwood Anderson returned to America she wrote to
him:

I wonder if you are still interested in doing an essay on me
... There is very likely to be a book of mine out this winter a
collection of things more or less chronological and to be
called 'Geography and Plays' . . . It has been suggested
that you do an introduction. Of course I would like that
because as I told you, you are really the only person who
really *knows* what it is all about.

Sherwood Anderson at once complied. 'It's a literary job I'd
rather do than any other I know of', and she was delighted and
moved by the result. Certainly he could not have written a more
appreciative or more charming introduction.
   It ends:

For me the work of Gertrude Stein consists in a rebuilding,
an entire new recasting of life, in the city of words. Here is
one artist who has even forgone the privilege of writing the
great American novel, uplifting our English speaking stage,
and wearing the bays of the great poets, to go live among the
little housekeeping words, the swaggering bullying street-
corner words, the honest working, money saving words,
and all the other forgotten and neglected citizens of the
sacred and half forgotten city.
   Would it not be a lovely and charmingly ironic gesture
of the gods if, in the end, the work of this artist were to
prove the most lasting and important of all the word slingers
of our generation!

The only exception Gertrude Stein could have taken to this
eulogy was that Sherwood Anderson addressed writers rather
than ordinary readers. For she maintained that her work was a
proper diet for the general reader if he would only take the
trouble to read it, whereas to Sherwood Anderson she was a
writers' writer. This was a friendship which endured; she spoke
of him always with affection and gratitude and praised his work,
although she criticized it too and he welcomed her criticism.
   In December 1921 she wrote to her 'best English friend', the
painter Harry Phelan Gibb, warmly thanking him for his faith
in her work, unwavering since the beginning, and his efforts to
make others share it. 'Things seem to be stirring my way a little

bit, I suppose some day I will be the acknowledged grandmother of the modern movement.'

This month a note from Sherwood Anderson was posted to her in Paris by Ernest Hemingway.

> Mr. Hemingway is an American writer instinctively in touch with everything worth while going on here and I know you will find Mr. and Mrs. Hemingway delightful people to know . . .

Hemingway, newly married to the pianist Hadley Richardson, had come to Europe in December 1921 as 'roving correspondent' of the *Toronto Star* with headquarters in Paris. They arrived via Spain, which greatly excited Hemingway although his passion for the bullfight was yet to come. It was Gertrude Stein who first talked to him of its drama.

After staying for a while at the Hotel Jacob and then visiting Switzerland and Italy, the Hemingways took an apartment near the place du Tertre and he sent out the sheaf of introductions given him by Sherwood Anderson, 'like launching a flock of ships'. He soon met many figures of literary Paris, including James Joyce and Ezra Pound, but the one he liked best at this time was Gertrude Stein.

She was equally pleased with him. 'He was an extraordinarily good-looking young man, twenty-three years old . . . rather foreign looking, with passionately interested, rather than interesting eyes. He sat in front of Gertrude Stein and listened and looked.' They talked and they walked and she visited the Hemingways' apartment and 'went over' everything he had so far written. He appears to have been very modest and quite prepared for both Ezra Pound and Gertrude Stein to blue-pencil his work, although he was not a beginner. Ever since his return from the war and the many operations his wounds entailed his one desire had been to turn his experiences into literature. He was a journalist only in order to earn a living, but although sometimes the necessity to send off 'this Goddam newspaper stuff' irked him he did his job well and was lucky in being employed by a paper which wanted lively stories and left the choice of subjects to their correspondent.

Hemingway was Gertrude Stein's first pupil and she much enjoyed the rôle of teacher. She wrote to Sherwood Anderson, 'He is a delightful fellow, I like his talk and I am teaching him to cut his wife's hair. He can learn to do it so much better than the barber', but these were not his only lessons. Her most famous dictum is, 'Hemingway, remarks are not literature', but there were many other pronouncements.

> Gertrude Stein rather liked the poems, they were direct, Kiplingesque, but the novel she found wanting. There is a great deal of description in this she said, and not particularly good description. Begin over again and concentrate, she said.

This was preaching what she practised.

Since the war both women had found themselves very tired and Gertrude Stein had undergone a minor operation. So in the late summer of 1922 they went off in 'Godiva' to Saint-Rémy and although the mistral was bad and the hotel not particularly comfortable stayed through the following winter, greatly enjoying the country they had come to love during the war—'the valley of the Rhône was once more exercising its spell over us'.

In these quiet months Gertrude 'worked with slow care and concentration, and was very preoccupied', as she 'meditated upon the use of grammar, poetical forms and what might be termed poetical plays'. In the new year she wrote *An Elucidation*,[1] 'her first effort to realise clearly just what her writing meant and why it was as it was'. But the reader's hope of illumination is frustrated; the work contains no explanation, only many examples of characteristic word-play.

> Suppose, to suppose, suppose a rose is a rose is a rose is a rose.
>
> To suppose, we suppose that there arose here and there that here and there there arose an instance of knowing that there are here and there that there are there that they will prepare, that they do care to come again. Are they to come again.

When spring came they went back to Paris.

[1] First printed in *transition*, April, 1927. Reprinted in *Portraits and Prayers*, Random House, New York, 1934.

This long winter in Saint-Rémy broke the restlessness of the war and the after war. A great many things were to happen, there were to be friendships and there were to be enmities and there were to be a great many other things but there was not to be any restlessness.

Geography and Plays[1] was now out, but even the Sherwood Anderson introduction did not bring the author the literary recognition she craved, although here and there a serious review appeared. Edith Sitwell gave the book faint praise in *The Nation and Athenaeum*, but in 1925, reviewing it again in *Vogue*, she hailed Gertrude Stein as an important pioneer and prophesied that no history of the English literature of that day would be complete unless it took full account of the work she was doing in bringing the language back to life.

In the early summer Gertrude Stein reported that Paris was very lively, 'but mostly with balloon ascensions and fairs . . . and 5000 Americans weekly'.[2] She was now a famous personality and people flocked to the rue de Fleurus not only to see the pictures, but to hear her talk, and Alice Toklas unobtrusively but firmly arranged the audiences.

Once again in *The Autobiography* there are lists of people. Hemingway was there of course. From time to time, in spite of Gertrude Stein's injunctions to give up journalism and write, the best advice, he said, that she ever gave him, he went away for his newspaper but he always came back. Presently there was a Hemingway baby with Gertrude Stein and Alice Toklas for its godmothers. There was another baby in their lives too, Picasso's, for the breach with him was healed. In 1924 she wrote *A Birthday Book*, which he was to have illustrated but never did, for his little son. She began it on her own birthday, February 3rd, 'Paulot' being born on the 4th.

February third Ulysses.
Who Ulysses. Who Ulysses. Who Ulysses.

[1] In the notes to *The Canticle of the Rose*, Macmillan and Co., 1949, Dame Edith Sitwell states that *Jodelling Song* on page 50 is founded on Gertrude Stein's *Accents in Alsace* (The Watch on the Rhine) contained in *Geography and Plays*.
[2] C.V.V.

February third, February third heard word heard shirred heard. Heard word. Who.

She often now used minute notebooks, but the birthday book was written in exercise books with illustrations on the cover and stories inside to educate the young. The first of these is *La Bourse Perdue*, but she had a fine collection of *menagères, colonies, sports* and so forth. The earlier exercise books had been quite plain.

Although she and Picasso were on good terms again her intimacy with Juan Gris still displeased him and her praise of his paintings still more. 'Juan Gris was the only person who Picasso wished away. The relation between them was just that.'

Another painter who interested her now was André Masson, then influenced by Gris. One of the things she loved about Paris was that there were always pictures to look at without having to look for them, and while Alice Toklas typed or occupied herself with domestic matters, she walked about the streets and visited galleries and dealers. And commented:

> The salons are mutally destructive, the independent is dying and its death is destroying the old salons. There is no more artistes français, new ones are springing up all claiming to be unique but nobody believes them. The logic of the french triumphs. If you can't épater the bourgeois you can't rebel and if you can't rebel you can't have tradition and so it tumbles together.[1]

To select from the lists of people who now crossed her path:

> We met Ezra Pound at Grace Lounsbery's house, he came home to dinner with us and he stayed and talked about japanese prints among other things. Gertrude Stein liked him but did not find him amusing. She said he was a village explainer, excellent if you were a village, but if you were not, not. Ezra also talked about T. S. Eliot. It was the first time any one had talked about T.S. at the house. Pretty soon everybody talked about T.S. Kitty Buss talked about him and much later Hemingway talked about him as the Major. Considerably later Lady Rothermere talked about him and

[1] C.V.V.

invited Gertrude Stein to come and meet him. They were founding the Criterion. We had met Lady Rothermere through Muriel Draper whom we had seen again for the first time after many years. Gertrude Stein was not particularly anxious to go to Lady Rothermere's and meet T. S. Eliot, but we all insisted she should, and she gave a doubtful yes. I [Alice Toklas] had no evening dress to wear for this occasion and started to make one. The bell rang and in walked Lady Rothermere and T.S.

Eliot and Gertrude Stein had a solemn conversation, mostly about split infinitives and other grammatical solecisms and why Gertrude Stein used them. Finally Lady Rothermere and Eliot rose to go and Eliot said that if he printed anything of Gertrude Stein's in the Criterion it would have to be her very latest thing. They left and Gertrude Stein said, don't bother to finish your dress, now we don't have to go, and she began to write a portrait of T. S. Eliot and called it the fifteenth of November, that being this day and so there could be no doubt but that it was her latest thing. It was all about wool is wool and silk is silk or wool is woollen and silk is silken. She sent it to T. S. Eliot and he accepted it but naturally he did not print it.

Then began a long correspondence, not between Gertrude Stein and T. S. Eliot, but between T. S. Eliot's secretary and myself. We each addressed the other as Sir, I signing myself A. B. Toklas and she signing initials. It was only considerably afterwards that I found out that his secretary was not a young man. I don't know whether she ever found out that I was not.

A Description of The Fifteenth of November, A Portrait of T. S. Eliot, was printed after some vicissitudes in the January 1926 number of *The Criterion*. Mr. Eliot wrote to Miss Stein humbly apologizing for the delay and adding, 'I am immensely interested in everything you write.' This naturally delighted her, particularly as she had just received a note from *The London Mercury*, 'Mr. J. C. Squire very much regrets that he doesn't understand Miss Stein's two stories', and she also records her pleasure in learning 'that Eliot had said in Cambridge that the work of Gertrude Stein was very fine but not for us.'

The T. S. Eliot portrait begins:

On the fifteenth of November we have been told that she will go either here or there and in company with some one who will attempt to be of aid in any difficulty that may be pronounced as at all likely to occur. This in case that as usual there has been no cessation of the manner in which latterly it has all been as it might be repetition. To deny twice. Once or twice.

And it ends:

He said enough.
He said enough.
Enough said.
He said enough.

After which comes the final passage about silken wool and woollen silk to which Miss Stein refers. This work was reprinted in *Georgian Stories*.

Returning to *The Autobiography*:

But to come back to Ezra. Ezra did come back and he came back with the editor of The Dial.[1] This time it was worse than japanese prints, it was much more violent. In his surprise at the violence Ezra fell out of Gertrude Stein's favourite little armchair, the one I have since tapestried with Picasso designs, and Gertrude Stein was furious. Finally Ezra and the editor of The Dial left, nobody too well pleased. Gertrude Stein did not want to see Ezra again. Ezra did not quite see why. He met Gertrude Stein one day near the Luxembourg gardens and said, but I do want to come to see you. I am so sorry, answered Gertrude Stein, but Miss Toklas has a bad tooth and beside we are busy picking wild flowers. All of which was literally true, like all of Gertrude Stein's literature, but it upset Ezra, and we never saw him again.

It is sometimes said by Gertrude Stein's detractors that social life at the rue de Fleurus was contrived to one end alone, the furtherance of her literary career. Her attitude towards Ezra Pound refutes this view, for he was at the time influential with several magazines and could certainly have aided publication.

[1] Scofield Thayer. Marianne Moore, the poet who later became managing editor, was a great admirer of Gertrude Stein's.

Through her letters one continues to get glimpses of inner and outer events:

> We have just been having a great time with the fete at Versailles for the benefit of the Palace. Juan Gris did the decor and the Russian ballet the rest, it was a typical French fete Juan Gris a Spaniard did the decor, Diaghilev a Russian the ballet—Astruc an Austrian Jew organised it and the audience was mostly American, as it ran to 1,000 francs per we saw it unofficially that is the decor. It made the palace quite nice, they even put in electricity.[1]

Elsewhere she speaks of watching Juan Gris directing the scene-painting of his décor for the Russian ballet at Monte Carlo: 'It is mostly done by an English woman who does it as if she were a lady gardener.'

As usual she was enjoying herself, 'happily hopefulness does succeed despair, nicely', and her rôle of critic and teacher was developing. About Carl Van Vechten's *Peter Whiffle*, published in 1922, she said 'You are indeed the most modern the least sentimental and the most gently persistent of romantics', and in 1923 she wrote at length to Sherwood Anderson about his new book *Many Marriages*:

> It's a fine piece of work and has in it some writing that I find far better than anything you have done before . . . On the other hand there is to my thinking a little too much tendency to make the finale come too frequently that is to say you the writer know a little too frequently that there is an ending. May I say that there should be a beginning a middle and an ending, you have a tendency to make it a beginning an ending an ending and an ending. Then there is perhaps a little bit too much tendency to mix yourself and the hero together, it is a little your weakness in your long things, you do a little tend to find yourself more interesting than your hero and you tend to put yourself in his place.

And Sherwood Anderson replied: 'Do you know I think it the most clear-headed criticism I have had and that you have its weaknesses and good points about rightly sized up.'

In the same spring Hemingway wrote to her saying that he had

[1] C.V.V.

been working hard and thinking hard about everything that she had said to him and as a result was probably going to give up journalism. He told her that the young American critics and their public were turning against both her and Sherwood Anderson but that he was sure that she would win them back. He urged Ford Madox Ford to include her among the contributors to *Transatlantic Review*, a magazine which he had recently started with the help of an American patron of letters. Early in 1924, as recorded in *The Autobiography*, he brought her good news:

> Hemingway came in then very excited and said that Ford wanted something of Gertrude Stein's for the next number and he, Hemingway, wanted The Making of Americans to be run in it as a serial and he had to have the first fifty pages at once. Gertrude Stein was of course quite overcome with her excitement at this idea, but there was no copy of the manuscript except the one that we had had bound. That makes no difference, said Hemingway, I will copy it. And he and I [Alice Toklas] between us did copy it and it was printed in the next number of the Transatlantic. So for the first time a piece of the monumental work which was the beginning, really the beginning of modern writing, was printed, and we were very happy. Later on when things were difficult between Gertrude Stein and Hemingway, she always remembered with gratitude that after all it was Hemingway who first caused to be printed a piece of The Making of Americans. She always says, yes sure I have a weakness for Hemingway. After all he was the first of the young men to knock at my door and he did make Ford print the first piece of The Making of Americans.

But Hemingway who found *The Autobiography* full of falsities certainly got over his weakness for Gertrude Stein.

Ford wrote to her a little sadly, saying that he had had the impression from Hemingway that her contribution was a long-short story, and had he known that it was a long novel, indeed three or four novels, he would have offered her a lump sum for the whole thing. Nevertheless he was prepared to publish it although there were of course complications.

The Transatlantic Review was in financial difficulties and uncertain of survival. Gertrude Stein's friend, Jane Heap, then editing the American *Little Review*, which published her first portrait of Juan Gris, arranged with Lady Rothermere for the serializing of *The Making of Americans* to be transferred to *The Criterion*. The *Transatlantic* did however survive for a time, and several chapters of the novel were printed in it, although Ford kindly said he would not stand in Gertrude Stein's way if she could get more money from *The Criterion*.

Meanwhile efforts to get *The Making of Americans* published as a book continued. Carl Van Vechten was enthusiastic, 'my feeling is that you have done a very great thing, probably as big as, perhaps bigger than James Joyce, Marcel Proust or Dorothy Richardson'. He added pertinently, 'To me, now, it is a little like The Book of Genesis. There is something Biblical about you, Gertrude. Certainly there is something Biblical about you.'

Eventually he succeeded in interesting Alfred A. Knopf in publishing it on a subscription basis. 'If he does the book he wants to do it *beautifully* and that will cost money: three or four volumes of large type, with possibly portraits of you by Davidson, Picasso, etc. as frontispieces. And signed by you. This will all cost money . . .'

Following her custom, however, although she was so eager to be published, before anything could be settled with Knopf Gertrude Stein cabled Van Vechten to take the script away from him and give it to Horace Liveright, whose Paris agent, a friend of Hemingway's, was certain of its success. Then after all Liveright decided not to publish it, and so it went on, until at last Gertrude Stein induced Robert McAlmon to include 'the monumental work' in his Paris-produced *Contact Editions* of contemporary authors. But this was by no means the end of disagreements and difficulties.

CHAPTER TWELVE

PERSONALITIES AND LECTURES

'Belley is its name and Belley is its nature.'
Mike Stein.

IN the summer of 1923 some weeks were spent with the Picassos in Antibes. With her gift of understanding, Gertrude Stein made friends with Picasso's mother in spite of the lack of a common language, and found Picasso very like her. It was a happy visit and while 'delighting in the movement of the tiny waves on the Antibes shore', she wrote several more portraits and *A Book Concluding with As a Wife Has a Cow a Love Story*[1] which was published by Kahnweiler with lithographs by Juan Gris and is now a collector's piece. Later he published *A Village*, illustrated by Elie Lascaux.

The following summer they decided to repeat the Antibes visit, but were seduced *en route* by the Rhône Valley. Alice Toklas had read in the *Guide des Gourmets* about Pernollet's Hotel at Belley, in the Bugey. The journey in 'Godiva' was anxious—Gertrude Stein did not like precipices—but presently they arrived in a pastoral landscape among woods and the rolling foot-hills of the Alps. Gertrude wrote to Picasso that they would go no further; they booked at the Pernollet for a few days and remained for months; their hearts were won; this was the countryside that they were to make their own.

Brillat-Savarin had been born at Belley, Lamartine had gone to school there and Madame Récamier came from the same region— all reasons, they felt, why the food should be good, but the hotel meals fell below their high standard. Every evening they ate its best dish, the local lake fish, *lavaret*, poached with brown butter, but for gourmet fare they explored the Haute Savoie. Gertrude Stein, who had passed her fiftieth year, was now in very good

[1] Éditions de la Galérie Simon. Paris, 1926.

health and had lost weight. 'Avery[1] said you were getting thin,' she told Van Vechten, 'we all do and well don't we.'

In the spring of 1924 they returned to the same hotel but to a different régime, the programme no longer one of leisurely writing and excursions, for *The Making of Americans* had been printed in Dijon and the proofs had to be read. It was beautifully produced by Maurice Darantière, but as the compositors were French and had not understood a word of the text, Gertrude and Alice had to check not only each line and word of nearly a thousand large pages, but every letter, and when a line had been left out 'the effort of getting it back again was terrific'.

The Pernollet had no garden so:

> We used to leave the hotel in the morning with camp chairs, lunch and proofs, and all day we struggled . . . Proof had to be corrected most of it four times and finally I broke my glasses, my eyes gave out, and Gertrude Stein finished alone.
>
> We used to change the scene of our labours and we found lovely spots but there were always to accompany us those endless pages of printers' errors.

This is all that *The Autobiography* says of the ordeal, but Miss Toklas to this day declares that it was simply frightful.

Gertrude Stein called *The Making of Americans* Carl Van Vechten's godchild. It is interesting to see that she was nervous now about its length.

> You know it is rather funny and youthful, there are moments when I think I should prune it out but then after all it was done as much done as it could be and after all these years I guess it will do. It is quite xciting, I don't know why it should be but it is that and its large thoughts I was not so young then but it does seem young are what hit me most.[2]

To Sherwood Anderson a postcard said, 'we are going on and on, it is a bit monumental and sometimes seems foolishly youthful now after twenty years, but I am leaving it'. And in a letter to him:

> It has been printed in France and lots of people will think

---

[1] Avery Hopwood, the playwright.   [2] C.V.V.

many strange things in it as to tenses and persons and adjectives and adverbs and divisions are due to the French compositors errors but they are not it is quite as I worked at it and even when I tried to change it well I didn't really try but I went over it to see if it could go differently and I always found myself forced back into its incorrectnesses so there they stand. There are some pretty wonderful sentences in it and we know how fond we both are of sentences.

In spite of this labour Gertrude Stein, working towards the period of her most difficult thinking, succeeded in writing new things. They returned to Paris in the autumn with the proofs nearly finished and before the end of the year the book appeared, although she and her publisher, Robert McAlmon, were no longer on good terms. The edition consisted of five hundred paper-bound copies and five in vellum. One copy went naturally to Carl Van Vechten. 'I have very much the feeling', she wrote, 'that it is you that have kept the interest of the public in it all these years and so well I am very fond of you anyway.'

New people claimed her attention. Among painters were three young Russians, the Berman brothers and Pavel Tchelitchew, introduced by Jane Heap.

> He was painting, so he said, colour that was no colour, he was painting blue pictures and he was painting three heads in one. Picasso had been drawing three heads in one. Soon the russian was painting three figures in one. Was he the only one. In a way he was although there was a group of them.

The group did not interest Gertrude Stein, but Tchelitchew did. For one thing he made amusing contributions to *les histoires*, always part of Left Bank living and as necessary a form of nourishment at the rue de Fleurus as good food and company, paintings and the printed word. 'He had already then a passionate enmity against the frenchman whom they called Bébé Bérard and whose name was Christian Bérard and who Tchelitchew said copied everything.'

For a time he was a close friend and it was through Gertrude Stein that he met Edith Sitwell and painted her portrait. The friendship broke but Tchelitchew is 'for ever *reconnaisant* for all she did for me. I was a Russian boy, a beginner. She made my name.' He told his friend Charles Henri Ford, who describes himself as one of Gertrude Stein's last 'finds', that she 'liked to take a chair and sit in a person's life'.[1] Ford was then editing the American review *Blues*, one of the little magazines Gertrude Stein admired because 'they gave their blood for literature', and published several of her short pieces.

At an exhibition of the Tchelitchew group she met the American composer George Antheil who asked if he might come and see her. It is a pity that he has not recorded his impressions of her; his descriptions of people in Paris at this time are so vivid.

> Satie was a most peculiar little old man, working in the day-time as a clerk in a post office, selling stamps and in the late afternoon and at night becoming a high and mighty potentate in the decisions of musical France.

And of the writers at the 'Shakespeare Bookshop':

> No one dressed even remotely like another. Hemingway, exponent of the rough and ready dressed like a lumberjack; T. S. Eliot, a bank official in London, dressed in a quiet brown business suit; Ezra Pound wore a bizarre outfit of tweeds designed by himself and sewn with bright blue square buttons; Ford Madox Ford draped himself in a tentlike suit of light grey tweeds; Wyndham Lewis wore a jet-black suit, hat and cape to match; Joyce wore white duck . . .[2]

And he goes on to describe as vividly the differences in the locution and accents of the literary lions of the day. But of Gertrude Stein, whom so many others have described, he only says, 'hearing Purcell in a Paris possessing its own Rameau was as difficult as getting Gertrude Stein to say that *Ulysses* was a great work'. Another friend now was the American painter Man Ray who took so many splendid photographs of her and Picasso and other outstanding figures of the day, and whose way of using lights fascinated her.

Through George Antheil, Gertrude Stein met Virgil Thomson

[1] Author's journal.
[2] *Bad Boy of Music*. Doubleday, Doran and Co., New York, 1945.

the composer, who was soon to become New York's leading music critic. He was then earning a precarious living by writing musical criticism for *Vanity Fair*. He had already set *Susie Asado*,[1] *Preciosilla*,[2] and *Capital Capitals*[3] to music which naturally inclined her to him. An acute observer and a witty talker he and Gertrude Stein found each other excellent company. In *Mémoires*[4] Elisabeth de Gramont gives a charming description of him at the rue de Fleurus, sitting quietly chanting Gertrude Stein's pieces while partaking of 'thé excellent avec de petits sandwiches'. And the author delighted in listening to her words framed by his music.

'There were many Gertrudes,' Virgil Thomson says, 'the neighbour Gertrude, a homely pleasant countrywoman, the Dr. Johnson Gertrude, laying down the law, the *homme de lettres*, *homme* not *femme*, the *salonière*, giving her opinion on everything, and Gertrude the hermetic poet, hard-working, humble . . . Not humble before the views of other people on her work, but humble before a piece of paper. And even more so before ideas of grammar, of composition. Hers was a work of method more than of communication. She would work at composition, at description, at narration, in a way in which no other writers have. One can compare this with Bach working at fugal technique as he wrote.'[5]

Virgil Thomson was an authority on Erik Satie, whose music Gertrude Stein liked, and he used to play it to her on the piano at his apartment. How appropriate this was, for sometimes when Virgil Thomson is writing about Satie's compositions he might be writing about Gertrude Stein's. 'They are as simple, as straightforward, as devastating as the remarks of a child. To the uninitiated they sound trifling. To those who love them they are fresh and beautiful and firmly right . . . It [Satie's music] is as simple as a friendly conversation and in its better moments exactly as poetic and as profound.'[6]

Although Gertrude Stein considered that she had outgrown music Virgil Thomson found her well grounded in it. She had

---

[1] *Geography and Plays*. 1922.   [2] Ibid.
[3] *Operas and Plays*. Plain Edition, 1932.
[4] Éditions Bernard Grasset. Paris, 1935.   [5] Author's journal.
[6] *The Musical Scene*. Alfred A. Knopf, 1947.

no musical talent, he says, although she still liked to play what she called sonatinas on the white notes, but her education in the classics had left its mark. She used words as composers use notes and phrased musically, which made him find her words 'right to write music under.' Before long he asked her to make him a libretto.

Virgil Thomson had many paintings by Christian Bérard which Gertrude Stein used to discuss endlessly with him. 'She could not find out at all what she thought about them.' Finally, borrowing the Roman Catholic Church's distinction between hysteric and saint, she decided that Bérard, who was to become the leading designer in the Paris theatre, was more hysteric than saint.

Through Virgil Thomson Gertrude Stein met the young poet and *homme de lettres* Georges Hugnet, for a time a close friend, and it was now too that Scott Fitzgerald was brought by Hemingway into the Stein orbit. On the eve of meeting her Fitzgerald wrote to Edmund Wilson of his disgust with American women in Paris, 'who have all (so they say) read James Joyce and who simply adore Mencken'. Gertrude Stein was a revelation to him. 'She looks like the Great Stone Face', he said and added to his friend Esther Murphy, 'What an old covered-wagon she is!' Scott Fitzgerald at once recognized the quality of Gertrude Stein's best work and did not change his view. Twenty years later, when his daughter was beginning to write, he pointed out the good influence reading *Melanctha* had had upon her style.

In May 1925 Gertrude Stein wrote to him from Belley, to which they now returned every summer, about his newly published novel *The Great Gatsby*:

> Here we are and have read your book and it is a good book. I like the melody of your dedication and it shows that you have a background of beauty and tenderness and that is a comfort. The next good thing is that you write naturally in sentences and that too is a comfort . . . You are creating the contemporary world as much as Thackeray did in his *Pendennis* and *Vanity Fair* and this isn't a bad compliment. You make a modern world and a modern orgy strangely enough it was never done until you did it in *This Side of Paradise*. My belief in *This Side of Paradise* was alright. This is as good

a book and different and older and that is always a pleasure . . .

Scott Fitzgerald replied:

Thank you very much. My wife and I think you a very handsome, very gallant, very kind lady and thought so as soon as
we saw you, and were telling Hemingway so when you
passed us searching your car on the street . . . He's a peach of
a fellow and absolutely first rate.

I am so anxious to get *The Making of Americans* & learn
something from it and imitate things out of it which I shall
doubtless do. That future debt I tried so hard to repay by
making the Scribners read it in the *Transatlantic* & convinced
one but the old man's mind was too old.

You see, I am content to let you, and the one or two like
you who are acutely sensitive, think or fail to think for me
and my kind artistically . . .

Presently Carl Van Vechten sent them 'quantities of negroes',
among them Paul Robeson. From *The Autobiography*:

Paul Robeson interested Gertrude Stein. He knew american values and american life as only one in it but not of it
could know them. And yet as soon as any other person came
into the room he became definitely a negro. Gertrude Stein
did not like hearing him sing spirituals. They do not belong
to you any more than anything else, so why claim them,
she said. He did not answer.

And now came Edith Sitwell.

I [Alice Toklas] remember so well my first impression of
her, an impression which indeed has never changed. Very
tall, bending slightly, withdrawing and hesitatingly ad-
vancing, and beautiful with the most distinguished nose I
have ever seen on any human being. At that time and in
conversation between Gertrude Stein and herself afterwards,
I delighted in the delicacy and completeness of her understanding of poetry. She and Gertrude Stein became friends at
once. This friendship like all friendships has had its difficulties
but I am convinced that fundamentally Gertrude Stein and
Edith Sitwell are friends and enjoy being friends.

And Osbert Sitwell:

> She always said he was like an uncle of a king. He had that pleasant kindly irresponsible agitated calm that an uncle of an english king must always have.

He was a great comfort to her in her stage fright when at Cambridge and Oxford in the spring of 1926 she gave her first lectures. She had promptly refused the first invitation from Cambridge, 'quite completely upset at the very idea', but a letter from Edith Sitwell, pointing out how much a visit to England would help the recognition of her work there, persuaded her to change her mind. This letter gave the disappointing news that Virginia Woolf had rejected *The Making of Americans* for the Hogarth Press, but Edith Sitwell expressed her conviction that so great a writer as Gertrude Stein would in the end triumph.

And so she agreed to go.

> She was very upset at the prospect, peace, she said, had much greater terrors than war. Precipices even were nothing to this. She was very low in her mind. Luckily early in January the ford car began to have everything the matter with it . . .
>
> One cold dark afternoon she went out to sit with her ford car and while she sat on the steps of another battered ford watching her own being taken to pieces and put together again, she began to write. She stayed there several hours and when she came back chilled, with the ford repaired, she had written the whole of Composition as Explanation.[1]

She intended to read the lecture and now everybody gave her advice. One aged French professor of history told her to talk as quickly as she could and never look up; another lecturer told her to talk as slowly as possible and never look down. She tried all the methods on anybody who came to the house and sometimes her friends read the lecture to her so that she could hear how it sounded.

[1] *The Dial*, October 1926. The Hogarth Press, 1926; *The Hogarth Essays*, Doubleday, Doran, 1928. Reprinted in *What Are Masterpieces*, The Conference Press, Los Angeles, 1940.

Meanwhile Alice Toklas made all the arrangements and ordered her a new dress and hat. Gertrude Stein told Van Vechten that she was a little nervous 'but I am all dressed anyway so that is always that'. Miss Toklas's protection went as far as taking her friend's passport to be stamped on the boat because such formalities troubled the already troubled author. 'She does not care to come down', Miss Toklas told the officials, and Gertrude Stein was left in peace.

Edith and Osbert Sitwell each gave a party for her, and the dreaded day came.

> Gertrude Stein was soon at her ease, the lecture went off very well, the men afterwards asked a great many questions and were very enthusiastic. The women said nothing. Gertrude Stein wondered whether they were supposed not to or just did not.
>
> The day after we went to Oxford . . . Gertrude Stein was feeling more comfortable as a lecturer and this time she had a wonderful time. As she remarked afterwards, I felt just like a prima donna.

And she enjoyed the hecklers and got the best of them in her hearty, good-natured way.

> The next day we returned to Paris. The Sitwells wanted us to stay and be interviewed and generally go on with it but Gertrude Stein felt that she had had enough of glory and excitement. Not, as she always explains, that she could ever have enough of glory. After all, as she always contends, no artist needs criticism, he only needs appreciation. If he needs criticism he is no artist.

To Van Vechten she reported:

> It was a nice adventure one of the nicest I ever had, real sympathy understanding and enthusiasm and so many admiring young men and my thing is good it is to appear in the Hogarth Essay series press and is to be called Composition as Explanation and in the discussions I was very bright and I am really very happy about it all.

Composition as Explanation, which Professor J. Isaacs has called 'the most perfect broadcast script I know', contains some of

Gertrude Stein's most provocative thinking and this apt comment on the contemporary in art:

> No one is ahead of his time, it is only that the particular variety of creating his time is the one that his contemporaries who also are creating their own time refuse to accept . . . In the case of the arts it [the refusal] is very definite. Those who are creating the modern composition authentically are naturally only of importance when they are dead because by that time the modern composition having become past is classified and the description of it is classical. That is the reason why the creator of the new composition in the arts is an outlaw until he is a classic, there is hardly a moment in between and it is really too bad very much too bad naturally for the creator but also very much too bad for the enjoyer, they all really would enjoy the created so much better just after it has been made than when it is already a classic . . .
>
> There is almost not an interval.
>
> For a very long time everybody refuses and then almost without a pause everybody accepts. In the history of the refused in the arts and literature the rapidity of the change is always startling. Not the only difficulty with the volte-face concerning the arts is this. When the acceptance comes, by that acceptance the thing created becomes a classic . . . The characteristic quality of a classic is that it is beautiful . . .
>
> Of course it is beautiful but first all beauty in it is denied and then all the beauty of it is accepted. If every one were not so indolent they would realise that beauty is beauty even when it is irritating and stimulating not only when it is accepted and classic. Of course it is extremely difficult nothing more so than to remember back to its not being beautiful once it has become beautiful.

Then she describes the progress of her own writing, 'a groping for a continuous present and for using everything by beginning again and again', stressing repeatedly that her development was the natural one for her epoch. Some of her statements are paradoxical such as, 'Everything being alike, everything naturally everything is different.' But Robert Bartlett Haas, who wrote the introduction to *What Are Masterpieces*, sees a development here of the Pragmatic attitude.

Preciosilla, included in the Hogarth Press edition of *Composition as Explanation* ends with the line, 'Toasted susie is my ice-cream.' Donald Sutherland remarks of this that it 'is a very slight heightening of what would be popular enough: Sunburnt Susie is my dish', and the phrase certainly became famous in America. In the same volume is the portrait, *Sitwell Edith Sitwell* —the name should surely be read the first time as two words— which opens, aptly for those remembering her parties in the twenties, 'In a minute when they sit when they sit around her'. And then there is *Jean Cocteau*, a whimsy written in the tiniest of notebooks, beginning:

> Needs be needs be needs be near.
> Needs be needs be needs be.

This portrait elicited a charming letter from its subject. 'Le pays perdu' is Jean Cocteau's version of Gertrude Stein's 'the land astray'; his English words are a quotation from the portrait.

> Gertrude l'admirable
> J'ai reçu ce soir votre grand sourire grammatical.
> Votre rose qui est dans une rose qui est dans une rose.
> Je ne vous vois pas, mais je vous aime, vous le savez, et
> J'habite avec vous le pays perdu.
> Hélas je comprends seulement à moitié (When half is May how much is May)!
> G. Stein, je suis fier de votre poème et je vous embrasse
> Jean[1]

Across the penultimate sentence he wrote 'mal', and at the end of the letter drew a little heart. It is interesting to note his version of 'rose is a rose is a rose', the line Alice Toklas had long ago found among her friend's scripts and embroidered on the linen and had engraved in a circle upon the letter paper.

It was pleasant returning to Paris with her laurels.

Mildred Aldrich was awfully pleased at Gertrude Stein's english success. She was a good new englander and to her, recognition by Oxford and Cambridge, was even more important than recognition by The Atlantic Monthly.

[1] From the Yale Collection, unpublished.

From Belley later that summer Gertrude Stein warmly praised Van Vechten's new book *Nigger Heaven*. Of the praise some of her own work was now receiving she said, 'I can eat it with a spoon or with a soup ladle or anything and I like it.' Other young American authors she dismissed with a line, 'McAlmon is pretty bad. Fitzgerald and Cummings are the best of the crowd, the rest are fairly weak in the head.'

In the autumn a bevy of new young men flocked to the rue de Fleurus. They could see the pictures in comfort now for there were electric radiators in the atelier.

> We were as our finnish servant would say getting modern. She finds it difficult to understand why we are not more modern. Gertrude Stein says that if you are way ahead with your head you naturally are old fashioned and regular in your daily life.

One of Gertrude Stein's favourites among these young men was Tchelitchew's friend, the writer René Crevel. 'He was young and violent and ill and revolutionary and sweet and tender. Gertrude Stein and René are very fond of each other, he writes her most delightful english letters, and she scolds him a great deal.' There was without doubt much maternal feeling in her relationships with young men. Another of these was Bravig Imbs, the young American writer, who ten years later recorded his memories of these days in *Confessions of Another Young Man*.[1]

He tells of the notes summoning him. 'Don't come tomorrow, do come Tuesday.' Of Alice Toklas weeding people out before they reached Gertrude Stein, of Alice's infallible memory and famous earrings—Picasso had at once called her a gipsy because of the large earrings and her elegant small feet. Imbs said that one dared not talk of James Joyce to Gertrude Stein, that she enjoyed setting people at sixes and sevens, that she had a glorious laugh, that she was serious, that she liked prose, and that she looked like a monk when she was discussing literature.

Of the relations between James Joyce and Gertrude Stein Alice Toklas says: 'They did not meet for many years. Friends were to bring him to see her and he didn't turn up. She didn't mind. Then

[1] The Henkle-Yewdale Press, New York, 1936.

she saw him at an Edith Sitwell reading at Sylvia Beach's book-shop, but they did not meet. Finally Sylvia Beach introduced them at a party of Jo Davidson's, but after Joyce had remarked that their names were often linked and she that they lived in the same quarter, they had nothing to say to one another. How could they have? Gertrude was never interested in *fin de série*. Even with Picasso, when he had got there and painted the twenty more, she didn't want the twenty. By then they had become beautiful. That didn't interest her. Nor the perfected thing. She wanted creation —the break and crash of it. That's all Joyce was, although brilliant, *fin de série*.'[1]

A characteristic turn of phrase. James Joyce has been called *fin de siècle* in the sense of being the culmination of a literary method rather than the creator of a new one, but *fin de série* has a flavour of Left Bank mischief. One should remember, however, that although Gertrude Stein lived on the Left Bank she never joined the vehement gatherings of foreign writers and artists on the *terrasses* of the Rotonde and the Dôme. Alice Toklas remembers her occasionally going in the early days to a café where her brothers played billiards, 'but', she explained:

> . . . if you see what I mean she was too good a bourgeoise and too good a bohemian for café life. It wasn't café conversation at the rue de Fleurus so there was no need to continue it at cafés.

They seldom went to restaurants in the Quarter either. When dining out they 'went across town', often to the Café Anglais. Nor did Gertrude Stein frequent the literary salons of Paris, she preferred to talk 'to *concierges* and neighbours', but she did now begin going to Miss Natalie Clifford Barney's Friday afternoons. Miss Barney, the American writer to whom Rémy de Gourmont's *Lettres à l'Amazone* are addressed, has had a literary and political salon since girlhood. At this time she was eager to foster a better '*entente*' between French and Anglo-Saxon *femmes de lettres*. She wrote to Gertrude Stein that she 'thought that *you, presented by yourself*' (the italics are Miss Barney's) would 'balance the French trio', which included Colette. In that gracious rue

[1] Author's journal.

Jacob house, Gertrude Stein might have met Rilke, for he too occasionally visited the Amazon, who wrote of him a *Reconnaissance Tardive*. Perhaps they would have had nothing to say to one another, but if they had exchanged reminiscences of their early days in Paris, they could have found out that far apart though they had travelled, each of them at the beginning had been vitally struck by the painting of Cézanne, and that Rilke too had discovered, as he wrote in 1907 to his wife:

> Artistic observation had first to make such a conquest of itself as to be able to see even in the horrible and apparently only repulsive that existence, which, together with all other exisence, has value. Aversion from any kind of existence is as little permitted to the creator as selection . . .

Rilke and Gertrude Stein meet however only in Miss Barney's memories of the many creators of the century who contributed to her own *Aventures de l'Esprit*.[1]

His denial of selection to the artist brings to mind Alice Toklas's answer when asked who, at this time, were Gertrude Stein's best friends. 'Nobody. Anybody. Everybody. She didn't have special friends. She liked people. They interested her and they were all of equal worth.'[2]

At the hotel in Belley she was introduced by Miss Barney to the duchesse de Clermont-Tonnerre, a great personality and a distinguished writer in her maiden name of Elisabeth de Gramont.

> We did have a great many parties in those days and the Duchess of Clermont-Tonnerre came very often.
>
> She and Gertrude Stein pleased one another. They were entirely different in life, education and interests but they delighted in each other's understanding. They were also the only two women whom they met who still had long hair. Gertrude Stein had always worn hers well on top of her head, an ancient fashion that she had never changed.
>
> Madame de Clermont-Tonnerre came in very late to one of the parties, almost every one had gone, and her hair was

[1] Émile Paul Frères, Paris, 1929. Miss Natalie Clifford Barney also wrote the foreword to Gertrude Stein's volume *As Fine As Melanctha*. Yale University Press, 1954.

[2] Author's journal.

cut. Do you like it, said Madame de Clermont-Tonnerre.
I do, said Gertrude Stein. Well, said Madame de Clermont-
Tonnerre, if you like it and my daughter likes it and she does
like it I am satisfied. That night Gertrude Stein said to me,
I guess I will have to too. Cut it off she said and I did.

I was still cutting the next evening, I had been cutting a
little more all day and by this time it was only a cap of hair
when Sherwood Anderson came in. Well, how do you like
it, said I rather fearfully. I like it, he said, it makes her look
like a monk.

As I have said, Picasso seeing it, was for a moment angry
and said, and my portrait, but very soon added, after all it
is all there.

With the new coiffure came a new habit of running her hands
through her hair. Elisabeth de Gramont describes her with her
head of a Roman centurion, seizing hold of her dark hair streaked
with grey as if to pull out her ideas, while another friend comments that whereas most people push their hair back she always
pushed hers forward. In spite of Picasso's second thoughts her
short hair did change her appearance, nor was she an exception to
the rule that cutting their hair off changes women's characters.
Shyness and doubt were shorn with her tresses. And she was becoming increasingly elegant, with a taste for handsome waistcoats
and beautiful cuff-links. Many years later Madame de Clermont-
Tonnerre wrote to Miss Barney: 'J'ai connu avec beaucoup de
joie dans des époques préhistoriques l'admirable Gertrude
Stein.'

In May 1927 she told Van Vechten that they were staying on in
Paris a little later than usual, 'and a beautiful spring it is. Hya-
cinths turn into wistaria alright . . . Working a lot as usual some
very funny little narratives . . . At the same time a very great grief
as my very very dear friend Juan Gris is dying.'

When Picasso condoled with her about Juan Gris's death she
told him bitterly that he had no right to mourn. 'You never
realised his meaning because you did not have it, she said angrily.
You know very well I did, he replied.' His death inspired her
to write of his gifts in *The Life and Death of Juan Gris*.[1] To quote
a few lines:

[1] *transition*, July 1927. *Portraits and Prayers*. Random House, 1934.

He had very early a very great attraction and love for French culture. French culture has always seduced me he was fond of saying. It seduces me and then I am seduced over again. He used to tell how Spaniards love not to resist temptation . . . He had his own Spanish gift of intimacy. We were intimate . . . As a Spaniard he knew cubism and had stepped through into it. He had stepped through it. There was beside this perfection. To have it shown you. Then came the war and desertion. There was little aid. Four years partly illness much perfection and rejoining beauty and perfection and then at the end there came a definite creation of something. This is what is to be measured. He made something that is to be measured. And that is that something . . .

CHAPTER THIRTEEN

NEW PASTURES

'One day we saw the house of our dreams across a valley.'
The Autobiography of Alice B. Toklas.

ANOTHER piece of Stein enterprise was now taking place. Michael and Sarah had for some years been living in rue de la Tour with their friend, Madame Osorio, and the three of them now decided to make a permanent home together in the suburbs of Paris. Visiting an exhibition of modern art in 1925, Mike and Madame Osorio were impressed by the work of Le Corbusier, then an unknown young architect. Through a sculptor friend whose house he had built, they got in touch with him and chose a site at Gârches. Mike was knowledgeable about building materials and alert in his supervision, with the result that *Les Terrasses* is in better condition today than many of the Le Corbusier houses of that period. And when the villa was finished in 1928 into it went the Stein Renaissance furniture and the twentieth-century pictures, except for the nineteen Matisse canvases tragically lost through having been lent to an exhibition in Germany shortly before the war. Gertrude who, although never wanting to live in a modern house herself, was interested in everything Mike did, drove out often to see her relatives at *Les Terrasses*.

At about the same time she and Alice Toklas found a second home. They had continued to go to Belley every summer and had begun to look in the district for a place of their own. One day they saw the house of their dreams across a valley. It was occupied by an army officer, but they approached the agent, a kindly old farmer, who told them '*allez doucement*', and before long the lieutenant went to Morocco and 'we took the house still only having seen it from across the valley and we have liked it always more'.

This, the house at Bilignin, a tiny hamlet three kilometres from Belley of ancient grey stone barns and cottages, unchanged to this day, was indeed to be to them and to the many friends who enjoyed their renowned hospitality an unfailing delight. A distinguished deep-roofed house, almost a little château, set on a hillside among poplars and acacias, it presents a discreetly railed and gated front to the village. On the other side, the one they knew so well from across the valley, is a *jardin de curé* with old, formal box-edged flower-beds flanked by a low, wide parapet, on which Gertrude Stein often sat, although it was Alice Toklas who said, 'I like a view but I like to sit with my back turned to it.' At the corners and in the centre of the parapet are large turreted summerhouses; above and beyond lie the vegetable gardens and below the land falls and rises again to the hills.

'It is a case of In the greenest of our valleys by good angels tenanted', Gertrude Stein wrote to Carl Van Vechten, and she begged him and his wife to come and 'eat our peas and beans which I am so actively cultivating and Alice is so actively picking and then so actively cooking'. Her cooking was superb and their table famous although by now Gertrude Stein was on a stringent diet and drank no wine.

Presently she reported, 'we bought ourselves a white caniche of two months which we call Basket to go with it [the house] and with us and I am working making sentences about the sentence and there we are.' This caniche was the famous poodle, Basket the first, whom the local children called Monsieur Basquette. Bravig Imbs claimed the distinction of finding him at the Bazar de l'Hôtel de Ville and putting him on a table for Gertrude Stein among yellow daisies and candles. Henceforward her letters seldom omitted Basket and presently Picabia added a tiny Mexican dog which they called Byron. 'Gertrude Stein always says that she only has two real distractions, pictures and automobiles. Perhaps she might now add dogs.' She wrote a portrait of Basket beginning 'A lizard is going up the wall with a grasshopper in its mouth'—she still liked to include the moment in her writing.

To the left, as one faces the garden, is a little, one-storeyed, Louis XVI salon with painted walls and here and in the garden Gertrude Stein went on writing. The libretto for Virgil Thomson, *Four Saints in Three Acts*,[1] was finished. She always liked saints and

[1] *transition*, June 1929. *Operas and Plays*, 1932. Random House, 1934.

had already written some pieces about them, so they were a natural choice of characters, and it was also natural, she explains in *Everybody's Autobiography*, 'that when I wanted saints that they should be Spanish Saints'.

> There are saints there have been saints in Italy and in France and even in Germany and I suppose in Austria, I do not know anything about them, but the important saints have been Spanish and Italian and that is natural enough, there must be really weather in which to wander in order to be a saint.
>
> A saint a real saint never does anything, a martyr does something but a really good saint does nothing and so I wanted to have Four Saints who did nothing and I wrote the *Four Saints in Three Acts* and they did nothing and that was everything.
>
> Generally speaking anybody is more interesting doing nothing than doing something.

Her four were Saint Theresa, an old favourite, and Saint Ignatius of Loyola whom William James liked, with Saint Settlement and Saint Chavez, who do not appear to be historical, as their respective confidantes. Besides these there is a small chorus of named saints and a larger one of unnamed. The opera has no plot and imaginary incidents in the lives of the saints provide the action in an imaginary scene of sixteenth-century Spain. Like her plays it is a landscape, and magpies are in the landscape, she tells us, magpies as she saw them at Avila, flat on the sky like the Holy Ghost as a bird in early Italian pictures.

Virgil Thomson was delighted with the libretto. He added two characters, the Compère and the Commère, representing the laity and arranged the part of Saint Theresa for two singers dressed alike, to which innovations the author readily agreed. She herself suggested that there should be a ballet and the composer decided on a Negro cast partly because of his admiration for the way Negroes speak English, but also because of their natural approach to religious themes.

Donald Sutherland points out that although the opera owes little or nothing to the chapter on saintliness in *The Varieties of Religious Experience* some of James's passages fit wonderfully well with it. 'This auroral openness and uplift gives to all creative ideal levels a bright and caroling quality, which is nowhere more marked than where the controlling emotion is religious. "The true monk", writes an Italian mystic, "takes nothing with him but his lyre."' Sutherland speaks further of the opera's 'pitch of beatitude and reckless gaiety'.

Recalling the way Gertrude Stein had come to live entirely in the present, 'where everything that came before her was attended to, not in a provisory way but completely, and with the finality of a Last Judgment', he suggests that this little description of saints from the opera could be used of herself:

> They have to be.
> They have to be.
> They have to be to see.
> To see to say.
> Laterally they may.

The script starts in the middle of a page of an exercise book and is called, '*Beginning of Studies for an opera to be sung*'.

> To know to know to love her so
> Four saints prepare for saints
> It makes it well fish.
> Four saints it makes it well fish.
> Four saints prepare for saints it makes it well well fish
>   it makes it well fish prepare for saints.
> In narrative prepare for saints.

The words seem simple, but the author worked hard to get this result, writing first such exercises as *Practice in Orations, Praises, Precepts*, and studying words in relation to a work which was to be both seen and heard.

As soon as she had finished this, she began *Lucy Church Amiably*,[1] *A Novel of Romantic beauty and nature and which Looks like an Engraving*, inspired by the Bilignin countryside and local church. The first page is headed *Advertisement* and is a kind of publishers' blurb.

> Lucy Church Amiably. There is a church and it is in Lucey and it has a steeple and the steeple is a pagoda and there

[1] Plain Edition, Paris, 1930.

is no reason for it and it looks like something else. Besides this there is amiably and this comes from the paragraph.

The beautiful theme sentence of the book follows:

> Select your song she said and it was done and then she said and it was done with a nod and then she bent her head in the direction of the falling water. Amiably.

She called it a pastoral novel and in it enjoys her countryside, often by simply listing its features:

> The beauties of nature hills valleys trees fields and birds. Trees valleys fields flocks and butter-flies and pinks and birds. Trees fields hills valleys birds pinks butter-flies clouds and oxen and walls of a part of a building which is up.

Not only was she writing but being published. This was largely due to the new *avant-garde* magazine *transition*, founded in the winter of 1926–7 by the Lorraine-American poet Eugène Jolas and his American wife, Maria. Jolas, who had recently been in America for six months and was preparing his *Anthologie de la Nouvelle Poésie Américaine*, naturally had excellent American contacts, besides those with European writers and visual artists. His wife, a linguist, did translations for *transition* and looked after the business and secretarial side. They invited Elliot Paul, a young American on the staff of the Paris *Chicago Tribune* of which Jolas was now City Editor, to be their assistant. Elliot Paul at once asked Gertrude Stein, whom he knew through Bravig Imbs, for a contribution for the first issue of April 1927. She gave him *An Elucidation*; it appeared with some words set in the wrong order, but this proved a boon, for it was then reprinted separately and issued as a *transition* supplement. During the next two years many examples of her work followed in this magazine including *As a wife has a cow a love story*, *Made a mile away*, *A hundred prominent men* and *Four Saints in Three Acts*. Gertrude Stein's titles in themselves are good reading.

The appearance of *transition* filled the *avant-garde* writers with hope, Gertrude Stein's only chagrin being the editors' enthusiasm for James Joyce. Finally, when Elliot Paul was no longer concerned with the magazine, she fell out with the Jolases on this account. She had no use for Joyce at all and said so roundly.

transition revived interest in her work. The same year new editions of *Three Lives* appeared in England and America, and in 1928 Payson and Clarke of New York brought out a volume of her short pieces under the title *Useful Knowledge*. Meanwhile, as she wrote to Carl Van Vechten who this year visited her, cementing their affection, 'there is even more of it face to face',

> ... we are all now that Virgil has left who was to do it translating Making of Americans only 60 pages but oh my, our little George Hugnet 20 years old hair is turning white with the struggle but it really does not sound so bad but it is a funny language not mine of course but the french ...

And to Sherwood Anderson:

> I am working fairly steadily on the sentence, I am making a desperate effort to find out what is and what isn't a sentence, having been brought up in a good old public school grammar and sentences are a fascinating subject to me. I struggled all last year with grammar, vocabulary is easier, and now I think before more grammar I must find out what is the essence of a sentence, sometimes I almost know but not yet quite ... otherwise we have been busy with a translation of 60 pages of Making of Americans, it was rather interesting particularly as my young translator knew no English.

Only six years before in *Operas and Plays* she had written 'I do hate sentences.'

The funniness of French did not prevent her from now trying her own hand at it in *Film: deux sœurs qui ne sont pas sœurs*, and being very proud when *La Revue européenne* published it with the note, 'Le premier texte écrit et publié en français par Miss Stein.'

The French translation of parts of *The Making of Americans* made by Georges Hugnet with the help of Gertrude Stein and her friends was published by him in 1929 in Éditions de la Montagne under the title *Morceaux choisis de La fabrication des Américains*. It had a Christian Bérard portrait of the author for frontispiece and in his preface Georges Hugnet wrote: 'Je ne sais pas Anglais mais j'ai traduit lettre par lettre et virgule par virgule.' He also said that the rhythm of the language reminded him of a chair in his childhood which played *Martha* when one sat on it. He then published *Dix Portraits*, containing the English text with translations of many of her portraits of artists and illustrations by Picasso, Tchelitchew, Bérard, Eugène Berman and others of her subjects. Picasso did produce his drawing this time, but about another project a little later she wrote: 'The trouble with asking Picasso is that he is just as liable to say yes as no but having said yes he is more than likely not to do anything.'

In 1930 Marcel Brion published a long article in *Échanges* called *Le Contrepoint poétique de Gertrude Stein*. It was the third number of this enterprising magazine, edited by Allanah Harper, and Gertrude Stein was in excellent company with Thomas Hardy, Thomas Mann, Bertrand Russell, Norman Douglas and Edith Sitwell.

Marcel Brion affirmed in this appreciation that whereas hitherto poets seeking to be musical had cultivated the vague and the atmospheric, 'in a word *le flou*', and had never thought of asking Bach to give them a lesson in style, Gertrude Stein's work in its crystalline integrity was comparable to a Bach fugue. He also found in it an analogy with the Mexican dance and observed that he had always been struck by the 'extraordinarily hard and strangely cruel side' there was to her art.

Gertrude Stein was delighted with this article. 'Of course', Alice Toklas commented. 'For what he said about Bach is true. She introduces her theme contrapuntally and turns to the minor key and has the same exactitude.'[1]

With all this going on and her new home and her old one, life for Gertrude Stein as the twenties drew to a close was full of activity and full of hope. 'We are very busy farming,' she wrote, 'we like farming, and we are busy being published we like being published.'

One may also remember that she was very busy doing nothing. Being a genius, she said, took up a great deal of time, and at Bilignin she spent much of it lying in a chair in the garden with her dogs on top of her, looking unblinkingly up into the sun.

Yet, although her interest in her own work was so intense that

[1] Author's journal.

it dominated her life, she was not in an ordinary sense self-centred. Had she been, she would never have exercised such magnetic power over those who came within her orbit. She had the gift, part of which was in her steady gaze, of making whomever she was talking or listening to feel that he was the most interesting person in the world. This was sincere; her interest in human beings was inexhaustible, and sometimes when she was talking— Thornton Wilder emphasizes this point—she was definitely inspired.

One friend of this period was Louis Bromfield, then living with his family at Senlis. Gertrude Stein took great pleasure in his beautiful arrangements of flowers and his taste for good food, and they discovered a 'community of language'. 'The more experienced I grow,' he wrote in 1931, thanking her for a note about his book *Twenty-four Hours*, 'the nearer I come to speaking your tongue.' He also declared 'that it was Gertrude Stein who formulated, however mysteriously, the American rhythm in writing, and she it is who is largely responsible for the fact that the writing of any American under forty is utterly different from the writing of any Englishman under forty'.[1]

By now, at fifty-five, she had influenced the lives and work of a great many writers and painters.

Gertrude Stein liked children and it is interesting to have their impression of her. Her friends Jane Heap and Margaret Anderson, the editors of *The Little Review*, had adopted Fritz[2] and Tom Peters when they returned to New York for the winter of 1925-6, they left the boys at the Gurdjieff Institute at Fontainebleau in charge of Gertrude Stein—or rather, as Fritz Peters puts it, 'of course Gurdjieff was in charge, but Gertrude was the watcher-over or something'. There are a few letters in the Yale files from the boys all beginning, 'Dear Alice and Gertrude Stein', and speaking of being 'so awfully busy cleaning, sowing grass seed, raking brush wood', and so forth.

In one letter Tom explains the complications of Mr. Gurdjieff's plans for combining the Russian and English Christmas on December 26th and wanting to have the boys 'in the Sprit of it'.

[1] *New York Herald Tribune*, Sept. 25th, 1932.
[2] Later the novelist Fritz Peters.

He suggests rather wistfully that he and his brother might go to the rue de Fleurus on real Christmas day. The letter ends:

> Please wire
> very urgent
>
> A very loving Fool that I am
>
> Tom

Gertrude Stein liked her exiled charges to have real American Thanksgiving and Christmas, and Alice Toklas used to produce delicious meals for them. For six months the boys visited them regularly and Gertrude Stein showed them Paris.

> She felt, [Fritz Peters writes] and it was in every way marvelous that she did, that two adolescents living in Paris should KNOW the city from every point of view. Every day with her meant some kind of excursion: to see the usual things such as Nôtre Dame, Sacré Cœur, Eiffel Tower, the bridges, the museums, the various quarters of the city, as well as visits to the homes of friends which included a great many of the writers, painters, and other artists living there at the time. . . . I would certainly say (and it has become clearer to me as the years have passed) that Gertrude's main contribution to my life was that of making the city of Paris . . . known to me better than I know any city in the world, and of having done it in such a way that all those ineffable things that are usually unavailable (especially to young people) became something of mine for life.

He says further:

> We were very startled when Jane told us Gertrude Stein was going to take care of us. We went the first time in trepidation. But she was wonderful to us, always gave us what we wanted, not what she wanted to give us.
>
> I didn't like sight-seeing much as a child, but I liked what she arranged for us. 'Go up to the top of Nôtre Dame and here's a red handkerchief to wave so I can see you've got there.'
>
> At the Louvre she told us one or two things we should look at but didn't go round with us. 'You must like what you like not what I like. Art is something you must live with.'
>
> Once she asked me what I thought of the pictures at the

rue de Fleurus. I began slowly explaining I didn't like Picasso's portrait of her. She cut in quickly: 'Remember you don't have to like them.' And she pointed a finger at me repeating emphatically: 'Remember.' Another time she found me looking at one of her books and asked me what I thought of it.

'It doesn't make sense.'

'You've more courage and intelligence than most people,' she said. 'No, it doesn't make sense. That's the point.'

I was a little scared of Alice. She came and went so mysteriously. And although she often came in bearing some wonderful cake or other concoction I gave Gertrude the credit for it. I knew Alice was doing it for her.

And then one day in 1926 he saw her for the last time in the garden at Fontainebleau.

She was very upset and had brought me a box of some special candy. I believe the break was caused by some disagreement with Jane and I don't believe she thought the Institute was a good place for us. But she never said a word against Jane or Gurdjieff. She only said she would never see me again. And we were all very unhappy.[1]

Gertrude Stein and Gurdjieff met once. 'She had nothing against him', Alice Toklas says. A memorable statement when so very much has been said.

Another little boy, who knew the ladies a few years later, had a somewhat different impression. This was Mike's grandson, Dan, who used to be brought in to call on them by his grandparents with whom he lived. The day would be too eventful altogether; the car-sick journey, the excitement of sail-boats and donkey rides in the Luxembourg gardens, and finally the fascination of his aunt's house. He found the outside grim, 'like my imaginings of a prison', but the inside was 'literally stuffed with a fascinating hodge-podge of *objets d'art*; incomprehensible paintings exploded in cascades of colour from the walls'.

One is apt to forget what an inveterate collector Gertrude Stein was. There was something oriental in her liking to 'literally stuff' her rooms, a taste which her old friends Claribel and Etta

[1] Author's journal.

Cone emulated in Baltimore. Gertrude Stein was not a purist in anything but words.

It is strange that young Daniel found those pictures so garish considering how much more sombre her Picassos and Gris were than the *fauve* masterpieces hanging in his grandparents' Le Corbusier house. For the rest he found his aunt's dogs fascinating, for he had none at home, but he was not allowed to play with them. And of his hostesses he writes:

> To my child's eyes Aunt Gertrude herself seemed formidable and unique. For one thing she spoke quite loud. Being rather timid I believe I was a little afraid of her. Alice Toklas, on the other hand, had a much more subdued voice and a generally calmer and more reassuring presence. Still I am convinced Gertrude was genuinely fond of me. She sent me little gifts and post cards. I treasured long a small vase with my name on it and BILIGNIN, the name of the *manoir* near Belley.

CHAPTER FOURTEEN

CRITICISM AND CONTROVERSY

'I asked her to invent a name for my edition and she laughed
and said call it Plain Edition. And Plain Edition it is.'
The Autobiography of Alice B. Toklas.

WITH the new decade new friendships developed. Edith Sitwell,
writing to say how delighted she was with *An Elucidation* in
transition, had suggested that Gertrude Stein should invite her
friend the Chilean painter, Alvaro Guevara, to the rue de Fleurus.
Now, just back from Bilignin in the autumn of 1930, and going
out to buy some nails at the bazaar in the rue de Rennes, she ran
into Alvaro Guevara, known as Chile, and his wife Méraude
Guinness. They invited her and Miss Toklas to tea to meet Sir
Francis Rose. Let him describe the meeting.

It was late afternoon; it was tea time. A noise (as of wild
caged animals) greeted me in the hall as the door was
opened . . . Soon the source of the noise became apparent
for Chile pushed me into the drawing room.
A big black and white spotted dog was chasing a little dog,
and a very big white poodle chased the spotted dog, and
another dog chased the poodle and round and round the
room they went, and Méraude was shouting and people
were struggling as people will struggle when dogs are
fighting, and everybody was being aimlessly perturbed and
agitated, that is every one who was on his feet, for one
woman sat at the table in the middle of the room quietly
eating a cake. She had her back to me, and her hair which
was turning grey was cut very short.
As Chile was a little perturbed by having to receive a new
guest and attend to a dog fight at the same moment . . . he
took the easy course and pushed me into a seat next to the
woman with the cake, mumbling something quite incomprehensible.

The cake slowly disappeared, the dog fight was over ... the woman turned to me and said 'You are Francis Rose?' I said yes. 'Do you want to see your pictures?' I felt very surprised and said yes. 'Well later,' she replied.

These were the first words I exchanged with Gertrude Stein before I knew who she was. Then Méraude told me and I met Alice. Since then I have loved them. I met Basket also, the first Basket, and Basket was the white poodle the champion of the noise ...

Until that tea party I did not know that Gertrude Stein had bought pictures of mine, so it was on this memorable day that my work and life became first connected with her. She did not talk much then but other people did ... and when the talking was over, we walked across the Boulevard Raspail to the rue de Fleurus.

I was ignorant then about the rue de Fleurus. I did not know of the great glamour it held for artists, for the great and famous, for above all the inquisitive and interesting young, the wild, the violent and the creative who had crossed its threshold, drunk Alice's wonderful tea and eaten her exotic petits fours. I came to it as to just a new house; the street was just a most ordinary Paris street, not one of the beautiful ones of the rive gauche. We went through a porte cochère with a shabby concierge's loge in which sat an old concierge wearing a postière's cap and blue workman's trousers ... the small flagged courtyard we crossed was shabbier and facing us was a large lockup studio, which might have been a garage or a work shop ...

The studio was higher than it was large. The furniture was heavy and renaissance; a great sofa and armchairs covered with horsehair filled the middle; two tiny Louis XV chairs stood near by; they were covered with jewel-like petit point tapestry, one in bright yellow, black and red, the other in green and white. These were the work of Alice B. Toklas from the designs Picasso had painted on the canvas. The atmosphere was like that of a cultured Spanish house ... but the walls! The walls were covered, tier over tier of paintings. One over the other until one could hardly see them near the ceiling. The whitewashed walls were just covered with paintings. Paintings the kind that only people who love paint will have. I do not mean pictures. I think when Gertrude

Stein wrote her essay on painting she expressed this when she said she loved painting, all painting on flat surfaces and in oil paint.[1]

Indeed, oil paint and particularly white oil paint delighted her, most of all as used by Spanish painters. Another thing she liked was *trompe-l'œil*. She had discovered in Italy that if she were specially pleased by the marble in some church, it always turned out to be real marble mixed up with a painted imitation. And a curtain or shutters depicted on a wall gave her more pleasure than the real thing although she never discovered why.

From the day of their meeting Francis Rose was devoted to her, and having previously read little of her work and found it unintelligible, he came now to believe that she was in her way as great a writer as Shakespeare. But she no longer had so strong a faith in painting as in her early days. On the first page of her current book, *How to Write*,[2] comes the line, 'painting now after its great moment must come back to be a minor art'. Writing was to her the highest achievement of man's imagination.

Another important new friendship was with Bernard Faÿ, a young professor of literature at the University of Clermont-Férrand, whom Bravig Imbs described as 'something between a saint and a captain of intellectual history'. Gertrude Stein had met him some years before and he had always been greatly interested in her work. Now they came to know one another well. She saw that he was destined for the Collège de France, and he was stimulated by her mind and, himself an historian of Benjamin Franklin, enjoyed her original views of American history. He translated parts of *Melanctha* and *The Making of Americans* into French and had them published, and later, in America, he both wrote and spoke about her work with enthusiasm.

These friendships with Francis Rose and Bernard Faÿ endured, but meanwhile others ended. In January 1931, with the new heading *Plain Edition* to her notepaper, she wrote:

My dearest Carl
　　Voilà pourquoi j'avais . . . well anyhow we have decided to publish ourselves, Alice is managing director I am author,

[1] From *Memories of Gertrude Stein* by Francis Rose. (Unpublished.)
[2] Plain Edition, 1931.

and we hope there will be purchasers, and so to be so best to you both, and will you Carl if you can do a notice somewhere or get somebody else to of the edition and the book, perhaps that would help, anyway it's a try and I am very happy about it. We have been having a hectic one might almost say lurid winter so far, there is this and many other things and then we have quarrelled beginning with Bravig Imbs going on through Tonny[1] and George Hugnet, ending with Virgil Thomson and now we don't see any of them any more, but we seem to be seeing almost everybody else such is life in a great capital, otherwise calm. Basket had distemper but he is now well, I am writing plays rather nice ones, Bernard Faÿ is translating me on Madame Récamier, that pleases me . . .

Bravig Imbs, however, would not be so easily dropped. In January 1931 he wrote:

> . . . If I have said, done, or written anything which has displeased or hurt either you or Alice, I am heartily sorry and beg you to forgive me . . .
>
> If I have become dull or uninteresting to you, that is another matter, and I recognise your right to drop me in such a case. . . .
>
> Losing friends is a sad matter for me, as I have so few of them, and to lose such friends as you and Alice have been, is doubly hard. I remember you said once that all the young men went away, and I wondered at your statement, for I could not believe it possible. Perhaps the young men should go away for their own sakes, but I do not feel or care to be one of them.

His loyal tenacity healed the breach but only for a while; then relations ended suddenly with a *coup de téléphone*. He was considered to have presumed upon their friendship.

Great hopes were now pinned to the *Plain Edition*. In spite of appearing in print more often, Gertrude Stein felt the need of a publisher who would produce her work regularly and help to build up a public for it. 'There are many Paris picture dealers', she wrote, 'who like adventure in their business, there are no publishers in America who like adventure in theirs.' Alice Toklas

[1] Kristians Tonny, the artist.

therefore decided to become a publisher herself and start by producing *Lucy Church Amiably*.

Advice poured in about how to get the book printed and distributed and before long it appeared bound in blue and looking, as its author wished, like a school book.

> It was easy to get the book put in the window of all the booksellers in Paris that sold english books. This event gave Gertrude Stein a childish delight amounting almost to ecstasy . . .

As Thornton Wilder says, 'there was always the little girl in her, so ready to be pleased and excited'.

The second work to be brought out in the *Plain Edition* was a poem containing some beautiful lines opening:

> In the one hundred small places of myself my youth
> And myself in if it is the use of passion,
> In this in it and in the nights alone.
> If in the next to to night which is indeed not well
> I follow you without it having slept and went . . .

This poem was what she called a 'reflection' of *Enfances* by Georges Hugnet. To begin with he was pleased and wrote, 'Admirable Gertrude . . . This isn't a translation, it is something else, *it is better*', but a few months later he was writing to protest about the proposed placing of their names on the prospectus which suggested a collaboration, 'when, don't you agree, there is no question of that'. She retaliated by having his *Enfances* printed in the magazine *Pagany* opposite her *Poem Pritten on Pfances of Georges Hugnet*. And the change in their relations inspired for the poem the best of all her titles, *Before The Flowers of Friendship Faded Friendship Faded*.[1]

There was no difficulty in selling the *Plain Edition* of a hundred copies, finely printed at Chartres on Antique Morval paper, and Gertrude Stein observed:

> They all seem nuts about it and I guess it is because I have in it for the first time kind of solved the problem of modern poetry which torments them all.[2]

Years later, in America, she asked Lindley Hubbell to read the

[1] *Plain Edition*, 1931.   [2] C.V.V.

lectures she was about to give and he started with one about poetry.

> Well, she sort of hung over my shoulder while I was reading it and when I reached a certain point she exclaimed, 'There! When I wrote that I was *frightened*, because I realized that I am the only person who has ever known what poetry is.'[1]

The third volume of *Plain Edition* was *How to Write*, a collection of obscure meditations with titles such as *Saving the Sentence, Regularly Regularly in Narrative, A Vocabulary of Thinking and Forensics*. A thousand copies were made by the Darantière Press at Dijon which had printed *The Making of Americans*, and the venture seems to have been financed with the proceeds of selling Picasso's beautiful early painting *Girl with a Fan*.

> A sentence is made by coupling meanwhile ride around to be a couple there makes grateful dubiety named atlas coin in a loan.
> This is what they all do . . .
> Regularly regularly in a narrative. A narrative is in revision a narrative is in division a narrative is in reconciliation a narrative is in a narrative is they is in they that the the that that is the and then . . .
> What is an argument. What are forensics. What are master pieces. What are their hopes. An argument is this. I have it. They reserve it. They do not answer at once. Forensics is this. Better come when it rains, better come when it rains, and rains, better come and puzzle that they have been within and it rains who have all by the time and not also to go.

It is difficult to get the flavour in short quotations. Throughout the quite long book the author sustains her thought, and sometimes one can follow, but often there are not enough clues to point the way.

Letters announced that *Plain Edition* was doing very well, 'Lucy is in considerable demand and Alice is a proud editor and I am an equally pleased author.'[2] For the next publications, *Operas and Plays*[3] and *Matisse Picasso and Gertrude Stein*,[4] Monsieur

---

[1] Letter from Lindley Hubbell to Jan Marfyak.
[2] C.V.V.   [3] Plain Edition, 1932.   [4] Plain Edition, 1933.

Darantière devised charming little volumes bound in tan paper, each in its own box. This was to meet the editor's request that *Plain Edition* should be inexpensive.

> After all Gertrude Stein's readers are writers, university students, librarians and young people who have very little money. Gertrude Stein wants readers and not collectors . . . she wants her books read not owned.

In 1931, *Axel's Castle* appeared. 'Gertrude Stein is a singular case', Edmund Wilson wrote. 'Widely ridiculed and seldom enjoyed she has yet played an important rôle in connection with other writers who have become popular.' He admitted that 'most of us balk at her soporific rigmaroles, her echolaliac incantations', but none the less declared, 'whenever we pick up her writings, however unintelligible we may find them, we are aware of a literary personality of unmistakable originality and distinction'.[1]

Gertrude Stein commented:

> Yes I have seen Bunny Wilson's book, thanks so much, I was not born in Baltimore, and I am not *german*, and I do make poetry which can be read otherwise I was pleased.[2]

That summer she wrote a revealing letter to the young American, Lindley Hubbell, about his poems:

> . . . every now and then there is a perfect harmony of sound and sense, and they are simple and they bear rereading, just how meaning is related to sound and just how you must conceive meaning so that sound does not count, is the thing that endlessly holds us, because of course if the meaning has a certain emphasis, then the sound separates itself and it all goes to pot, and if the sound sounds then the meaning is annoyed, and after all the meaning is reliable only if it creates in and by itself the sound, and yet there should be no sound, well it's all very difficult, but then it is what we do. I am at present trying a long narrative poem, I always had a passion in my youth for the long dull poems of Wordsworth and Crabbe and I want to do a long dull poem too and a bare one, and perhaps I am but anyway your sympathy and appreciation mean a lot to me and I know mine do to you.

[1] W. H. Allen; London, Charles Scribner's Sons, New York, 1931.
[2] C.V.V.

The following spring she gave him some characteristic advice:

> . . . and I like the idea of your writing a novel make it long
> enough and go very slow sometimes and go pretty fast some-
> times but keep going . . . it is in getting your emotion to have
> imagination and your observation to have the same value of
> imagination but after all all that there is to do is as the french
> say continuez and that you will do.

Before the break with Robert McAlmon she had given him
similar counsel:

> I have been reading Village . . . your style is getting more
> adequate and more simply merged in your material and you
> are entirely right to write a lot, like Trollope you ought to
> write a lot. It is in that way that completion will come to
> you.

And referring to his writer wife, Bryher, '. . . it is strange that
you have it in common to absolutely need the classic french
advice, continuez'. Advice which Gertrude Stein took herself.

Lindley Hubbell reciprocated about the book which baffles so
many readers:

> I finished How to Write and liked it a lot. It is, if I count
> right, your eighteenth book, and what an interesting pro-
> cession they make, from Three Lives to How to Write.

He then admits that one of the essays in it, *A Vocabulary of
Thinking*, was the first of her writings that he found difficult,
'the unit of form is so huge'. He goes on to praise the beauty of
her Hugnet poem, and ends with a remarkable comparison between her work and Joyce's.

> . . . most people say that you and he are the only two creative
> writers in English today. It is interesting because you and he
> started at about the same point (*Dubliners* isn't as good as
> *Three Lives*, but it *is* good) and from that point you started
> in exactly opposite directions; he towards greater com-
> plexity and you towards greater simplicity. And his is a
> blind alley, because the more complicated you get the more
> incomprehensible you become, until you reach a point where
> you are entirely incomprehensible (he's reached it. And I
> have to laugh at people who say that *Work in Progress* is

witty. He has no more wit than a trout.) But the road which you took can't end until you reach the thing-in-itself. And whether there is a thing-in-itself I don't know, and neither do you. But at any rate, it's a long road, open under the sky and good healthy travelling. The result is that everyone who has followed him has become sterile and finally stopped writing altogether; and everyone who has followed you— well, everyone who writes stories for Harpers or Scribners or the Atlantic is following you, so there can't be any harm in it!

How different is the view of Robert McAlmon in his book *Being Geniuses Together*.[1]

> They are as unlike as the North Pole is from the Equator. Joyce knows words, their rhythms, colour, associations, capacity to evoke, their histories and their emotional significations. Stein fumbles and mauls them, and gradually something emerges as so much mud emerges into some sort of form in the hands of a maladroit child. Stein's wit is sluggish; Joyce's is almost too quick, constant, and, around a limited range of experience, variable. They have in common only a tendency to withdraw themselves from the horde, to make themselves precious, but that tendency is indeed light with Joyce, and would not be in him at all if it were not that his eyes do not allow him to be as gregariously free and easy as he would like to be. He is not afraid of being unmasked, for he is sure of himself, and I have never known him to boast without immediately withdrawing it in a 'What do we all know about it?' manner. That cannot be said of poor Gertrude.

Thus differently did her work affect these two young writers, although it is only fair to remember that McAlmon also said that she had qualities which commanded admiration. He was entirely mistaken in thinking that she was unsure of herself; like all artists she often doubted her ability to realize her vision, but in that vision and the supreme importance of it she had from the beginning complete conviction. Another view comes from Moholy Nagy:

[1] Secker and Warburg, 1938.

Gertrude Stein's seemingly primitive stammering, her repetitive childlike statements hide sharp criticism. It is a canny
form of attack in the guise of sancta simplicitas. Hiding in
the skin of the innocent, unsophisticated, she often offers
the most shocking of all statements, the Truth.[1]

As for her wit, Alice Toklas maintains that this is a purely
English quality which Gertrude Stein could not have, though she
had her particular brand of humour, while Donald Sutherland
says that she had 'a gift for extremely broad and reckless farce'.
In any case she could be beautifully funny. And it was a taste for
rather mischievous fun which now induced her, as a rest from
exhausting philological meditations, to write 'as simply as Defoe
did the autobiography of Robinson Crusoe' *The Autobiography of
Alice B. Toklas.*

[1] *Vision in Motion.* Paul Theobald, Chicago, 1947.

CHAPTER FIFTEEN

THE AUTOBIOGRAPHY OF ALICE B. TOKLAS

'So I am an American and I have lived half my life in Paris, not the half that made me but the half in which I made what I made.'

What Are Masterpieces.

'Although I never do think anything is going to happen things were happening, Roosevelt was being elected, the opera was going to be given, the Autobiography was selling, everybody wanted to know me.'

Letter to Carl Van Vechten.

HAD she not been so tired and had the fall of 1932 not been so long and lovely, luring the friends to stay on at Bilignin, perhaps *The Autobiography* would not have been written. But there were portents too of good luck, and Gertrude Stein was superstitious. 'Anything is a superstition and anybody rightly believes in superstition. Because it is certain that what has been is going on.' And when things were not going well she observed that anyway one can always wear something by mistake inside out. In this case conditions were favourable and in about six weeks she wrote herself in to fame.

It has been well said by Robert Bartlett Haas in his introduction to *What Are Masterpieces* that in what she chose to call *The Autobiography of Alice B. Toklas*, Gertrude Stein became her own Boswell. But her feat was subtler than that: she created a to-the-life study, a kind of film, of Alice Toklas in the act of being her Boswell. Told in the first person the conversational style is that of Miss Toklas; on every page one hears her turn of phrase, recognizes her sharp or gentle observation, her swift sizing up of everything and everybody. At the same time one has a clear impression of Gertrude Stein herself, hears her conversation and her laughter, watches her many activities, and is aware too of her being quite endlessly indolent while Miss Toklas is being endlessly diligent.

One feels the women enjoying a fine rich life and warmly welcoming anybody who can add to it while ruthlessly expelling the rest.

On the opening page of the first exercise book is written *Autobiography of Alice Babette Toklas, Thirty* [crossed out] *Twentyfive* [substituted] *years with Gertrude Stein*. And the script ends: 'Yours sincerely Alice B. Toklas', but these first ideas were discarded. In fact, Miss Toklas never liked even the 'B.', and always said so.

'The book is full of the most lucid and shapely anecdotes,' says Donald Sutherland, 'told in a purer and more closely fitting prose, to my sense, than even Gide or Hemingway have ever commanded.' The punctuation, in spite of her dislike of it, is conventional, and except for the book's achievement in making the past the present it does not follow her own dictates. It is therefore a little ironic, even a little sad, that it should be this work, clever though it is, that brought her the glory she had always craved.

She tells how, as soon as she got back to Paris, the Picassos came to the rue de Fleurus and she began translating the book aloud to them.

> So I began at the beginning with the description of the room as it was and the description of our servant Helen. You made one mistake said Pablo you left out something there were three swords that hung on that wall one underneath the other and he said it was very exciting. Then I went on and Fernande came in.
>
> I was reading he was listening and his eyes were wide open and then suddenly his wife Olga Picasso got up and said she would not listen she would go away she said. What's the matter, we said, I do not know that woman she said and left. Pablo said go on reading. I said no you must go after your wife, he said oh I said oh, and he left . . .[1]

And once again there was a silence between Picasso and Gertrude Stein for a couple of years.

The Autobiography's success was immediate. Her agent in Paris, Mr. W. A. Bradley, had no difficulty in selling the book to Harcourt Brace and Company and she at last achieved her ambi-

[1] *Everybody's Autobiography.*

tion to be published in the *Atlantic Monthly*. Just a year before
Ellery Sedgwick had written once more regretting that the magazine could not publish her work:

> Those vedettes who lead the vanguard of pictorial arts are
> understood, or partly understood, over here by a reasonably
> compact following, but that following cannot translate their
> loyalties into a corresponding literature . . .

Now, in February 1933, he wrote:

> There has been a lot of pother about this book of yours, but
> what a delightful book it is, and how glad I am to publish
> four instalments of it! During our long correspondence, I
> think you felt my constant hope that the time would come
> when the real Miss Stein would pierce the smoke-screen with
> which she has always so mischievously surrounded herself.
> The autobiography has just enough of the oblique to give it
> individuality and character, and readers who care for the
> things you do will love it . . .
> Anything that we can do to help the success of the book,
> as well as the serial, will certainly be done.
> Hail Gertrude Stein about to arrive! . . .

The 'pother' refers to characteristic differences of opinion
between publisher, author, agent and magazine about the instalments for the *Atlantic Monthly*. However these duly appeared and
the book was published in August 1933. All difficulties were light
now for Gertrude Stein. She had always felt that fame would be
pleasant but not that it would be quite so pleasant as this. 'I am
most pleased with everything', she told Van Vechten. 'I
love being rich, not as yet so awful rich but with prospects, it
makes me all cheery inside I don't know why it should but it
does.'

In the following letter she speaks of receiving the new edition
of *Three Lives*. 'I solemnly read the good Anna, one was young
and sweet and solemn, powerfully solemn in those days.' And
presently, from Belley, she tells of her new work: 'I am doing a
long book all about four eminent Americans and the first one is
Grant it is beginning well, I am at last getting used to my fame
and am beginning to work.'

Carl Van Vechten, who had become as keen a photographer as writer, was enchanted with the success for which he had worked so hard and long, and begged her to come to America and be photographed. Congratulations poured in; one postcard saying 'I wonder if you know you are more discussed in Hollywood these days than Greta Garbo?'

Among painters Francis Picabia and Francis Rose were now the two who most interested her. 'One might say they were both called Francis and anybody called Francis is elegant unbalanced and intelligent and certain to be right not about everything but about themselves.'

Picabia had conceived the idea that a line should have the vibration of a musical sound and was struggling to express his conception. Gertrude Stein wrote of him as the painter who was 'going to be the creator of the vibrant line', and Picabia, like Francis Rose, found that his conversations with her about painting did him 'enormous good'. In 1933 he painted a picture of her, bare-shouldered in an Indian blanket against a mountain background.[1]

But it was Francis Rose whom she called her real discovery, 'I care a lot for both works and man.' He painted the Bilignin house from across the valley as they had first seen it and also both his hostesses. One drawing, part of a design for a mural entitled 'Homage to Gertrude Stein', shows her sitting on a rock, her hand on top of her head holding down her thoughts. In 1932 she sponsored his first exhibition in Paris and later wrote a preface to the catalogue for his London show. Her taste in painting was more romantic now than in earlier days.

In June 1933 Virgil Thomson wrote to her from Paris about *Four Saints in Three Acts*:

> I find on working over the opera and orchestrating that I should very much like to make a few simple cuts. You offered me that privilege at the beginning of our collaboration and I didn't care to avail myself of it . . . I should like to eliminate for example a few of the stage-directions as sung, especially where they are repeated frequently . . . to replace them with an instrumental passage of the same length and time. This

[1] In the Gertrude Stein Collection, Yale Collection of American Literature.

makes a rather amusing effect and is as if an instrument were saying the words that somebody has just sung . . .

Before long it was arranged for the opera to have its première in Hartford, Connecticut, early in 1934. Virgil Thomson wrote from New York:

> The cast of the opera is hired and rehearsal is begun. I have a chorus of 32 and six soloists, very, very fine ones indeed. Miss Stettheimer's[1] sets are of a beauty incredible, with trees made out of feathers and a sea-wall at Barcelona made out of shells and for the procession a baldachino of black chiffon and bunches of black ostrich plumes just like a Spanish funeral. St. Teresa comes to the picnic in the 2nd Act in a cart drawn by a real white donkey and brings her tent with her and sets it up and sits in the door-way of it. It is made of white gauze with gold fringe and has a most elegant shape. My singers, as I have wanted, are Negroes, and you can't imagine how beautifully they sing. Frederick Ashton is arriving from London this week to make choreography for us . . . Everything about the opera is shaping up so beautifully, even the raising of money (it's going to cost $11,000), that the press is champing at the bit and the New York ladies already ordering dresses and engaging hotel rooms . . . Rumors of your arrival are floating about . . . and your presence would be all we need to make the opera perfect in every way.

And Gertrude Stein commented to Van Vechten:

> . . . just had a charming letter from a colored boy all about the opera, his feelings were hurt because it would appear they said in the newspapers they chose the Negroes as singers because they would not giggle and he said why should they giggle since of course they would understand.

The first of the many reports of the première was from the faithful Carl Van Vechten:

> Four Saints, in our vivid theatrical parlance, is a knockout and a wow. I cabled you when I got home from the invited dress rehearsal last night (I mean you were invited to buy

[1] Florine Stettheimer, 'Perhaps the greatest fantasiste, living in an apartment as spindly as her paintings . . . where the dining-room curtains are made of gold chocolate paper.' *New York*, Cecil Beaton, Batsford.

seats). It was a most smart performance in this beautiful little theatre. People not only wore evening clothes, they wore sables and tiaras . . . I haven't seen a crowd more excited since Sacre du Printemps. The difference was that they were pleasurably excited. The Negroes are divine, like El Grecos, more Spanish, more Saints, more opera singers in their dignity and *simplicity* and extraordinary plastic line than *any* white singers could ever be. And they enunciated the text so clearly you could understand every word. Frederick Ashton's rhythmic staging was inspired and so were Florine's costumes and sets. Imagine a crinkled sky-blue cellophane background, set in white lace borders, like a valentine against which were placed the rich and royal costumes of the saints in red velvets, etc. and the dark Spanish skins . . . The manager who is taking it to New York expects it to be a success and I am sure it will be *something* . . . I really think you should see, hear and feel Four Saints . . . .

What an astonishing elaboration to arise from Gertrude Stein's simplicity!

In her reply she spoke of her pride at getting a fan cable from an unknown in New York addressed Gertrude Stein, Paris, and asked for 'photos of my name in electricity'.

A letter from Alfred Harcourt, of Harcourt Brace and Company, describes a performance of the opera in New York:

The house was crowded last night with a really distinguished audience. Toscanini was in the orchestra chair behind me, and I noticed that he seemed completely absorbed in the performance and applauded vigorously.

It must be a good satisfaction to you to have had at last real recognition from an audience in America. I am delighted to have had some small share in it.

And Virgil Thomson contributed:

. . . all agree my music makes you palatable to otherwise not-having-any's. That's the literary group, the musicians all find that my music is not much without your words.

Demands for her presence increased and it was suggested that she should go over on a lecture tour. After all these years, W. G. Rogers, 'The Kiddie' of Nîmes in the First World War, was in

THE AUTOBIOGRAPHY OF ALICE B. TOKLAS' 179

touch with her again and visited her at Bilignin. He and Mr.
Bradley planned how best to make a success of such a venture
in the coming fall, although in the end Miss Stein dispensed with
managers other than Miss Toklas. Everyone was enthusiastic
about the project except one friend who wrote:

> . . . I don't at all approve of your going to America. I think
> that you should follow your usual serene habits and allow
> America to come to you. In other words the oracle on the
> mountain's top should *stay* on the mountain top. You and
> Alice will be like two Rip van Winkles over there. It's too
> *late* to take this step. [1]

But she decided, although not lightly, to go. She was finding
fame delightful but upsetting. On the one hand there was the
simple pleasure of spending, 'first I bought myself a new eight
cylinder Ford car, and the most expensive coat made to order by
Hermes and fitted by the man who makes coats for race horses for
Basket and two collars studded for Basket. I had never made any
money before in my life and I was most excited.' The telephone
was put in both at the rue de Fleurus and at Bilignin and a bath-
room installed in the country house. 'Up to this time we had
bathed in a rubber tub and had the water brought in from the
fountain. In France you do not have a pump you have a fountain.'
And instead of 'just having one servant we had a couple, a man
and a woman, and we spent a very hectic summer with them'.

For the Italians whom they brought from Paris did not like
the rural ways of Bilignin and there were many tiresome changes
of servants (at some point one who arrived looking like a Modigliani and left looking like a Rubens), until the advent of Trac,
the first of several Indo-Chinamen who was much loved and
photographed. There are countless snapshots of those tranquil
summer days—Picasso standing by the parapet against the view,
Gertrude sitting on it singing her favourite ditty, *The Trail of the
Lonesome Pine*, and a host of other friends, the women in big shady
hats—all but Gertrude, short-cropped, bare-headed, gazing into
the sun.

Now came the Pernollet tragedy, described with serene objecti-

[1] Janet Scudder.

vity in *Everybody's Autobiography*. The hotel in Belley had become famous for its food, but the family had had many troubles, culminating in the tuberculosis of one of the sons, a boy whose painting Gertrude Stein encouraged. One morning Madame Pernollet's body was found in the courtyard to which she had fallen from a high window. The family did not tell the clients but carried straight on with their business. This incident led to the writing of an abstract piece, *Blood on the Dining-room Floor*, an example of the creative artist's ability to remain aloof from personal involvement, which in Gertrude Stein was very marked.

Meanwhile, although she speaks of a long time when she was not writing, she had finished *Four in America*,[1] one of her major works. This was published in 1947, the year after her death, with an illuminating and moving introduction by Thornton Wilder which must be read by any serious student of Gertrude Stein's work. It ends:

> She said to me once: 'Everyone when they are young has a little bit of genius, that is they really do listen. They can listen and talk at the same time. Then they grow a little older and many of them get tired and they listen less and less. But some, a very few continue to listen. And finally they get very old and they do not listen any more. That is very sad; let us not talk about that.' This book is by an impassioned listener to life. Even up to her last years she listened to all comers, to 'how their knowing came out of them'. Hundreds of our soldiers, scoffing and incredulous but urged on by their companions, came up to Paris 'to see the Eiffel Tower and Gertrude Stein'. They called and found bent upon them those gay and challenging eyes and that attention that asked nothing less of them than their genius. Neither her company nor her books were for those who have grown tired of listening. It was an irony that she did her work in a world in which for many reasons and many appalling reasons people have so tired.

The opening page of *Four in America* runs:

> If Ulysses S. Grant had been a religious leader who was to become a saint what would he have done.

[1] Yale University Press, 1947.

If the Wright brothers had been artists that is painters
what would they have done.

If Henry James had been a general what would he have
had to do.

If General Washington had been a writer that is a novelist
what would he do.

Even now, when she found that by writing a book that 'has
a money value', she had in a way become public property, she
kept her integrity, her tenet that, to quote Thornton Wilder,
'at the moment of writing one rigorously excludes from the
mind all thought of praise and blame, of persuasion or conciliation. In the early days she used to say: "I write for myself and
strangers." Then she eliminated the strangers; then she had a great
deal of trouble with the idea that one is an audience to oneself,
which she solves in this book with the far-reaching concept: "I
am not I when I see."'

Yet she frankly admitted that what she wanted more than
anything was praise, and always for each drop of praise she had
received a bucketful of derision. All the more admirable that now,
when she was winning so much sweet praise with a book that
asked less of its readers, she should, once over the shock of fame,
continue with a work some of whose pages 'bristle with Miss
Stein's most idiosyncratic expressions'.

At the same time she was writing little things. One page of a
1934 notebook is interesting, in view of coming history. It is
written in French—she says in *Everybody's Autobiography*, 'I talk
French badly and write it worse'—'Qu'est que je pense de la
France. Je pense pas de la France, je l'aime je la defende je l'habite.'
But she was soon to say some very wise things about her adopted
country.

Back in Paris, 'everybody invited me to meet someone and
I went. I always will go anywhere once and I rather liked doing
what I had never done before, going visiting and meeting the
people who make it pleasant to you to be a lion. . . . We did not
yet use a tiny engagement book and look at it in a near sighted
way the way all the young men used to do as soon as they were
successful but we might have.'

Inevitably she quarrelled with her agent. 'I am always ready to sign anything a bank tells me to sign but everything else fills me with suspicion. I wanted the Four in America printed and he wanted me to sign a contract for another autobiography.'

'With a Frenchman quarrelling', she wrote, 'is another matter. Combat is so natural to them that quarrelling is not really anything.' But with Mr. Bradley it was everything. She said she would not go to America and lecture, 'I do want to get rich but I never want to do what there is to do to get rich', and he said she was upsetting all his carefully made arrangements. They never met again.

Altogether the prospect was upsetting. 'As I say I am a person of no initiation [sic], I usually stay where I am.' And since the war there had been no break in her customary routine. However by July 1934 she was writing:

> I am slowly but steadily getting pleased about getting over there and so is Alice, we begin to talk about it quite now as if we were going and even beginning to feel confident about it.

And she wrote *Meditations on being about to visit my native land*, and her six lectures, *What is English Literature, Pictures, Plays, The Gradual Making of the Making of Americans, Portraits and Repetition, Poetry and Grammar*.[1] Into these lectures she poured ideas, ideas, as Donald Sutherland says, 'expressed as they are had', but also for the first time she gave some explanation of the aim and method of her writing. She read the lectures aloud to Bernard Faÿ, now a professor of the Collège de France, and others of her friends, 'in France everybody reads everything aloud'.

> . . . and now we really were going to America . . .
> We decided to have all our clothes made in Belley and we did. That is one of the nice things in France if you are anywhere near Lyon you can get very good clothes made. Near Paris is not so good, Paris is a capitol [sic] and anywhere near it is suburban, but once you are away and anywhere near Lyon, there is good cooking and good dressmaking. So we had all our clothes made in Belley, I went on writing my lectures and everything was getting ready, I was not worried any more, worrying is an occupation part of the time but it can not be an occupation all the time.

[1] *Lectures in America*. Random House, 1935.

We had a special case made for the lectures, they make very good things in Belley, and this fitted exactly and we packed everything we could find to pack . . . Of course I had many new shoes, I am very fond of new shoes, I do not care a great deal for new clothes, I have to let them hang a long time before I can wear them but I do like new shoes and at Chambery they made me a great many of them.

And indeed the American photographs show Miss Stein wearing not the well-known sandals but neat bar shoes.

So at last everything was done, including the settling of Basket and Pépé in a temporary home, and on October 17th, 1934, Gertrude Stein and Alice Toklas sailed on the S.S. *Champlain*.

CHAPTER SIXTEEN

LECTURES IN AMERICA

'So then there we were and we were liking it lecturing and everything. Almost always liking it very very much. I was always eating honeydew melons and oysters and an egg and green apple pie before lecturing, and I was enjoying everything.'

Everybody's Autobiography.[1]

THEY enjoyed the journey. Boat travel had improved since they last crossed the Atlantic; thirty years, Gertrude Stein said, is not much but it is thirty years. And apart from the comfort, 'it was the beginning of travelling being a celebrity and all the privileges attached to that thing. Everybody had always been all right to us but this was being a different thing.'

On October 24th they arrived and Gertrude Stein found Staten Island 'awfully pretty it was so white and green', but the silhouette of New York disappointed her, it did not look high enough. Then there on the quay was the Kiddie waving, and there was everybody else and the press and the photographers and soon she was answering a lot of questions but asking a lot too, because she had to know who everybody was and where they came from. Then she was somewhere else on the boat, 'and they said I was broadcasting', and presently they were at the Algonquin Hotel, where they found they had four rooms instead of the one they had expected, and there were flowers and friends and more photographing and talking with reporters, and 'by that time we were excited'.

The first dinner at the Algonquin interested them enormously. They had wondered, while Gertrude Stein was making up her mind whether or not they should go to America, how they would find the food. A young man from the Bugey, recently returned from a short visit to the States, had told them that he

[1] This chapter is based on the description of the American visit in *Everybody's Autobiography.*

found the food stranger than the people or their homes. Gertrude liked the food but found it moist so wine did not go well with it, whereas French food was dry—not even the sauces being very moist. She thought this might have something to do with the climate and the heated houses, 'in France where there is always lots of humidity food has to be dry'.

After dinner they walked in the streets and found the lights beautiful, and people said how do you do to them just as if they were in Bilignin and when they went into a fruit store the man greeted Miss Stein by name. 'He was so natural about knowing my name that it was not surprising and yet we had not expected anything like that to happen.' And then as they were watching the elevated railroad which 'looked just like it had ever so long ago . . . we saw an electric sign moving around a building and it said Gertrude Stein has come and that was upsetting . . . to suddenly see your name is always upsetting . . . I like it to happen . . . but always it does give me a little shock of recognition and non-recognition. It is one of the things most worrying in the subject of identity.' And finally, 'after the thirty years we went to sleep in bed in a hotel in America. It was pleasing.'

Random House had arranged to publish a collection of short pieces, *Portraits and Prayers*, to coincide with her visit. On the day that it came out with a Van Vechten photograph of her on the cover she was walking down Fifth Avenue with Alice Toklas, Max White and Lindley Hubbell when a young Negro woman smiled at her and pointed to the book in a shop window. New York was full of pleasures of this kind and as soon as she met her publisher, Alfred Harcourt, she said to him, 'remember this extraordinary welcome that I am having does not come from the books of mine that they do understand like the Autobiography but the books of mine that they did not understand, and he called his partner and said listen to what she says, and perhaps she is right.'

For a month they stayed in the city and found it very nice being a celebrity, 'a real celebrity who can decide who they want to meet and say so and they come or do not come as you want them'. Dealing with invitations was not quite so simple, except when they refused everything, 'but Alice Toklas felt that when the women writers asked us to tea we had to go, she feels that way from time to time. . . .'

The mail became bigger every day. One early letter came from William Saroyan in San Francisco:

> My visit to my native land is very pleasant too. I still cannot figure out how it happened and why I should be so very lucky. Everyone seems to have forgotten what a miraculous thing it is to be alive but I am afraid I won't begin to forget until I am dead and after that I will be a long time forgetting . . .
>
> Some critics say I have to be careful and not notice the writing of Gertrude Stein but I think they are fooling themselves when they pretend any American writing that is American and is writing is not partly the consequence of the writing of Gertrude Stein and as the saying is they don't seem to know the war is over. Even when a writer has never read the writing of Gertrude Stein if he writes America his work will show something maybe differently but show it just the same that is already in the writing of Gertrude Stein. So help me. . . .

Lecturing had begun at once. On the first day she was terribly nervous and felt sure something was the matter with her throat and she would be unable to speak. A doctor reassured her and she was never nervous again. Carl Van Vechten was a support in everything, and now christened himself and Alice Papa and Mama Woojums with Gertrude as Baby Woojums. He was asked to introduce her for the first lecture, but rightly assumed that she would not wish to be introduced. Having refused him made it simple for her never to accept anyone else. '. . . it was silly everybody knew who I was if not why did they come and why should I sit and get nervous while somebody else was talking. So it was decided from then on that there would be no introduction nobody on the platform a table for me to lean on and five hundred to listen.'

She liked college audiences best, 'they inevitably are more flattering', but wherever the lectures were given they were a success. And they remain interesting and often enlightening reading.

She continued to wander around the streets. 'The way the people moved on those broad side-walks in New York was very different from the way they move in Paris and I like to go with them . . .'; 'The ten cent stores did disappoint me but the nut stores not'; and the people in the drug stores fascinated her, 'I was always going in to buy a detective novel just to watch the people sitting on the stools. It was like a piece of provincial life in a real city.' And going to places for her lectures outside New York, although train travel was unchanged and bad, she found everything interesting.

> In going to Philadelphia we first saw again the wooden houses the American wooden houses and American grave-yards and American country . . .
> The wooden houses of America excited me as nothing else in America excited me . . . I do like a flat surface that is the reason I like pictures and do not like sculpture and I like paint even if it is not painted and wood painted or not painted has the colour of paint and it takes paint so much better than plaster. In France and in Spain I like barracks because they have so much flat surface but almost I liked best American wooden houses and there are so many of them an endless number of them and endless varieties in them. It is what in America is very different, each one has something and well taken care of or neglect helps them to be themselves each one of them. Nobody could get tired of them and then the windows they put in. That is one thing any American can do he can put windows in a building and wherever they are they are interesting . . . Of course the skyscrapers have lots of them and it is that that makes them interesting, sky-scrapers is a wrong name because in America there is no sky there is air but no sky of course that has a lot to do with why there really is no painting in America no real painting . . .

So it went on and meanwhile Gertrude Stein was more care-fully protected than ever by Alice Toklas. She saw the people whom she wished to see and those whom she had to see, but there were others, among them relatives and former friends, for whom she had no time. They left therefore a good many hurt feelings in their wake; there are stories of cool nods in the street to former intimates, of remarks such as 'you must come to Paris if you want to see me', of formal notes signed 'Alice B. Toklas, secretary'. Occasionally there was trouble over some professional engagement, but on the whole things went smoothly.

Of her visit to Cambridge, where she stayed one night and spoke at Radcliffe and at Harvard, she wrote:

> It was funny about Cambridge it was the one place where there was nothing that I recognised nothing. Considering that I had spent four years there it was sufficiently astonishing that nothing was there that I remembered nothing at all . . . I lost Cambridge then and there. That is funny.

Now came news that *Four Saints* was to have a short run in Chicago, and naturally Gertrude Stein very much wanted to see it.

> They telephoned there is plenty of time if you come by airplane. Of course I could not do that we telephoned back, why, not, they said, because I never have, we said, we will pay you your trip the two of you forward and back, they said, I want to see the opera I said but I am afraid.

Finally she agreed to fly if Carl Van Vechten went with them.

> We went on doing what we were doing and then one day we were to meet Carl and fly and we did very high. It was nice. I know of nothing more pleasing more soothing more beguiling than the slow hum of the mounting. I had never seen an airplane near before not near enough to know how one got in and there we were in. That is one of the nice things about never going to the movies there are so many surprises . . . Reading does not destroy surprise it is all a surprise that it happens as they say it will happen. But about the airplane we had known nothing and it was an extra-ordinarily natural and pleasant thing much more simple and natural than anything even than walking, perhaps as natural as talking . . . And so we liked it and whenever we could we did it. They are now beginning to suppress the noise and that is a pity, it will be too bad if they can have conversation, it will be a pity.

Indeed when, after they had been in the air for a while, Alice Toklas anxiously asked Gertrude Stein how she was feeling, she answered tartly: 'Do not interrupt my pleasure.'

She now began to formulate her theory that twentieth-century painters painted as they did because they were born into the air age. She wrote of this first in *Everybody's Autobiography*, but developed the theme poetically in the last passage from the book *Picasso*.

> One must not forget that the earth seen from an airplane is more splendid than the earth seen from an automobile. The automobile is the end of progress on the earth, it goes quicker but essentially the landscapes seen from an automobile are the same as the landscapes seen from a carriage, a train, a waggon, or in walking. But the earth seen from an airplane is something else. So the twentieth century is not the same as the nineteenth century and it is very interesting knowing that Picasso has never seen the earth from an airplane, that being of the twentieth century he inevitably knew that the earth is not the same as in the nineteenth century, he knew it, he made it, inevitably he made it different and what he made is a thing that now all the world can see. When I was in America I for the first time travelled pretty much all the time in an airplane and when I looked at the earth I saw all the lines of cubism made at a time when not any painter had ever gone up in an airplane. I saw there on the earth the mingling lines of Picasso, coming and going, developing and destroying themselves, I saw the simple solutions of Braque, I saw the wandering lines of Masson, yes I saw and once more I knew that a creator is contemporary, he understands what is contemporary when the contemporaries do not yet know it, but he is contemporary and as the twentieth century is a century which sees the earth as no one has ever seen it, the earth has a splendor that it never has had, and as everything destroys itself in the twentieth century and nothing continues, so then the twentieth century has a splendor which is its own and Picasso is of this century, he has that strange quality of an earth that one has never seen and of things destroyed as they have never been destroyed. So then Picasso has his splendor.

Of the production of *Four Saints* she says: 'I was less excited about that than I had expected to be. It was my opera but it was so far away.' But further:

> It looked very lovely and the movement was everything

they moved and did nothing, that is what a saint or a doughboy should do they should do nothing, they should move
some and they did nothing it was very satisfying.

So Florine Stettheimer was able to write to her, 'I am so pleased
you decided that our production . . . was not the way you do not
like it.'

Flying was now the natural way to travel and thus they 'came
home', to the Algonquin in New York. Presently Alfred Harcourt invited them to the country for the week-end and took
them to see the Yale-Dartmouth football game. This was her
first experience of motoring in America. She was surprised to
find how slowly and law-abidingly Americans drove compared
with the French. 'I was fascinated with the way everybody did
what they should.'

In New York Carl Van Vechten gave a party for them of
'all the Negro intellectuals that he could get together'.

I know they do not want you to say Negro but I do want to
say Negro. I dislike it when instead of saying Jew they say
Hebrew or Israelite or Semitic I do not like it and why should
a Negro want to be called coloured. . . . he may not
want to be one that is alright but as long as he cannot change
that why should he mind the real name of them. Ulysses
Grant says in his memoirs all he learned when he was at school
was that a noun is the name of anything . . . I have stated
that a noun to me is a stupid thing, if you know a thing
and its name why bother about it but you have to know its
name to talk about it. Well its name is Negro if it is a Negro
and Jew if it is a Jew and both of them are nice strong solid
names and so let us keep them.

So the New York months passed. Bennett Cerf gave a luncheon
party 'to have all of us meet all of us', and there was Alexander
Woollcott, 'Miss Stein you have not been in New York long
enough to know that I am never contradicted', but they got on
very well partly because they both had poodles. At Katharine
Cornell's they had 'the best lemon pie . . . that was ever made
anywhere', and everywhere there was something to enjoy.

They flew back to Chicago and it was winter. 'I had not seen
winter for many years and Alice Toklas had never seen it. We

liked it.' Here—one of the most important events of the tour—
'Thornton Wilder happened'.

> We never met him until we went to Chicago, we might have
> met him earlier because he had been in Paris at the same time
> as all those of his generation, but Thornton always likes to
> think of himself as older which so nicely makes him younger
> now than any of his generation.

They stayed in Chicago for two pleasant weeks and went to
the opera and concerts, which took Gertrude Stein back to her
youth, 'as if Europe had not been', and also spent an evening in
the homicidal squad car during which they just missed the only
homicide that happened that night but saw a walking marathon.
'A most xtraordinary thing, they are like shades modern shades
out of Dante and they move so strangely and they lead each other
about one asleep completely and the other almost, it is the most
unearthly and most beautiful movement I have ever seen it makes
the dance nothing at all.'[1] She describes the marathon vividly
again in *Everybody's Autobiography* with more emphasis on its
horror.
During this visit to Chicago she had her first experience of
teaching, the result of a violent argument about the nature of
ideas with two professors who challenged her to take their class.
It gave her 'a funny feeling' to be teaching instead of lecturing
but the experiment was so successful that she was invited to come
back and give a course.

> I began to talk and they . . . began to talk and pretty soon
> we were all talking about epic poetry and what it was, it was
> exciting we found out a good deal . . .

All the students talked, even those usually silent, and her explanation of this to her hosts is particularly interesting in view of
her often quoted last words.

> . . . I said you see why they talk to me is that I am like them
> I do not know the answer, you you say you do not know
> but you do know if you did not know the answer you could
> not spend your life in teaching but I I really do not know, I

[1] C.V.V.

really do not, I do not even know whether there is a question let alone having an answer for a question.

From Chicago they proceeded to Wisconsin, Minnesota, Michigan, Indiana and Ohio, lecturing most of the time at universities. They were pleased to find themselves flying over Pittsburgh, over Allegheny where Gertrude Stein was born; and so over Virginia and the Potomac to Washington and from there by train to Baltimore.

Here Gertrude was on familiar ground and felt happy. They spent Christmas at the house of her cousins the Julian Steins at Pikesville on the outskirts of Baltimore. She was really fond of these relatives as were they of her; the only difficulty was that Mr. Stein's health was failing, and Gertrude's fame was such that wherever she went, in spite of the vigilance of Alice Toklas, she was besieged by callers and reporters while the telephone never stopped ringing.

Nevertheless Mrs. Rose Ellen Stein remembers the visit with the greatest pleasure and says that despite a little self-importance Gertrude was still a simple person and sincerely interested in others. 'A young man came to see her,' she reminisced, 'shy and awkward and keen on her writing. In five minutes Gertrude knew all about his wife and children and had him perfectly at ease.' Mrs. Stein added: 'I never found her particularly clever, but bright and fun and darling to be with if she liked you. She was always governed by her likes and dislikes, and protected and ruled by Alice of whom she was even a little afraid in a pleasant kind of way. Gertrude was by nature a lovely person.'[1]

She saw few of her many relatives still living in Baltimore, but she did see Aunt Fanny and Uncle Eph, the sculptor, both of whom were about eighty and 'just as they had been', and also her cousin Helen Bachrach. She renewed acquaintance too with the Scott Fitzgeralds. He regretted not seeing her quietly. 'I was somewhat stupid-got with the Christmas spirit,' he wrote, 'but everyone felt their Christmas eve was well spent in the company of your handsome face and wise mind—and sentences "that never leak".'

Their next visit was to Washington.

[1] Author's journal.

We were staying with someone and we were all asked to tea at the White House and we went I had never been before.

We were the only ones asked to tea, we went upstairs not downstairs and in a passage way we had tea a passage way which was a hall. Mrs. Roosevelt was there and gave us tea, she talked about something and we sat next to some one. Then later two men came through from somewhere going to somewhere, one quite an old one and the other one younger. Mrs. Roosevelt asked them if they would have some tea they said no and they stood and I asked some one who was next to me who are they and she said it was Mr. Howe and I had heard of him and then they went on away and Mrs. Roosevelt said yes they were all writing the message to Congress that was going to be given next day and they were all writing it and each one and any one was changing it and then we went away.

For New Year's Eve a friend drove them into Virginia, where they 'ate spoon bread and little tenderloins of pork and hot bread on the James river', which in view of her enthusiasm for the Civil War Gertrude Stein found specially exciting.

So back to New York to repack and on to Springfield, Massachusetts, where W. G. Rogers, the Kiddie, and his wife were living. Rogers was editing a paper and he drove his old friends all over New England in the snow, while Gertrude Stein lectured at countless schools and colleges and wondered that no better method of winter driving had been invented than those tyre chains which were always breaking or skidding.

During this part of her tour she thought a great deal about education. The two colleges whose students most interested her were both missionary-training places and not concerned with culture or with the other professions. This she found surprising and significant. One thing that puzzled her was that American men in general should think that success was everything when they knew that eighty per cent of them were not going to succeed.

A letter from Smith College, Northampton, gives a snapshot of her reception as a lecturer:

> . . . Amherst was awfully nice, the next morning the students went around collecting faculty opinions and the football coach said yes I'd like to have Gertrude for the tackles but

I don't know whether she would be good to call the signals and then reflectively but I guess Alice B. would do that, and another one said, I was dead against her and I just went to see what she looked like and then she took the door of my mind right off its hinges and now it's wide open.[1]

After New England the southern journey began, 'and I was interested, after all there never will be anything more interesting in America than the Civil War never'. To Richmond, to Charlottesville, where she spoke to the Raven Society and was given a key to Poe's room in the university which she henceforward carried in her pocket.

On then by car to North Carolina, South Carolina, 'every state was exciting', although all through the Carolinas it rained. In Charleston they had the best food yet and met DuBose Heyward, 'a gentle man . . . like his Porgy'. 'We liked you in Charleston, tremendously,' he wrote, 'even if we did not always understand you.' From here they flew to Atlanta and drove through Georgia. 'There on the roads I read Buy your flour meal and meat in Georgia. And I knew that that was interesting. Was it prose or was it poetry I knew that it was interesting . . .' She had already been enchanted by the rhyming couplets used for radio advertising, and here were quatrains on the roadside billing a shaving cream.

Alabama, and by plane to New Orleans which reminded them of a provincial town in southern France, and where they joined Sherwood Anderson, who took them about in his car, and met Marc Connelly, the author of *Green Pastures*.

'New Orleans hot and delicious', she wrote, and described how they had been shown

> the social register of the bawdy houses and a charming little blue book with the simple advertisements of the ladies by themselves and we have eaten oysters à la Rockefeller and innumerable shrimps made in every way and all delicious and we were taken to visit the last of the Creoles in her original house unchanged for 100 years . . . all very lovely and lively . . .[2]

By way of Tennessee and Arkansas to St. Louis next, where

[1] C.V.V.   [2] Ibid.

Gertrude Stein saw General Grant's house and was surprised to find it quite a small cabin. Here too they ate very well; they remembered every detail of the food everywhere, and it was quite a gourmet voyage.

This was the end of the southern trip. They flew back to Chicago where Thornton Wilder lent them his apartment and Alice Toklas kept house, trying recipes from the many American cook books she had collected, while the differences from French *ménage*, such as the invisible arrival of the milk, continued to surprise and please her. Meanwhile Gertrude Stein settled down, wrote some excellent new lectures 'about organisation and inside and outside', and hired a drive-yourself car which gave much pleasure. One did not have to pass a test in Illinois, and cars could be left all night in the street without lights. Moreover, when one morning her car was completely invisible for snow, the janitor simply brushed it off and it went, and when they had a puncture the garage sent another car with newer tyres and took the old one away. 'Everything in America is just as easy as that . . . We liked it.'

In the new lectures[1] she once again expressed her conviction that repetition was a form of insistence and emphasis found in all living, and her preoccupation with immediate existing. She explained the 'passionate need' she felt of words 'taking care of themselves by themselves', without being enfeebled by punctuation or other extraneous help, and she commented on national characteristics of literature, what 'the life of every one in that nation makes it be'.

> I do know about English literature that it has been determined by the fact that England is an island and that the daily life on that island was a completely daily life . . . Americans and English use the same language but the Americans have not a daily living as any Englishman does and can have.

And Americans wanted 'no narrative to soothe'; everything has to be exciting, 'to move as everything moves'. She had already asserted in the earlier lecture *How Writing is Written*[2] that in the

[1] *Narration*. Four lectures by Gertrude Stein with an introduction by Thornton Wilder. The University of Chicago Press, 1935.

[2] *The Oxford Anthology of American Literature*, 1938.

twentieth century events were so continuous that they were no longer exciting. People were not now interested in what happened but in existence, and so it was 'quite characteristic that in The Making of Americans, Proust, Ulysses, nothing much happened'.

These lectures too were enthusiastically received and Gertrude Stein spent many happy hours talking with the students. 'I liked all of them, Thornton had chosen them not only those who were interested in literature, but those interested in philosophy and history and anything, which made it much more varied and interesting.'

This was, she reminds us, the first time that she had worked with a group of students since her Radcliffe days and the experiments in automatic writing. About these everyone constantly asked her, for although she had come to the conclusion then that there was really no such thing as automatic writing, people insisted on attributing her style to that early experience. This was an annoyance. She had thanked Sherwood Anderson the year before for laying that ghost by what he wrote of her writing, yet here it was still walking.

Of her talks with the students Gertrude Stein wrote:

> There is a bother about that you get more familiar with a thing when you say it than when you write it, when you say it you repeat it when you write it you never do because when you write it is in you and when you say it they hear you. After two weeks I wondered if I heard what I said or if I only heard them hearing what I said.

This touched her preoccupation with the artist's necessity to be unconscious of any audience and her concern with the inside and the outside. If talking and writing renounced their individuality and came 'near being one', inside and outside were for her confused and purity in danger of being lost.

At this time, February 1935, *transition* published as a supplement a pamphlet entitled *Testimony against Gertrude Stein*, signed by Braque, Eugène and Maria Jolas, Henri Matisse, André Salmon and Tristan Tarza.

Their complaint was that in *The Autobiography of Alice B. Toklas* Gertrude Stein had claimed to be intimately concerned with 'the genesis and development of such movements as Fauvism, Cubism, Dada, Surrealism, transition etc.' whereas in fact her knowledge of them was superficial and she represented the epoch and its personalities 'without taste and without relation to reality'.

Matisse was particularly angry because Gertrude Stein said his wife had a face like a horse. He also took exception to the way in which she described Madame Matisse's devotion to his daughter and deplored Gertrude's failure to mention Sarah Stein, 'the really intelligently sensitive member of the family'. He also referred to her 'sentimental attachment' to Picasso and went on to affirm that she had not kept her promise to help Juan Gris.

Tristan Tzara, who had never been a close friend, was malicious about the characters of both Miss Stein and Miss Toklas and declared that the former's connection with art was solely due to the weight of her pocket-book. Braque said that she had entirely misunderstood Cubism, 'which she sees simply in terms of personalities'.

> In the early days of cubism [he wrote], Pablo Picasso and I were engaged in what we felt was a search for the anonymous personality. We were inclined to efface our own personalities in order to find originality. Thus it often happened that amateurs mistook Picasso's paintings for mine and mine for Picasso's. This was a matter of indifference to us because we were primarily interested in our work and in the new problem it presented.

Braque also mentioned that he had been embarrassed by the war-time visit to him of Miss Stein and Miss Toklas because their strange appearance provoked so much curiosity, and added that none of the group had read her work until *transition* began to make it known in France. 'Now that we have seen her book, *nous sommes fixés.*'

André Salmon chiefly confined himself to pointing out the inaccuracy of Gertrude Stein's description of the Rousseau banquet, while Marie Jolas gave the facts about the founding and editorship of *transition* and touched on Gertrude Stein's anger with

Eugène Jolas when she considered that he was neglecting her in favour of James Joyce.

Asked if Gertrude Stein minded this attack Alice Toklas said:

> Mind—*that?* Oh no. She knew none of them knew any-thing about her work. How could Matisse judge when he couldn't read a word of English? That wasn't one of the things I had to hide from her.

The fact that Matisse did not read English was scarcely relevant, for the *Testimony* was not written until after the publication of Bernard Faÿ's French translation of *The Autobiography*. But Matisse declared that her translator seemed not to have under-stood either her or the things she was talking about. Leo Stein also, although privately, declared that the book was far from truthful.

That Gertrude Stein took *transition*'s obloquy lightly is borne out by this letter:

> Being a really truly college professor is hard work, parti-cularly when you have never been one before. . . .Thornton is a darling . . . Alice wrote you all about the manifesto and I suppose you have seen it, what I enjoyed was Salmon's statement that he was drunk only in appearance to impress the American ladies and so he ought to be happy that he fooled them instead of complaining that they were fooled, apparently Paris is amusing itself greatly about it all it seems to have made them forget politics for a brief moment and my French publishers are naturally very pleased . . .[1]

One cannot get the true flavour of the gossip in *The Autobio-graphy* or of *transition*'s refutation unless one remembers that both were part of *les histoires*, without which artists' Paris would have been a duller if a kindlier place. But there was more to it than this. These artists and the editors of *transition* felt that it was essential to issue a statement which would avert the danger of *The Autobio-graphy* with all its inaccuracies being taken in the future as docu-mentary evidence of the period.

In *Everybody's Autobiography* Gertrude Stein says of the matter:

> It was funny about The Autobiography of Alice B. Toklas,

[1] C.V.V.

writers well I suppose it is because writers write but anyway
writers did not really mind anything any one said about
them, they might have minded something or liked something
but since writing is writing and writers know that writing is
writing they do not really suffer very much about anything
that has been written. Beside writers have an endless curiosity about themselves and anything that is written about
them helps to help them know something about themselves
or about what anybody else says about them. Anything
interests anybody who is writing but not so a painter oh no
not at all. As I told Picasso the egotism of a writer is not at
all the same egotism as the egotism of a painter and all the
painters felt that way about The Autobiography of Alice B.
Toklas. Braque and Marie Laurencin and Matisse they did
not like it and they did not get used to it. . . .

. . . Matisse I never saw again but Braque yes twice and
Marie Laurencin once.

Hemingway, however, although a writer, never forgave
Gertrude Stein for *The Autobiography*'s 'falsities'.

She and Marie Laurencin, who had not been one of the mani-
festo signatories, continued to meet, always by chance and always
greeting each other with an embrace as 'Chère Gertrude' and
'Chère Marie', and the painter later made a charming portrait of
the second Basket. Marie Laurencin explained that painters never
liked comments on their past because they only lived in what they
could see and they could not see their past. Having meditated on
this view, Gertrude Stein goes on:

> Braque was another thing. Braque was a man who had a
> gift of singing and like all who sing he could mistake what he
> sang as being something that he said but it is not the same
> thing. When I say he sang I mean he sang in paint, I do not
> believe he sang otherwise but he might have, he had the
> voice and the looks of a great baritone.

When the busy weeks in Chicago were over they flew to
Texas where they saw *Porgy* acted by an amateur Negro cast. It
was natural, Gertrude Stein says, that it should be done very well,
'it is not acting it is being for them, and they have no time sense
to be a trouble to them'.

> And then we left for California very early in the morning,
> it was strange our going to California where we both had
> come from . . . As we landed at Los Angeles there were of
> course a lot to see us there.

They went to Pasadena where Gertrude Stein hired a new
Ford car, 'a much better one than they had given me in Chicago'.
Here she met Saroyan and was disappointed to discover that he
had not invented the title *A Daring Young Man on the Flying
Trapeze*. 'I could have known everybody else did but there it is
I do know lots but there are lots of things I do not know.'

Among those at a dinner party given for her at Beverly Hills
were Charlie Chaplin, Anita Loos, and Dashiell Hammett whom
she had specially asked to meet.

> Of course I liked Charlie Chaplin he is a gentle person like
> any Spanish gipsy bullfighter he is very like my favourite
> one Gallo who could not kill a bull but he could make him
> move better than any one ever could and he himself not
> having any grace in person could move one as no one else
> ever did, and Charlie Chaplin was like that, gipsies are intelli-
> gent I do not think Charlie Chaplin is one perhaps not but
> he might have been, anyway we naturally talked about the
> cinema, and he explained something. He said naturally it was
> disappointing, he had known the silent films and in that they
> could do something that the theatre had not done they could
> change the rhythm but if you had a voice accompanying
> naturally after that you could never change the rhythm you
> were always held by the rhythm that the voice gave them.
> We talked a little about the Four Saints and what my idea
> had been . . . After dinner they all gathered around me and
> asked me what I thought of the cinema, I told them what I
> had been telling Charlie Chaplin, it seemed to worry them
> but almost anything could worry them and at last I found out
> what was bothering them they wanted to know how I had
> succeeded in getting so much publicity, I said by having a
> small audience, I said if you have a big audience you have no
> publicity, this did seem to worry them and naturally it would
> worry them they wanted the publicity and the big audience
> . . . yes alright the biggest publicity comes from the reallest
> and the reallest has a small audience not a big one, but it is

really exciting and therefore it has the biggest publicity, alright that is it.

To this passage from *Everybody's Autobiography* Thornton Wilder adds his recollection of what Gertrude Stein said to the Hollywood film director, Mamoulian, on the same question.

> Now listen: you think that I'm a fool and that I write nonsense. I assure you that if I wrote nonsense you wouldn't have heard of me. Lots of people write nonsense and we don't hear of them. My publicity comes from the fact that one person in a great many hundred has said that I write something of value. Now we all want to read and hear something of value. People go about saying 'This is the best book I've ever read' or 'that is the best movie I ever saw', but we don't really hear conviction in it. You people in the movies need publicity, but you have to pay for it. You get little waves of publicity and then it dies down and you have to pay for some more. The only publicity that matters comes from one person in a great many hundred saying—and meaning it—that they have read something of value.[1]

This is what Gertrude Stein did sincerely believe. She never admitted that her personality had anything to do with her growing fame.

> And then we in our Ford car left for our California, this had been California of course but not our California the California we had come from and we drove off the next morning to go travelling for ten days and no lecturing just travelling, we had a good time.

She wrote to Sherwood Anderson of the excellence of American highways and the joy of going up all the hills without changing gear. The San Joaquin Valley was their first destination, 'naturally this was interesting because Alice Toklas' pioneer grandfather had owned all his land there', and then they visited the Yosemite where neither of them had ever been. There it was very high and, although it was now April, wintry, but they enjoyed being taken by the Director of the Valley to see 'the big trees'.

The thing that was most exciting about them was that they

[1] Author's journal.

had no roots did anybody want anything to be more interesting than that that the oldest and the solidest and the biggest tree that could be grown had no foundation, there it was sitting and the wind did not blow it over it sat so well. It was very exciting. Very beautiful and very exciting.

Thence to Monterey where Alice Toklas had spent her youthful holidays, but which was new to Gertrude Stein. They looked for Sherman's Rose where Alice used to stay with an old Spanish woman, but some millionaire had moved the whole lovely adobe house to another site.

> Then slowly we came into San Francisco it was frightening quite frightening driving there and on top of Nob Hill where we were to stay, of course it had not been like that and yet it was like that, Alice Toklas found it natural but for me it was a trouble yes it was . . .

In the hotel they found even more flowers than there had been everywhere else and from all their windows were views of the bay, and Gertrude Atherton was there to welcome them and make the arrangements.

'My dear people,' Gertrude wrote to the Julian Steins,

> Here we are and the streets are steep yes they are, I knew they were, but my gracious yes they are, and the newspapers are full of the Oakland girl who had made good, in a big way, I love that, and now our American visit is almost over and we are very sad. No we don't want to go home that is to France no we want to go on as we are, we do like the lap of luxury and the pleasant adulation, it is nice—the flowers and what flowers . . .

Gertrude Atherton's arrangements included what promised to be 'the most notable cocktail party' in San Francisco for years. Not one refusal was received to the vast number of invitations and the numbers were only limited by the hostess's desire that everyone should have a chance of talking to the guest of honour. Mabel Dodge (now Luhan) was at this time staying at Monterey but she again was someone whom Gertrude Stein was now not seeing.

All this was delightful, but she did not enjoy going back to see East Oakland.

Ah Thirteenth Avenue was the same it was shabby and over-
grown the houses were certainly some of those that had been
and there were no bigger buildings and they were neglected
and lots of grass and bushes growing yes it might have been
Thirteenth Avenue when I had been. Not of course the house,
the house the big house and the big garden and the eucalyptus
trees and the rose hedge naturally were not any longer
existing . . .

Childhood scenes plunged Gertrude Stein into meditations
about the past, identity, memory and change. 'What is the use
of having been if you are to be going on being . . . ?'

I did not like anything that was happening. Later much later
all that went to make The Geographical History of America
that I wrote, what is the use of being a little boy if you are
going to grow up to be a man.

She does not mention Leo while writing about the Californian
visit, although he is mentioned in other parts of *Everybody's
Autobiography* where there are descriptions of her childhood. But
one can see that old emotions connected both with the good and
with the bad times in her early life were stirred, and in a letter to
Sherwood Anderson she admitted that she loved California less
than Alice Toklas did. So there was a certain relief for Gertrude
when, after a little more speaking and a lot more visiting, they
turned East again. Once more the flight was an enchantment;
they had by chance seen the first big aeroplane flying off to Hono-
lulu and Gertrude Stein commented, 'I would like to go around
the world in an airplane. I never did want to do anything and
now I want to do that thing.'

She liked crossing the Salt Lake region best, 'it was like going
over the bottom of the ocean without any water in it and I
was very satisfied with it after all it is nice to know the difference
between the ocean with water and the ocean without water in it'.

To Omaha, where Gertrude Stein walked about in the night,
liking it, 'but I did like being everywhere everywhere where I was
I never very much wanted to be in any other place than there',
and a last night in Chicago and then New York, where the
Rockefeller Centre building was finished and she was welcomed

as warmly as ever. Everything was a pleasure and the climax of the tour was perfect.

Before we went on the Champlain I asked Bennett Cerf about my writing, I always want what I have written to be printed and it has not always happened no not mostly happened and now I timidly said something to him, he said it is very simple whatever each year you want printed you tell me and I will publish that thing, just like that I said, just like that, he said, you do the deciding, and so we happily very happily went on to the Champlain.

This, Gertrude Stein's last view of her native shores, was on May 4th, 1935.

CHAPTER SEVENTEEN

BEING A GENIUS

'Any time is the time to make a poem.'
Everybody's Autobiography.

As they approached Le Havre the *Normandie* on her trial trip ran all round them several times.

> She was a pleasure and it was a nice day as we came nearer and there we were back again in France. Of course but that we had expected was that everything looked little and littler than it had looked. Come back to anything is always a bother you have to get used to seeing it as it looks all over again until it looks as it did which it does at last.[1]

As they ran through the cities of Northern France Gertrude Stein thought how beautiful the old parts of European cities were, but 'as the new parts in America are more beautiful than the new parts in Europe perhaps the American cities are more beautiful than the European. Interesting if true.'

> And then we had to see the place we had always had as home and then we had to gather in Basket and Pépé and then we left for Bilignin, it was to begin again being as we always had been although of course it was not the same thing.

> Settled down in Bilignin I became worried about identity and remembered the mother goose I am I because my little dog knows me and I was not sure but that that only proved the dog was he and not that I was I.

> To get this trouble out of my system I began to write The Geographical History of America or The Relation of Human Nature to the Human Mind and I meditated as I had not done for a very long time not since I was a little one about the contradiction of being on this earth with the space limiting and knowing about the stars in an unlimited space

[1] *Everybody's Autobiography.*

that is that nobody could find out if it was limiting or limited and now these meditations did not frighten me as they did when I was young, so that was that much done.[1]

All her friends in the neighbourhood had to have the tour described to them and her American mail made it clear that whereas before it she had been an object of interest and curiosity she was now an important literary figure. Henry Miller, for instance, sent her his *Tropic of Cancer*, 'if you have anything good or bad to say about it I should be pleased to hear it'. Wendell Wilcox thanked her for interesting Harcourt Brace in his script, and many young writers acknowledged her influence. James Laughlin, for example, a very young American who came from Lausanne to visit her, said that the more he thought and wrote about her work, the more he knew what a sloppy thinker and hopeless writer he was, 'but I have come to feel that I can rely on you, and on your work, that I can be sure to find it always hard at the center and moving on the surface'.

Thornton Wilder was the most communicative of new followers. From Vienna in September of this year he wrote:

Dear Friends:
    I cast myself out into the open seas of friendship and hope to be supported and understood. So: there are long long stretches of the *Four in America* where I don't understand a word . . . The movement of the poetical opening [of the Fourth Section, *George Washington*]—the autumnal mood—*that* I got and then I was lost. The Grant I followed best of all and it is full of beauties—on religion and war and America, though even that slips away from me in the last quarter. The first part of Henry James was the clearest of all, because there I could follow the ideas from memory of your expressing them in other places. So that degree to which I can express my happiness and confidence in the whole of the work, is bound up with my mortification and my rueful apology of my inadequacy to so much of it.
    Anyway it's no news to you that I am a slow-poke plodder in so many ways, still stuck in the literal XIXth Century; but very proud every time I feel I have made more progress and have been given more and more flashes of insight into

[1] *Everybody's Autobiography.*

the endlessly fascinating individual expression which is Gertrude's style.

Before long she sent him the script of *The Geographical History Of America*,[1] and he exclaimed:

> What a book! I mean WHAT a book! I've been living for a month with ever-increasing intensity on the conceptions of Human Nature and Human Mind, and on the relation of Master-pieces to their apparent subject-matter. Those things, yes and identity, have become cell and marrow in me and now at last I have more about them. And it's all absorbing and fascinating and intoxicatingly gay, even when it's terribly in earnest . . .
>
> Don't be mad at me if I say again there are stretches I don't understand. This time it doesn't seem important that I don't understand, because there's so much that I do understand and love and laugh at and feed on . . .

Certainly Gertrude Stein had not rested on her laurels. Before she returned to Paris she had finished this book which, to quote Thornton Wilder's introduction, 'says what it knows: a work of philosophy, a work of art, and a work of gaiety'. Still with absurdities of layout she mocked pompousness and pedants, and avoided punctuation as a hindrance to understanding. 'A comma by helping you along holding your coat for you and putting on your shoes keeps you from living your life as actively as you should live it . . . A long complicated sentence should force itself upon you, make yourself know yourself knowing it.'

Yet there is more punctuation in this book than in some of her earlier works, and although Gertrude Stein insists on the difference between the written and the spoken word, may not the shorter phrasing derive from her practice in speaking? For its subject matter one can turn to *Play I Characters*: 'Identity, human nature, human mind, universe, history, audience and growing.' To this list one must add money, masterpieces, romanticism and the flatness of America, all which she had been pondering.

The names of many people are woven into the text too and some of the meditations are addressed to 'Thornton'. This passage bears on her use of the word as a unit:

[1] Random House, 1936.

I found that any kind of a book if you read with glasses and somebody is cutting your hair and so you cannot keep the glasses on and you use your glasses as a magnifying glass and so read word by word reading word by word makes the writing that is not anything be something.

This book shows the extraordinary patience of her method of transcribing thought. Here is an example of its general style, the page numbers appear arbitrary, one of the author's gaieties in part of the book, for many of her 'pages' make up the printed one.

Is there any difference between flat land and an ocean a big country and a little one.

Is there any difference between human nature and the human mind.

Poetry and prose is not interesting.

What is necessary now is not form but content.

That is why in this epoch a woman does the literary thinking.

Kindly learn everything please.

That autumn she saw Picasso after a gap of two years.

When I saw him again I said how did you ever make the decision and keep it of leaving your wife. Yes he said you and I we have weak characters and no initiative and if I had died before I did it you never would have thought that I had a strong enough character to do this thing. No I said I did not think you ever could really do a thing like that, hitherto when you changed anything somebody always took you away and this time nobody did and how did it happen. I suppose he said when a thing is where there is no life left then you either die or go on living, well he said that is what happened to me.

When he got rid of his wife he stopped painting and took to writing poetry. Everything does something I suppose and this is what that did . . .

When I first heard that he was writing poetry I had a funny feeling . . . one does you know. Things belong to you and writing belonged to me, there is no doubt about it writing belonged to me. I know writing belongs to me, I am quite certain and no matter how certain you are about anything about anything belonging to you if you hear that somebody says it belongs to them it gives you a funny feeling.

Thornton Wilder was in Paris, visiting the rue de Fleurus for the first time, and he and Alice Toklas went over with Gertrude Stein 'to listen all evening to Pablo Picasso's poetry'.

The poems were in French and Spanish and he translated the Spanish ones into French for them.

> We both had put on our glasses to do this reading he to read and I to look on while he was reading. In France they always read everything aloud they read more with their ears than with their eyes but in reading English we read more with our eyes than with our ears.

Gertrude Stein and Thornton Wilder both said it was very interesting and they all talked about how beautiful words look when written and how one can have only one language. When Picasso next saw her he asked what Wilder had said about his writing.

> . . . he said that certain descriptions that you make have the same quality as your painting. Oh yes said Picasso and he did find it interesting. Yes I said and he did find it interesting. And then we talked some more. And you Gertrude he said you do not say much of anything. Well you see Pablo I said you see the egotism of a painter is an entirely different egotism than the egotism of a writer.

Her meditations on grammar had nothing to do with writing grammatically.

John Brown, in his *Panorama de la Littérature Contemporaine aux États-Unis*,[1] reports her as also saying to Picasso over the matter of his poems: 'Vous n'avez jamais éprouvé de sentiment pour aucun mot. Les mots vous ennuient plus qu'autre chose. Comment pouvez-vous donc écrire?' However, after she had translated her lecture on painting to him and he had not looked much at the pictures on her walls, she told him 'drearily' to go on writing.

> Yes he said that is what I am doing I will never paint again very likely not I like the life of a literary man, I go to cafés

[1] Gallimard, 1954.

and I think and I make poetry and I like it. It is most interesting I said and then for a little while we did not see each other again.

They soon did, however. In 1936 she wrote to W. G. Rogers:

> We have been leading a hectic life, Paris I do not know why but this year Paris is its nice old self and everybody knows everybody and everybody is talking and painting is once more a subject. Paris is never quite itself unless painting is its subject.

Now that Picasso was alone, his old friend Sabartes and his wife had come to live with him. Gertrude Stein tells of an evening when the three of them brought an American to the rue de Fleurus and the Picabias and Marcel Duchamp and Georges Maratier were there. 'Nobody had been invited but everybody came . . . and everybody would have been just as well pleased not to meet everybody but then one cannot bother about that.'

Picasso and Picabia had on identical ties and shoes and Gertrude Stein made them stand back to back so that she could measure them. They 'are about the same height which is not a high one and they are about the same weight which is a fair one . . . but they do not look like one another no they do not'.

On another occasion Picasso asked if he might bring Dali, 'and we arranged an evening and Dali and his wife came but Picasso did not bring him and soon you will see why I did not know why then'. The reason she gives is that Dali's wife was Russian and Spaniards and Russians, according to Gertrude Stein, although superficially attracted are fundamentally incompatible. Of Spaniards she produces this gem: 'They do not hear what you say nor do they listen but they use for the thing they want to do the thing they are not hearing.'

And she goes on:

> And then it came to me it is perfectly simple, the Russian and the Spaniard are Oriental, and there is the same mixing. Scratch a Russian and you find a Tartar. Scratch a Spaniard and you find a Saracen.
>
> And all this is very important with what I have been saying about the peaceful Oriental penetration into European

culture or rather the tendency for this generation that is for the twentieth century to be no longer European perhaps because Europe is finished.

Painting in the nineteenth century was French at the end of the nineteenth century it became Spanish, Spanish in France but still Spanish, and philosophy and literature had the same tendency, Einstein was the creative philosophic mind of the century and I have been the creative literary mind of the century also with the Oriental mixing with the European.

Thus, jovially, writing *Everybody's Autobiography* in 1936, she put herself where she believed that she belonged. 'It is funny', she several times observed, 'being a genius', and as was her habit she analysed the matter and described how the knowledge that she was a genius had gradually grown in the old days with Leo. But he had his own view.

He said it was not it it was I. If I was not there to be there with what I did then what I did would not be what it was . . .

He did not say it to me but he said it so that it would be true for me. And it did not trouble me and as it did not trouble me I knew it was not true and a little as it did not trouble me he knew it was not true.

But it destroyed him for me and it destroyed me for him.

It is funny this thing of being a genius, there is no reason for it, there is no reason that it should be you and should not have been him . . . no no reason at all.

In discussions with Picasso she tried to work it out:

What is a genius . . . Really inside you if you are a genius there is nothing inside you that makes you really different to yourself inside you than those are to themselves inside them who are not a genius . . .

What is a genius. If you are one how do you know you are one . . .

They have not given us a clear answer but they knew that they were.

From the discussion of the Oriental penetration into European culture she proceeds:

However here is Dali waiting to come and his Russian wife with him.

Dali has the most beautiful moustache of any European and that moustache is Saracen there is no doubt about that . . .

After this, with diversions of course, as other thoughts come to her, she gives clearly enough her opinions of Juan Gris, Dali, Miro and Chirico. She speaks of the 'natural ignorance' of the Spaniard and says that Picasso liked Dali because he, in the same way as himself, based everything on this native ignorance. In her view Miro was nice and excited everybody by his painting, but as he had nothing to follow his ignorance up with, Dali went on exciting people more. Gertrude Stein never liked surrealism but she recognized the energy of Dali's big early pictures and enjoyed writing about him.

He painted a picture and on it he wrote I spit upon the face of my mother, he was very fond of his mother who had been a long time dead and so of course this was a symbolism. He knew about Freud and he had the revolt of having a notary for his father and having his mother dead since he was a child. And so painting this picture with this motto was a natural thing and it made of him the most important of the painters who were surrealists. Masson's wandering line had stopped wandering and he was lost just then, Miro had found out what he was to paint and he was continuing painting the same thing, and so Dali came and everybody knew about him . . . Having done anything you naturally want to do it again and if you do it again then you know you are doing it again and it is not interesting. That is what worries everybody, anybody having done anything naturally does it again, whether it is a crime or a work of art or a daily occupation or anything like eating and sleeping and dancing and war . . . A painter has more trouble about it than any one. Most people at least do not see what they have just done a writer does not see what he has just written, a musician does not hear what he has just played, but a painter has constantly in front of him what he has just painted, his walls are covered with it . . . I am often sorry for them. I know that I am the most important writer writing today but I never have any of my books before me naturally not, but they have all the time naturally everything they have just done right in front of them.

The account of Dali's visit ends thus:

We talked a great deal together but we neither of us listened very much to one another. We talked about the writing of painters, Dali had just brought me a poem he had written about Picasso, and I said I was bored with the hopelessness of painters and poetry. That in a way was the trouble with the painters they did not know what poetry was. Dali said that if it were not for the titles of Chirico's pictures and his own nobody would understand him . . . and as for Picasso's poems, they had finally made it possible for him to understand Picasso's paintings. Oh dear I said.

The Left Bank was much the same as ever.

As for Gertrude Stein's own writing, in *Everybody's Autobiography* she was concerned with 'narration' and 'content'. Walking about Paris with Thornton Wilder on the eve of his return to America she explained to him that she had really written poetry and really written plays and really written thinking but that so far she 'had not simply told anything'. This, in other words narration, she knew she must now do, and Thornton Wilder agreed with her. As for content, in her former book she had already stated its necessity, and replying to a letter from W. G. Rogers stressing its importance, she now wrote:

Yes I know what you mean and of course it is the content so much so that I have been meditating whether one can do content without form I tried to do it and I am still trying it well not without some form but with negligible form, I am trying to do it now in the autobiography sometimes it almost happens, I am very interested in the way any painter today can do line an almost perfect line and it is not interesting.

Towards the end of the book a doubt of her democratic use of words arises:

I had always wanted it all to be common-place and simple anything that I am writing and then I get worried lest I have succeeded and it is too common-place and too simple so much so that it is nothing . . .

Early in 1936 Gertrude Stein was once more invited to lecture at Oxford and Cambridge. Lord Berners, who was considering setting one of her plays to music for a ballet, invited her and Miss Toklas to Faringdon House in Berkshire, while Sir Robert and Lady Abdy asked them to Cornwall. 'Of course we went we always like to go.'

This time Miss Stein preferred the Cambridge audience to the Oxford one, but the whole trip was as usual a success. She wrote to Rose Ellen Stein:

> . . . . I came over to lecture in Oxford and Cambridge and it has gone off very well, it is very sweet the way the American boys in these colleges look upon me as the American flag . . . We have been staying in some beautiful houses . . . one of the pleasantest was Lord Berners the musician who is a charming person and there was hardly ever a moment when we were not all lords and ladies but we liked it, there was so much beautiful needlework and so many orchids that Alice was all pleased and so was I, glory is pleasant, it may not be lucrative but it is pleasant, and per-haps it will be lucrative, who shall say?

And in *Everybody's Autobiography* she observed:

> In English novels a baronet is always villainous or peculiar and sometimes both, I have in my life known two baronets and they are not at all villainous, they are gentle and sweet but they are peculiar, Bertie Abdy is one and Francis Rose is the other one, I came to know them about the same time but not together no naturally not together.

The Abdys took their guests sightseeing, among other places to Dartmoor Prison, which Americans always want to see. In Gertrude Stein's case there was a special interest as it comes so often into the Edgar Wallace thrillers she enjoyed.

Now there was danger in the air, and when they got back to Paris Alice Toklas began making copies of all the unpublished manuscripts to send to Carl Van Vechten for safe-keeping. In March 1936 Mike cabled from San Francisco advising his sister to send her pictures to America. She did not comply, but even before the outbreak of the Spanish Civil War she had noticed a change in the mood of Paris. The French had at last, she says, after the restlessness of war and post-war conditions, settled down to their proper occupations of conversation and chess, although much of the talk was of revolution and nothing could save the lost generation.

> It was the hotel keeper [Pernollet] who said what it is said I said that the war generation was a lost generation. And he said it in this way. He said that every man between the ages of eighteen and twentyfive becomes civilized. If he does not go through a civilizing experience at that time in his life he will not be a civilized man.

And Gertrude Stein adds:

> I had known the generation made by the war and the generation made by the peace I used to call them the children of the armistice.

So she watched the storm rising.

> And then just as conversation had begun again and checkers and economising and there were quite a few poodles to be seen and it looked as if everything was going to begin again it did not begin. Instead there began to be on all the walls political posters and everybody instead of commencing began to stop and silently read them. When French people read political posters they do not converse about it or about anything. They have been through so many things and they know that it makes trouble for them that naturally when they read them they just silently read them. It is like the women in Bilignin the farmers' wives the first thing they asked me when we came down this summer it was well before the Spanish revolution they asked me is there going to be a civil war oh dear is there going to be civil war . . .

In July 1936 the Spanish war broke out,

> . . . and that scared everybody really scared them . . . because it was so near and so frightening and also anything foreign may cause foreign fighting and Frenchmen like fighting but they do not want a war again not now no . . .

The women felt better . . . they felt the men seeing what was happening over the border and realising that civil war was really like that would settle down and be just simply Frenchmen again.

As for Gertrude Stein's own feelings:

All the time that I am writing the Spanish revolution obtrudes itself. Not because it is a revolution but because I know it all so well all the places they are mentioning and the things there they are destroying . . . When we were in England before the nineteen-fourteen war and just at its beginning the Whiteheads worried me they were so much more interested in the destruction of libraries and buildings in Belgium than they were in the war and why not, now I understand why not . . .

She was comforted by remembering that all through history works of art have been constantly destroyed and yet more remained than she could ever want to look at.

Here Gertrude Stein is characteristically self-centred and limited to personal experience, but her honesty in accepting the limitation is equally characteristic. Knowing Spain, she could imagine the destruction going on there, but in *Four Saints* she made Saint Theresa 'not interested' when asked what she would do if by touching a button she could kill three thousand Chinamen. 'After all you have to be able to imagine a thing to know it is there and how could Saint Theresa imagine the three thousand Chinamen when she was building convents in Spain.'

She does not mention the tragic human side of the Spanish war. It may be that in her dread of being distressed she did not encourage her imagination in this direction. However, although so many of her friends were Spanish painters and so much artist blood of every nationality was spilled for Spain on the other side, she was herself inevitably a supporter of Franco. Revolutionary in her art, she was reactionary in politics, and the liberal outlook did not appeal to her. She never forgot a remark of Maurice Grosser's to the effect that many liberals and intellectuals, 'the kind of people who believe in progress and understanding', felt themselves to have had unhappy childhoods. She lists Leon Blum as one of such people, while as for herself 'I never had an un-

happy anything. What is the use of having an unhappy anything.'
Leo Stein, on the other hand, she says, although he had had everything, 'was gradually remembering that his childhood had not
been a happy one'. 'If Leo had been English,' Alice Toklas once
remarked, 'he would have been on the *Manchester Guardian*.'
Nevertheless she mocks dictators whatever their politics.

> There is too much fathering going on just now and there
> is no doubt about it fathers are depressing. Everybody now-
> a-days is a father, there is father Mussolini and father Hitler
> and father Roosevelt and father Stalin and father Trotzky
> and father Blum and father Franco is just commencing now
> and there are ever so many more ready to be one. Fathers
> are depressing. England is the only country now that has not
> got one and so they are more cheerful there than anywhere.
> It is a long time now that they have not had any fathering
> and so their cheerfulness is increasing.

And to W. G. Rogers she wrote:

> . . . I hate to acknowledge it but in America from the 1st to
> the 2nd Roosevelt there has been a steady tendency to dictator-
> ship, we limit the time of the rule of the dictator but con-
> gress has been tending to be a yes congress . . .

Other comments on the European situation in her letters to
W. G. Rogers in 1936 include:

> . . . poor Miro he was here the other afternoon and so sad,
> he was allowed to leave Barcelona because he was to have a
> show in Paris but they would not let his wife and child come
> they said it would look like flight.

> . . . they are all envious of Italy because everybody there can
> live and be quiet and everybody xcept the few who make
> the noise want to live a little while and be quiet, and nobody
> thinks you can live or be quiet under communism.

> . . . here everybody thinks you have to be either red or
> white and I am not sure they are not right and certainly
> white is bad but not as bad as red.

> Down in Belley . . . one old duck was listening to gauche
> and droite and finally he said well anyway one always does
> keep one's pocket book in one's right hand pocket.

And she speaks of Russia wanting bourgeois art, Hitler none
at all, Mussolini anything that will help Italy, while in France
under Monarchy and Empire all the great writers were members
of the Academy and since the Third Republic there were none.
'So as my grandfather used to remark there is a great deal to be
said on both sides.' Going steadily on with *Everybody's Autobiography* through the mounting tension she reflects:

> Of course in France you never know it may be anything
> it might be another republic or soviets not so likely red very
> red or rather pink often quite pink, a king not so likely but
> perhaps a king . . .

She was also thinking more than she had since childhood about
God and the stars and space, characteristically pointing her cosmic
meditations with such observations as, 'The French have a funny
phrase. All these vast sums that everybody votes now-a-days to
do anything they call astronomical.'

All the talk about taxes and millions and billions worried her
and she wrote a number of short pieces about money, three of
which appeared in *The Saturday Evening Post*. In *Everybody's
Autobiography* she says:

> I have been writing a lot about money lately, it is a fas-
> cinating subject, it is really the difference between men and
> animals . . .
>
> About every once in so often there is a movement to do
> away with money. Roosevelt tries to spend so much that
> perhaps money will not exist, communists try to live with-
> out money but it never lasts because if you live without
> money you have to do as the animals do live on what you
> find each day to eat and that is just the difference the minute
> you do not do that you have to have money and so every-
> body has to make up their mind if money is money or if
> money isn't money and sooner or later they always do
> decide that money is money.
>
> The Jews and once more we have the Orientalising of
> Europe being always certain that money is money finally
> decide and that makes a Marxian state that money is not
> money. That is the way it is if you believe in anything
> deeply enough it turns into something else and so money
> turns into not money. That is what mysticism is . . .

Then too there was counting.

> There is no difference between men and animals except that
> they can count and never has there been so much counting
> as is going on at present. Everybody is counting, counting
> is everybody's occupation . . .
> Counting is the religion of this generation it is its hope and
> its solution.

And she notes the sadness of the people.

> They are being organised and it makes them sadder, well I
> suppose they might just as well be sadder as not. After every-
> body gets sad enough then they will try something else, and
> anyway people can't just go on being sadder or there would
> be no will to live . . .

But presently in Paris:

> . . . everybody cheered up because of course there was Mrs.
> Simpson. Everybody needs being excited by the story of Mrs.
> Simpson at least once a year, it cheered up the gloom of
> organisation, and the difference between sovietism and
> fascism, and new deals and sit down striking, . . . a funny
> American . . . who taught a great many people painting
> . . . used to say remember every room has its gloom and the
> great thing is to find the colour that will cut that gloom.
> Well organisation has its gloom and the only thing for a
> long time that really cut that gloom was Mrs. Simpson and
> King Edward and the abdication.

1936 was the year too of the Paris Exposition and Gertrude
Stein was invited to be on the picture selection committee for the
Petit Palais. She found it strange to be discussing paintings with
collectors and critics and councillors instead of with artists, but
as usual she enjoyed herself—and she had her own way in the end.

> Naturally I got excited I was surprised at so many things,
> that they would like Bonnard and Segonzac that was natural
> Bonnard is a good painter and Segonzac a bad one but they
> both are in what they call the tradition and the tradition is
> naturally easy enough to like so that in liking it there is no
> strain, that was alright but what did astonish me was that
> they had to accept but not with acquiescence Picasso and
> Braque and Derain but that they all accepted without any

trouble Modigliani now why I asked every one, that was a puzzle to me, finally an under-director of museums answered me, he said it is simple Modigliani combines Italian art with Negro art and both these arts are admitted by every one and as there is nothing else in Modigliani naturally nobody takes any exception. I myself would never have thought of that explanation but it is undoubtedly the correct one. Then of course I tried to introduce Picabia but to that there was no exception he was greeted by a universal no, why not I asked them because he cannot paint, they said, but neither everybody said could Cézanne, ah they said that is a different matter. Furthermore he is too cerebral they said, ah yes I said abstract painting is alright, oh yes they said, but to be cerebral and not abstract that is wrong oh yes they said, I found it all very interesting. And then the voting was very interesting, it reminded me of Matisse's description long ago of how they voted the first time he was on a jury for the autumn salon. They began with the a's and everybody looked very carefully and they refused some but they accepted a great many and then the president said but gentlemen remember that the space is limited you must be more exigeant and so they looked a little less long and refused a great many and that went on and then the president said but gentlemen after all we must fill the Grand Palais and you are refusing a great many and so they did not look at all long at any of them and they accepted most of them. Voting is interesting. Well anyway, they began to vote at least they said they did but not and of course I wanted a room for Juan Gris and they said yes yes and I said but you have not voted it and they said oh yes we did and I said when oh just now they said and somebody else said oh no and they said oh yes well all I want is that they give it to him I said are you certain that they will and the director of the museum said oh yes and that is what was called unanimous voting, well anyway after all I got to like the director of the museum . . . I am lending lots of Picassos of course but he is going to put in two Picabia paintings, you can vote for anything but you can always add anything which is a pleasant thing, that is the reason that Stalin has just announced that there must be a democratisation again of Sovietism, that is a natural thing that it is necessary so soon again.

Pictures are interesting and there are a very great many of them in France.

In a letter to W. G. Rogers she referred to Tal-Coat as 'the present white hope'. He painted her portrait in 1937 and with it won the Prix Blumenthal.[1]

Throughout these events Gertrude Stein and Alice Toklas moved as usual between the rue de Fleurus and Bilignin, and visitors, many of them new American friends, constantly descended at both places. Alexander Woollcott, one among many well-known guests, characteristically preluded his arrival with a request that the white poodle be made 'pure as the drivelling snow'.

In April 1937 they paid another visit to England for the première of *A Wedding Bouquet*, the ballet by Lord Berners and Frederick Ashton from Gertrude Stein's play *They Must. Be Wedded. To their Wife*, written in 1931 and published the following year in *Operas and Plays*. Constant Lambert was the conductor. Ninette de Valois directed and Margot Fonteyn, Robert Helpmann and Harold Turner were among the dancers.

They went to Sadler's Wells for the dress rehearsal, the first rehearsal Gertrude Stein had ever seen, and the whole thing delighted her. She liked them doing it again and again and felt that it was very right for everybody else to be working while she sat still.

> It is quite true what is known as work is something that I cannot do it makes me nervous, I can read and write and I can wander around and I can drive an automobile and I can talk and that is almost all, doing anything else makes me nervous.

And so another new experience, the first night of one of her own works.

> . . . I was not nervous but it was exciting . . . English dancers when they dance dance with freshness and agility and they know what drama is, it all went so very well, each time a musician does something with the words it makes it do what they never did do . . .

[1] Baltimore Museum of Art.

I like anything that a word can do. And words do do all they do and then they can do what they never do do.

This made listening to what I had done and what they were doing most exciting.

And for the first time Gertrude Stein was on the stage bowing. She knew then that the ballet had been a success, but she still wished a little wistfully that they would do one of her plays as a play. 'I wonder can they.'

And then we went somewhere and we met every one and I always do like to be a lion, I like it again and again, and it is a peaceful thing to be one succeeding.

Everybody's Autobiography ends with them flying back to Paris, gathering everything together and setting off for Bilignin:

That was a natural thing, perhaps I am not I even if my little dog knows me but any way I like what I have and now it is today.

Liking what she had and welcoming each today were two happy expressions of her continued 'loving being'.

CHAPTER EIGHTEEN

'THE WINNER LOSES'

'War is never fatal but always lost.'
Wars I Have Seen.

AT the beginning of 1938, below the monogram on the letter-paper, 'Rose is a rose is a rose', the old address was crossed out and a new one written in. 'You see by the above that we are moving,' Gertrude Stein wrote to Sherwood Anderson, 'I guess 27 got so historical it just could not hold us any longer and so the landlord wanted to put his son in and we might have made a fuss but we were kind of pleased and now we are very pleased.'

Rue Christine, called after the Queen of Sweden who once resided there, is a tiny street off rue Dauphine running down to the river at Pont Neuf, and Gertrude Stein makes an illuminating comment in *Paris France*:

> So from 1900 to 1930 those of us who lived in Paris did not live in picturesque quarters even those who lived in Montmartre like Picasso and Braque did not live in old houses, they lived in fifty year old houses at most and now we all live in the ancient quarter near the river, now that the twentieth century is decided and has its character we all tend to want to live in seventeenth century houses, not barracks of ateliers as we did then. The seventeenth century houses are just as cheap as our barracks of ateliers were then but now we need the picturesque the splendid we need the air and space you only get in old quarters. It was Picasso who said the other day when they were talking about tearing down the insalubrious parts of Paris but it is only in the insalubrious quarters that there is sun and air and space, and it is true, and we are all living there the beginners and the middle ones and the older ones and the old ones we all live in old houses in ramshackle quarters. Well all this is natural enough.

Familiarity does not breed contempt, anything one does every day is important and imposing and anywhere one lives is interesting and beautiful.

Clearly the friends were untroubled by leaving their old home after more than thirty years, but naturally the move was tiring. In her letters to W. G. Rogers, Gertrude Stein speaks of plumbers and curtains and clearing out drawers, 'my head just went round and round with fatigue and Alice did not know any longer that she could sit she lost the habit and just went on being on her feet, golly it was awful . . . '

She also remarks 'Picasso and we are all chummy again and we all like that', and in the midst of the confusion, from which she was certainly as far as possible protected, she began writing her book about him. She wrote it first in French and told Rogers, 'there are going to be lots of dates and foot-notes just like a real book. Escholier [the French editor] insisting upon that, so I am letting them put them in not having the habit . . . '

By springtime she was telling her friends that they were so settled in their new life that they hardly knew the old one ever existed and speaking of the delight of walking up and down the banks of the Seine and watching the sky from their flat roof. They were so much enjoying the light and air of Paris that they had not their usual impatience to get to Bilignin.

In *Everybody's Autobiography* Gertrude Stein says that once Picasso and she used to dream of the pleasure it would be if a burglar came to steal not silver and money but his painting or her writing. And now, when this might have happened, when both of them had become living legends, she wrote *Picasso* which refuted the charge of her detractors that she knew nothing about the art of her time. There can be no better description of it than Donald Sutherland's:

> The book is a wonder of complete and ample realization. While in perfect command of all the personal history and the aesthetical argumentation that accompanied the creation of the Picasso legend, she gives only the essence of his person, as he himself in painting her portrait had given only the essence of Gertrude Stein, and she manages to convey the quality of his paintings as real and exciting experiences, with-

out poetizing them and without a great fuss of critical explanation or justification.

The book was written again in English and at once bought in London by Batsford while, to the distress of Bennett Cerf of Random House, Scribner's acquired the American rights. After *The Autobiography of Alice B. Toklas, Picasso* is probably the best-known work. It does not contain examples of her more idiosyncratic writing, yet expresses her contemporaneousness which made her recognize twentieth-century art and greatly contribute to it. She explains how the real creator, not being like other people too busy with the business of life, is sensitive enough to understand how people are thinking and living and changing, and how a war, be it a war of notions or a war of cubism, changes everything.

A creator is not in advance of his generation but he is the first of his contemporaries to be conscious of what is happening in his generation.

Picasso was followed in 1938 by *Dr. Faustus Lights the Lights,*[1] a new opera commissioned by Lord Berners. In this libretto, although it is more logical than many of the plays and very entertaining, she returned to the repetitive style. By the time it was finished the war had begun and Lord Berners told her sadly that he could not write the music, 'all inspirational sources seem to have dried up', and reluctantly suggested that she should send the script to Virgil Thomson. She also sent it to Random House hoping that it would compensate for the loss of *Picasso*, but they declined to publish it. In the end it was the young American composer, Richard Banks, who wrote the incidental music for the posthumous production at New York's Cherry Lane Theatre in 1951.

Next came a children's book, *The World is Round,*[2] the American edition illustrated by Clement Hurd, the English one by Sir Francis Rose, who had recently returned from a long tour in Indo-China during which he kept in touch and was greatly encouraged by Gertrude Stein's confidence in his work.

[1] Rinehart and Co. Inc., 1949.
[2] William R. Scott Inc., New York, 1939; Batsford Ltd., London, 1939.

The World is Round is a prose-poetry story of a little girl called Rose who climbs a blue mountain carrying a blue chair and has many adventures. Gertrude Stein in her directness and simplicity understood children and could write for them, as Donald Sutherland says, 'without being instructive or patronizing, sentimental or cute'. He calls this book 'a narrative for children and philosophers', and that is what delightfully it is. Three years later she wrote another book, which small children enjoy, *The First Reader*,[1] also beautifully decorated by Francis Rose.

> The daily bird was all excited. He had heard a word. It might have been worm the word he heard but it was not. The word he heard was po-ta-toe. Sweet po-ta-toe, a lovely word, a sweet word, that was the word the daily bird heard. And he said hoe, no they mean hoe or ho and he said ha no they mean tea and he said toe oh yes toe, toe is that so. And then he said no it is not so it is potatoe and he smiled and smiled and said oh potatoe sweet potatoe that is so.

Towards the end of 1938 Basket died. Carl Van Vechten was not the only person to whom he had seemed 'an immortal dog'. In *Paris France*, written the following year, Gertrude Stein describes how she and Alice Toklas could do nothing but cry, 'and finally every one said get another dog and get it right away'.

> Henry Daniel-Rops said get another as like Basket as possible call him by the same name and gradually there will be confusion and you will not know which Basket it is. . . .
> And then I saw Picasso, and he said no, never get the same kind of a dog again never . . . Why said he, supposing I were to die, you would go out on the street and sooner or later you would meet a Pablo, but it would not be I and it would be the same. No never get the same kind of a dog, get an Afghan hound . . .
> So we tried to have the same and not to have the same and then at last we found another Basket, and we got him and we called him Basket and he is very gay and I cannot say the confusion has yet taken place but certainly le roi est mort vive le roi, is a normal attitude of mind.

Picasso was reconciled to the new Basket because, although pure

---

[1] Maurice Fridberg. Dublin, London, 1946.

poodle, he had something of the stance of an Afghan hound, and Gertrude Stein reflects:

It is rather interesting that the Frenchman said have the same and the Spaniard said no don't have the same. The Frenchman does realise the inevitability of vive le roi but the Spaniard does not recognise the inevitability of resemblances and continuation.

She did not expect the war, although as the months passed the views expressed to her friends modified. In an undated letter to W. G. Rogers she wrote:

Maybe there is going to be a war but as France Germany Switzerland and Italy do none of them want a world war perhaps there will not. France will not fight unless she or her possessions are directly attacked, she is not going to fight for that piece of troubled map of Europe, that is constantly changing fortunes and has done so for hundreds of years . . . also France will not fight for England and America, unless they conscript and have an army, she will not again use up her manhood while the Anglo Saxons filled with their ideas slowly prepare to come in, after she is in, and as Germany and Italy will perhaps not attack her, she will not be in a war. Hitler does not want a war, because he does not like blood being an Austrian and not a german, and because he knows once the army was in power he would not last long, Italy can do nothing alone, and England if she does not conscript cannot fight . . . the only people who seem to believe in fighting are Americans, and I guess Europe is a bit cynical about that, since we are the only people who would make anything out of a war instead of losing everything . . . They say here that American business men have sent over $9000000 to propagande for war, I hope it is not true . . . it kind of makes one sad, we did not fight for China, but we want France and England to fight for Slovaks and Albania, well there is no use getting heated up about it, I do like my country to have the beau role and just now it does sound a bit of a sordid story.

In 1939, now sixty-five years old, Gertrude Stein went on writing small things, including a piece in French on superstitions.

Inside this script lies a small loose sheet of her handwriting: 'What is important is that you are one of the rare writers in America who is not haunted by the spoken word. You write the written word and the written word speaks, the spoken word written never speaks.'

This opinion, whether of another's writing or her own, is interesting, for much has been said about Gertrude Stein's use of speech idiom. John Brown, for example, in *Panorama de la Littérature Contemporaine aux États-Unis*, takes the view that in order to give language freedom and movement Gertrude Stein deliberately wrote as one speaks. He goes so far as to say that she is the only American author who has used 'le langage parlé *à chaud*', even Hemingway in spite of Stein influence having converted it into literature. Certainly to many of us she appears to write the spoken word.

In the summer she began writing *Paris France*, opening it with the simple statement: 'Paris, France is exciting and peaceful.' This is an uneven piece of work, lucid and whimsical, containing many acute observations and not a little wisdom.

For the summer they moved as usual to their country house. Not only did they now know intimately every member of each family, only about twenty in all, in the little hamlet of Bilignin, but they had many friends in Belley and its neighbourhood. Through her magnetism and her warm interest in other people's lives, Gertrude Stein had achieved something very rare for a foreigner in France. She was accepted in both bourgeois and aristocratic families, *au fait* with their affairs, consulted about their problems, in fact treated as a loved and respected aunt. And concerned as these French people were with their own anxieties as the war drew near, they had time to worry about the situation of these two American women of Jewish birth. And they bear witness today to their courage.

Gertrude Stein tells what happened in *The Winner Loses, A Picture of Occupied France*, written in 1940 and boldly published in *The Atlantic Monthly* in November of that year. It appeared again as an Appendix to *Wars I Have Seen*,[1] the whole of which book she wrote during the Occupation, leaving it until the

[1] Random House, New York, 1944; B. T. Batsford Ltd., London, 1945.

Liberation in her handwriting, which she thought unlikely any German could read.

We were spending the afternoon with our friends, Madame Pierlot and the d'Aiguys, in September '39 when France declared war on Germany—England had done it first. They were all upset but hopeful, but I was terribly frightened; I had been so sure there was not going to be war and here it was, it was war, and I made quite a scene. I said, 'They shouldn't! They shouldn't!' and they were very sweet, and I apologised and said I was sorry but it was awful, and they comforted me—they, the French, who had so much at stake, and I had nothing at stake comparatively.

Whereupon she characteristically explains how she did not care about Poland—any more than she had cared about Belgium in 'the other war', but she did care desperately about France. However, once the panic was over, they 'settled down to a really wonderful winter'.

They did not make up their minds to stay, they just found themselves staying. One swift run to Paris was made in the car to arrange their affairs, collect a few pictures and their winter clothes and, as far as the floors of the apartment allowed, to lay down on them the most precious of the other paintings. Back at Bilignin Gertrude wrote to Rogers:

> ... I never did think there would be another war for me to see and here we are, well if there is one I would of course rather be in it than out of it, there is that something about a war, we are for the present staying here, we have done everything we can for everybody and they for us, and now we have come back to our normal life of gardening and digging and writing, and then we have had a radio installed, I never listened to one before, there is a deplorable amount of music going on in the world, if they would suppress most of it perhaps the world would be more peaceful.

It was the first time since childhood that she had spent a winter in the country and she loved it. There was snow and moonlight, and she dug and sawed wood for the fires and took long walks with Basket the second in the daytime and by night, coming to be able to see very well in the dark. And every week she bought a quantity of English books from Chambéry and Aix so that she was never short of a supply of detective and adventure stories. She also had a book of astrological predictions, *The Last Year of War*, which for a while gave everybody a good deal of comfort and amusement.

In the last months of 1939 she was still writing *Paris France* and the war slides quietly into its pages as she walks around the countryside talking with everybody as she always had. Even in the streets of Paris she would stop to ask workmen what they were doing or to discuss their wares and affairs with the marketers. Now one hears 'the farmers the gentle farmers' telling her how once everybody thought it was only kings who brought misery on people, but that democracy had shown them it was the *grosses têtes* anywhere any time. One sees the shadow falling: 'Ah yes the village is sad, the men are all gone and one of the women passing said ah yes and now once again it is evening, well yes once again it is it is evening.' And at the same time French living goes on, so that when they are all agitatedly waiting for important news, and at last the telephone rings, it is quite natural that it should be Mère Mollard announcing that her *quenelles* have turned sour on her. It was equally natural that Dr. Chaboux of Belley should kill a hare in the road with his car and the American ladies be invited by Madame Chaboux to partake of jugged hare at which dish she was expert. War or no war, cooking was important.

For ten years now, as Alice Toklas tells us in her *Cook Book*,[1] the vegetable gardens at Bilignin had been her joy, 'working in them during the summers and planning and dreaming of them during the winters'. By the time the war came her loving labours had been rewarded with plentiful supplies of excellent vegetables and fruits, and the cellar was stocked with a delicious dry white wine which compensated in the cooking for the lack of dairy produce. Besides, Gertrude Stein would come home from a walk with an egg when no one else could get one, and until under the Occupation fishing was forbidden, there was plenty of fish to be had from the Rhône and the Lac-de-Bourget.

One has the impression that in the changed conditions both women were more themselves than ever, Alice Toklas endlessly

[1] *The Alice B. Toklas Cook Book.* Harper and Brothers, 1954.

concerned with the household and the care of her friend, 'it took me an hour to gather a small basket [of *fraises des bois*] for Gertrude Stein's breakfast', and the writer ever faithful to the word.

> I like words of one syllable and it works out very well in the French order for general mobilisation. The printed thing gives all the detail and then it says the army de terre, de mer et de l'air. That is very impressive when you meet it in every village.

And so, before the French armistice with Germany, they lived quietly on. In that first spring the men of the village had leave for agriculture and everyone everywhere was digging. And in Belley there were many soldiers for whom Alice Toklas helped to make cakes with the Mixmaster that had been sent them from America.

Then came the first war tragedy to touch them:

> . . . our servant and friend Madame Roux had her only son, who was a soldier, of course, dying of meningitis at Annecy, and we forgot everything for two weeks in her trouble and then we woke up to there being a certain uneasiness.

If la veuve Roux was their friend, Miss Stein was a hundred times hers. Old, ill, living alone in the most primitive way, she still gasps her praises while tears run down her face. 'Oh, comme elle était bonne pour moi! Elle m'a sauvé la vie!' She knew them all, Picasso and Picabia—'but he's dead now, isn't he?'—and le Baron Rose, 'do you know him?' 'And have you seen Miss Toklas recently?' 'Ah ce Baskette, il est parti. Miss Toklas est seule maintenant. Comme moi, toute seule.'

'Yes, I did everything, even worked in the garden. My son did the vegetables. Oh, you should have seen the garden in those days! So beautiful. Always, always flowers. And Miss Toklas cutting fresh ones every morning although the old ones were not faded. Working in the garden in her big gloves.'

'And Miss Stein too?'

Madame Roux was shocked.

'Ah, non, madame, elle ne faisait que ses livres. Elle était génie.

Simply, like that, the village accepted her as a genius who

wrote books, although it was admitted that she also walked a great deal with her dogs. And she did, in fact, attend to the cutting of the box hedges, finding this almost as soothing an occupation as sawing wood. She told herself that by the time she had finished them all the war would be over.

Talking to the people who knew her in her country life, one finds a new Gertrude Stein. In Paris and New York and to a lesser extent in London she is a subject of interest, curiosity and controversy. In Belley and Bilignin she is a subject of affection and respect. She is warmly remembered at the Hôtel Pernollet, where she and Picabia took an interest in Jean Pernollet's painting, 'She taught me very much by what she said.' And in the Belley shops and brasserie and the post office 'elle venait souvent bavarder au guichet'. Yes, whatever was happening and whatever anxieties she may have had, Gertrude Stein's interest in ordinary people was unflagging. And one remembers that although she could be ruthless, with simple people and with children she was always kindly and gracious.

Madame Chaboux, the widow of the doctor, both of whom were close friends of Gertrude Stein's, still lives in Belley, with Carl Van Vechten's photograph of her against a faded background of stars and stripes on her crowded writing-table. 'Regardez, elle est toujours avec moi. Chère Gertrude! Chère Gertrude! Comme elle m'a manqué.' She finds it very moving to talk about her and the old times. How she saw her almost every day, coming striding from Bilignin with Basket and walking up into the flat and throwing her hat, 'un morceau de paille ou un morceau de feutre', on the floor and sitting down for a gossip. And if one called on her, even at an inconvenient moment, her welcome was always warm and her laugh enchanting.[1]

Then Tuesdays began. Every night in bed Gertrude Stein consulted her book of prophecy and everybody telephoned to know what it said. The dates it gave were right, only the events should have been bad for the Nazis, whereas, as a farmer's wife put it, 'Ils avancent toujours, ces coquins-là.'

It was a Tuesday when the first air attack came, Tuesday when Amiens fell, 'And the next Tuesday was the treason of the Bel-

[1] Bilignin and Belley conversations from the author's journal.

gian king.' Every Tuesday Paul Reynaud announced in a tragic voice that he had grave news to tell.

> And he always announced it the same way, and always in the same voice.
> I have never listened to the radio since.
> It was so awful that it became funny.
> Well, not funny, but they did all want to know if next Tuesday Paul Reynaud would have something grave to announce.
> And he did.
> 'Oh dear, what a month of May!' I can just hear Paul Reynaud's voice saying that.

Quietly she tells how they 'had all gotten careless about lights, and wandering about', but now as the enemy advanced and bombers and parachutists were more active they were strict about the black-out and stayed at home. Yet in that terrible May of 1940 she produced *To do a book of alphabets and birthdays*, for children, 'and I did get so that I could not think about the war but just about the stories I was making up for this book'. She walked outside in the daytime and up and down the terrace in the evenings thinking about writing and forgetting the war, 'except for the three times a day when there was the French communiqué, and that always gave me a sinking feeling in my stomach, and though I slept well every morning I woke up with that funny feeling in my stomach'.

She could not, however, ignore the war for long. Even in the families of that tiny hamlet there were casualties, and in June the book of predictions continued to give the days of crucial events, 'only they were not the defeat of Germany but the downfall of France'. It all reminded her of Shakespeare, of *Macbeth*'s woods marching and *Julius Caesar*'s 'Ides of March'; 'the twentieth century was just like that and nothing else'.

When, on the tenth of June, Italy came into the war, they were really frightened, '—well, here we were in everybody's path'. They telephoned to the American Consul in Lyon who promised to see to their passports and told them to leave at once, and they had the car prepared and made arrangements for Madame Roux to look after Basket, although adjuring her not to sacrifice herself to him. Madame Roux told them that the village was upset at the idea of the ladies leaving, 'and so were we'.

Twice they went to Lyon and they also consulted the Préfet at Bourg, and all the authorities told them to go, but still they could not make up their minds. There was so much to consider, the country they loved, their house, Basket, food and familiarity— and the perils of the road. Returning a second time from seeing the American Consul, at a village near a little lake not far from Belley they encountered their friends Dr. and Madame Chaboux calmly paying for their year's fishing rights. Pressed for advice the doctor considered that it was better for the ladies to stay where they were than to risk themselves among strangers— although he was well aware of the danger they would be in if the Germans came to the village.

> 'Thank you,' we said, 'that is all we need. We stay.'
>
> So back we came and we unpacked our spare gasoline and our bags and we said to Madame Roux, 'Here we are and here we stay.'
>
> And I went out for a walk and I said to one of the farmers, 'We are staying.'
>
> 'Vous faites bien,' he said, 'mademoiselle. We all said, Why should these ladies leave? In this quiet corner they are as safe as anywhere, and we have cows and milk and chickens and flour and we can all live and we know you will help us out in any way you can and we will do the same for you. Here in this little corner we are en famille, and if you left to go where?—aller où?'
>
> And they all said to me, 'Aller, où?' and I said, 'You are right—aller, où?'
>
> We stayed, and dear me, I would have hated to have left.

When they settled down again, Gertrude Stein decided not to read the prediction book any more and not to listen to the radio. She walked and wrote and read and cut the hedges, 'even the very tall one on a ladder', and Alice Toklas began making raspberry jam.

But if Gertrude Stein did not listen to the news, she read Marshal Pétain's speeches and devoted a number of exercise books to a translation of *Petain's Paroles*. She remembered him as the hero of Verdun and the relsover of the army mutinies and believed in his patriotism even when not liking his way of expressing it. In *Wars I Have Seen* she gave not only his views but those of such French who while not wanting a German victory did not want a British one either, and observed that 'in France there has always been a party that although they knew they could not stand the Germans felt that they should collaborate with them.'

So she recorded:

> Well anyway there was the armistice Pétain made it and we were all glad in a way and completely sad in a way and we had so many opinions. I did not like his way of saying I Philippe Pétain, that bothered me and we were in the un-occupied area and that was a comfort . . . A great many people complained that France was divided in two but it really was not it was for a very little while and then it gradually began to grow together again, others said there should not have been an armistice at all they should have gone to Africa and continued the fight but that was foolish-ness there were no industries no anything in Africa except a little food and a very small army, no Pétain was right to stay in France and he was right to make the armistice, in the first place it was comfortable for us who were here and in the second place it was an important element in the ultimate defeat of the Germans. To me it remained a miracle and I was always asking everybody why did the Germans grant it, why, it would have been so easy for them to take the whole why did they only take the half, it would have been easier for them to attack England from Egypt than across the channel, why did they grant the armistice . . .

In time she found an answer to satisfy her, that the Germans had come along so fast that they had lost their breath, and their plans for keeping everything repaired as they went had broken down. They had to wait and by the time they were ready it was too late.

It is hardly necessary to point out that there was no pro-German feeling in Gertrude Stein's approval of the armistice. She adored France and in spite or perhaps because of her ante-cedents she had always detested the Germans. So much so, indeed, that Alice Toklas was nervous about what would happen when

Gertrude Stein saw a German. But nothing happened. Even when they were billeted in their house the Germans remained, as to many of the French, invisible.

Bernard Faÿ, the French professor who had made translations of her work and been a frequent guest at Bilignin, took office under Vichy as Director of the Bibliothèque Nationale. After the war he was convicted of collaboration. In a letter to a friend at this time Gertrude Stein declared that Faÿ had never worked against the Free French and that he had helped many people including Jews and the Resistance, and affirmed:

> No his difficulty is the question of Free Masonry, there he made himself bitter enemies, and he certainly did certain things that he should not have done, but that he ever denounced anybody, no, that I do not believe. In fact I know he did not, he was a monarchist, he was a churchman, but he was a passionate patriot, always, about that there is no doubt, really not, you see living in an occupied country is very complicated, and that is what I have tried to make people understand in my play *Yes Is For A Very Young Man*.[1],[2]

Here speaks loyalty to a friend, and on his side Bernard Faÿ did what he could to ensure the safety of these two women and of Gertrude Stein's pictures during the Occupation.

In pouring rain, the armistice notices were pinned up and when the shock was over people began their normal lives again. One day they went in as usual to Belley:

> . . . and there they were.
>
> All the time they were here they were not spoken of as anything except they, *eux*.
>
> It was impossible, but there they were, and we were seeing them.

For although this was unoccupied territory, Belley, as a small well-found town close to the recent fighting, had been chosen for an army headquarters.

Gertrude Stein sat in the car while Alice Toklas went shopping:

> It was strange sitting there watching the people up and

[1] Written 1944-5. Published as *In Savoy*, Pushkin Press, London, 1946. *Last Operas and Plays*, 1949.   [2] Private collection, unpublished.

down on the main street of Belley, like all country towns; there are always a good many people going up and down on the main street of a country town, and now added to it were these familiar and unfamiliar German soldiers, familiar because we had seen their photographs in illustrated papers all winter and unfamiliar because we never dreamed we would see them with our own eyes.

They did not look like conquerors; they were very quiet. They bought a great deal, all sugar things, cakes and candies, all silk stockings, women's shoes, beauty products and fancy soaps, but always everlastingly what the American soldiers in the last war called 'eats'—that is, anything sweet—and anything that looked like champagne.

They went up and down, but they were gentle, slightly sad, polite; and their voices when they spoke—they did not seem to talk much—were low, not at all resonant.

Everything about them was exactly like the photographs we had seen except themselves; they were not the least bit like we thought they would be. They admired Basket II and said to each other in German, 'A beautiful dog.' They were polite and considerate; they were, as the French said, correct. It was all very sad; they were sad, the French were sad, it was all sad, but not at all the way we thought it would be, not at all.

The French, the girls and boys and the older men and older women, who also went up and down about their own affairs, had that *retenue* that is French—they neither noticed nor ignored the Germans. In all the three weeks that the Germans were in Belley there was no incident of any kind.

When the Germans left [Belley and other places] they thanked the mayors and congratulated them upon the extraordinary discipline of their populations. The Germans called it discipline, but it was not—it was the state of being civilised that the French call *retenue*.

Everybody went on working and waiting for them, for *eux*, to go. Gertrude Stein makes it sound like a dream. 'And then miles and miles of them went away and they were gone.' And everybody breathed again and everybody began to talk again, 'not about anything in particular, but they all just began to talk again'. And the men from whom nobody had heard for so long began writing and then began coming home, and gradually everybody realized that although a great many Frenchmen were prisoners, very few were dead. 'Everybody forgot about being defeated, it was such a relief that their men were not dead.'

One follows the train of events and the periods of eventlessness, so accurately observed, so clearly remembered and livingly described first in *The Winner Loses* and then in *Wars I Have Seen*.

In 1940 she also wrote *Ida, A Novel*[1] which had nothing to do with the war. In this she returned to the dear problems of identity and how to write. The heroine has a double identity: 'There was a baby born named Ida . . . And as Ida came, with her came her twin, so there she was Ida-Ida.'

When *Ida* was published Bennett Cerf wrote in the blurb: '. . . here it is, presented faithfully to you by a publisher who rarely has the faintest idea of what Miss Stein is talking about, but who admires her from the bottom of his heart for her courage and for her abounding love of humanity and freedom'. This calls to mind Donald Sutherland's perfect pronouncement, 'one has to like freedom in order to like Gertrude Stein's work at all'. Of *Ida* he writes that it is really the story of what Gertrude Stein called a 'publicity saint', that is a person who does nothing and is not connected with anything but who holds the public attention simply by being and becomes a legend.

> Ida is a sort of combination of Helen of Troy, Dulcinea, Garbo, the Duchess of Windsor, and in particular 'Gertrude Stein'. The extraordinary thing about the book is that it manages to maintain a level and atmosphere of legend, this legend being a fascinating mixture of Homer and Hollywood and the daily press.

It is also like a fantastic dream or a surrealist film, and fascinating from beginning to end.

'There was nothing funny about Ida but funny things did happen to her.' She wanders along with her dog Love, joins in a revivalist meeting and a walking marathon, wins the world prize at a beauty competition, writes letters to herself as her twin, gets married a number of times, goes round the world and settles down at Washington.

[1]Random House, 1941.

Once upon a time there was a city, it was built of blocks and every block had a square in it and every square had a statue and every statue had a hat and every hat was off.

And there are poetic passages:

The road is awfully wide,
With the snow on either side.
She was walking along the road made wide with snow.
The moonlight was bright. She had a white dog and the dog looked gray in the moonlight and on the snow. Oh she said to herself that is what they mean when they say in the night all cats are gray.

As for the portrait of Ida:

Ida woke up. After a while she got up. Then she stood up. Then she ate something. After that she sat down.
That was Ida.
It is difficult never to have been younger but Ida almost was she almost never had been younger.

Was this not perhaps true of Gertrude Stein? And this too:

Ida never spoke, she just said what she pleased. Dear Ida.

And most of all:

Ida decided that she was just going to talk to herself. Anybody could stand around and listen but as for her she was just going to talk to herself.

With the end of 1941 came Pearl Harbour. Early in February Gertrude Stein wrote to W. G. Rogers:

. . . the first days of the attack of the Japs was perfectly awful, Alice and I were pretty done up, it does not seem that it could be worse than an attack on France but I do suppose that after all one's native land is more one's native land than any other native land.

She told him that she was reading *War and Peace* and finding it 'just like today'. There is no sign of personal anxiety although she and Alice Toklas were now to the Germans enemy aliens. In a perfection of understatement she writes in *Wars I Have Seen*:

We had recently quite a number of difficult moments.

America had come into the war, our consul and vice-consul in Lyon with whom we had gotten very friendly . . . had been interned first at Lourdes and then taken to Germany . . .

Jewish in name and Jewish in appearance and speaking French with a strong American accent they stayed indomitably on.

In February 1943 the lease of their beloved *manoir* ended and the owners demanded possession. For the first, indeed for the only time in her life Gertrude Stein went to law, but she lost the case and friends found a house for them at Culoz, further up the Rhône. On the eve of moving with 'our electric water heater and our bathtub and our electric kitchen stove and our refrigera tor', not to speak of a number of pictures, Miss Stein's lawyer, who had just seen the former *sous-préfet* of Belley at Vichy, told the two women that they must leave immediately for Switzerland or else they would be sent to a concentration camp.

I felt very funny, quite completely funny. But how can we go, as the frontier is closed, I said. That he said could be arranged . . . You mean pass by fraud I said, Yes, he said . . .

So she went home,

. . . and Alice Toklas and I sat down to supper. We both felt funny and then I said, No, I am not going we are not going, it is better to go regularly wherever we are sent than to go irregularly where nobody can help us if we are in trouble, no I said, they are always trying to get us to leave France but here we are and here we stay.

And taking Alice Toklas by the arm, for the latter had not like her friend the habit of walking at night, she went back to Belley and told the lawyer her decision. He then offered to hide them in a house up in the mountains,

and I said well perhaps later but now I said tomorrow we are going to move to Culoz, with our large comfortable new house with two good servants and a nice big park with trees, and we all went home, and we did move the next day. It took us some weeks to get over it but we finally did.

Considering the precariousness of their position it was an amazing decision to make. They moved on the very day that the

Germans occupying the southern zone arrived in Belley, 'one cold winter day', Alice Toklas relates in her *Cook Book*, 'all too appropriate to our feelings and the state of the world'.

Ah, there would be another garden, the same friends, possibly, or no, probably new ones, and there would be other stories to tell and to hear. And so we left Bilignin, never to return.

CHAPTER NINETEEN

WAR AUTOBIOGRAPHY

'. . . and as long as there is no peace we are at war.'
Wars I Have Seen.

WHILE Alice Toklas mourned her garden, grief more poignant than any fear of the enemy, Gertrude Stein, whose love of the present was not confined to her writing, enjoyed the amenities of Le Colombier, 'a nice big modern house alone against a mountain with a lovely park all full of bushes and big trees, and firs'. With the house went Clothilde and Olympe, 'two sisters no longer young', one of them a very fine cook and the other a very good maid and both of them knowing all about enemies, 'in war and in peace . . . It sounds like the same thing but it is not.'

The fine cook was, however, not much help at first, for she announced that she could not cook with the scanty supplies the coupons permitted, and she was not encouraged when she was told that these would be supplemented by what Miss Toklas calls 'the blessed black market'. However, one way and another they managed to make themselves comfortable and to go steadily on with their own way of living.

It has been suggested, for people naturally wonder how they came safely through the war, that after the move to Culoz the two women remained in hiding at the back of the house, while the neighbours conspired to conceal their presence. Certainly when, in the late summer of 1943, Germans were billeted at Le Colombier they were given quarters as far as possible from their hostesses' rooms, and equally certainly, at a time when denouncing was widespread, nobody denounced them but they were by no means invisible. A passage in *The Alice B. Toklas Cook Book* explains their position. Parcels of cakes were being sent them from a shop in Belley:

I went to the bus stop to retrieve the first one. Intending to be discreet, she had addressed it to The Two American Ladies in Culoz. Not one of the two hundred and fifty Germans and their officers stationed at Culoz suspected our nationality, the French authorities having destroyed our papers and done everything possible to protect us. There was nothing to do but to hope for the best and to take the bus over to Belley to warn Madame Peycru neither to put either of our names on the package nor to mention our nationality. The conductor of the bus would leave it at the café where one of us would pick it up.

But what could be more conspicuous than Gertrude Stein walking some twelve kilometres with a great white poodle to fetch 'bread that was not dark' and such commodities? Sometimes, when she had a lot to carry, she and Basket boarded the crowded bus, but in spite of her years she walked these long distances continuously. During the war years she had grown much thinner, but she made light of this, remarking that it was far worse for the Frenchman dwindling without his cheese and his wine. No, Gertrude Stein was neither invisible nor did she keep silent in spite of her accent. The two American women lived in exactly the same way as the French people round them.

> Everything is dangerous and everybody casually meeting anybody talks to anybody and everybody tells everybody the history of their lives, they are always telling me and I am always telling them and so is everybody, that is the way it is when everything is dangerous.
> Life and death and death and life.

Wars I Have Seen is a kind of journal from the time of the move to Culoz in February 1943 until the return to Paris in December 1944. On the cover of the first exercise book is written 'An emotional autobiography', crossed out and underneath 'I am really writing my autobiography.' The first page is headed: 'Gertrude Stein's War Autobiography.'

Certainly this book, while lacking the poetic quality of the imaginative works, gives us more of the author herself than any other single volume. She dips back and forth in her experience, at one moment reliving her own childhood with Leo in California, 'during this kind of war you know what children think',

at the next watching the children of the Bugey playing at com-
mandos, at maquis, at *abris*. We glimpse again the uneasy adolescent, the happy student, the eager pioneer, and see how the one
has developed into the other and all of them into this rich-
natured, mature woman. Now, when she was nearly seventy, her
interest in the bottom nature of human beings, her love of the
contemporary, of the immediate present, and her passion for the
English word had brought her to the point when, in danger of
death or worse—and she was not, as she later said, made for
suffering—she sat, although often 'feeling funny', writing down
everything she saw, heard, thought and felt during the final
phases of the war.

She regarded the whole era, beginning possibly with Edward's
abdication, as a plunge back into mediaevalism, and she wondered
how the royal family had the temerity to call anybody who had
a chance of coming to the throne George, as every time England
had a king of that name misfortune fell. But although she joked
she was deeply serious. 'Mediaeval means, that life and place and
the crops you plant and your wife and children, all are uncertain.' And jew-baiting and denouncing and imprisonment and
torture were the most mediaeval practices of all. She also considered anti-semitism out of date, for whereas once Jews had been
international financiers, 'since industrialism, all the Jewish money
in the world is only a drop in the bucket and all of it together
could never buy anybody to make war or make peace, not a bit'.
Everybody, she said, knew this, but 'the countries who like to
delude their people' chose not to know it, and the Jews themselves
kept up the illusion for fear of losing their importance.

With regard to money she observed that you never could tell
who was going to help you. After America came into the war it
was naturally difficult for her to get funds, 'and nobody among
my old friends nobody asked me if we were in any trouble'.
But although 'French people are awfully careful of their money,
so careful and so hard', a young silk manufacturer from Lyon
who had bought a house in the neighbourhood and was interested
in literature, provided funds and would not take a cheque or any
note of acknowledgement. In the end she sold a picture, 'quietly
to some one who came to see me', and paid him back.

So by means of description, anecdote and reflection, Gertrude Stein wheels us along with her through the seasons of nature and the seasons of war. Like the French prisoners from Germany whom she quotes she saw the armistice as a pause and not an end, and long before the outcome could be known shared the faith these men had expressed in daily greetings while in prison, 'good morning and how long before the Germans are going to be defeated'. Adolescence according to her was mediaeval and childhood was legendary; behind the mediaeval catastrophe that had struck France down she saw the pristine France of legend. This was the France, she said, that the French really believed in, and it would rise like the phoenix from the ashes.

She goes on with her living and writing these chronicles. There is more content now and less direct concern with herself. She tells how the French like good fighters so much that the Vichy radio announcer cannot keep his pride in the Russians out of his voice; she wonders 'if Laval and the rest of them think they are right now in 1943'; she encourages the young men who come to say goodbye before being taken to Germany as hostages to think of themselves as students, 'you can learn their language and read their literature and contemplate them as if you were travellers and still know them to be enemies'. And when they have gone she comments, 'Oh dear me one cannot sleep very well', and meditates, 'The idea of enemies is awful it makes one stop remembering eternity and the fear of death.' And again and again the cry breaks, 'So many are prisoners, prisoners, prisoners everywhere.'

With the coming of summer she observes that 'every day the feeling is strengthening that one or another has been or will be a traitor to something', and describes the little wooden coffins, sometimes with a rope inside them, sent to suspects. 'Of course they had to find a reliable carpenter to make the coffins but they did find him.'

Yet, through the sadness and the darkness, one feels the invisible force growing, the dragon's teeth ready to burgeon just as the grapes were already being tended for the Victory wine and Alice Toklas had a cache of raisins and candied peel for a Liberation cake. Even when the Germans were billeted on them and it was 'funny to be Americans and to be here in France and to have that', it was very different from 1940 for 'the Germans not being conquerors any more nobody feels conquered'.

After the Germans had gone, Italians were billeted in the house. One welcome factor of their visit was that they sold Alice Toklas black-market cigarettes; lack of tobacco, as there was no ration for women, being one of her trials. 'The Italian tobacco', she writes in the *Cook Book*, 'was agreeable, convenient and plentiful; our young maid found the soldiers equally so.' Moreover the two officers billeted at Le Colombier afterwards sent them three pounds of Parmesan cheese, a welcome gift although by then the food situation was easier. Once they had suddenly realized that they were hungry but this had not been mentioned, although afterwards Alice Toklas confessed to a dream of a long silver dish floating in the air with three large slices of succulent ham upon it.

'And so going on.'

> Everybody is getting sombre, the winter weather and the war not over, everybody is getting sombre and a little dreary, in the summer they think it will be over this year but now that the fifth winter has commenced nobody can believe that it will ever be over. Nobody. The only thing that cheered anybody was the speech of General Smuts, against France, it made everybody feel alive, he said France was dead and as France does naturally rise from the ashes it made everybody feel very much alive. Naturally nobody was grateful to General Smuts but I was because everybody cheered up and it is better to have everybody cheered up rather than not. Decidedly yes.

In fact, even in darkest winter, everyone was beginning to think about unconditional surrender.

> Nobody in Europe had ever heard of that, there are always conditions there have to be conditions, life in Europe is conditional and the word unconditional surrender is like a new thing, jazz or automobiles when they were new or radio, it is something new, and the Europeans like something new.

The thanklessness of refugees does not escape her notice:

> There are so many refugees, roughly speaking one might

say everybody is a refugee . . . this Culoz is a little town of two thousand inhabitants and there are lots of them, Alsatians and Lorrainers and Poles and Americans, several besides us, working people that somehow are Americans and any town is like that and French quite a few French and Belgians, and anything else and lots of Persians . . . and every refugee is certain that he likes neither the climate the landscape the earth in which they garden nor the mosquitoes and if he does not say so certainly his wife does she most certainly does.

Besides these there were a great many Jewish refugees, French and every other kind, and a floating population of young men escaping from forced labour by continually changing their abode . . . 'oh dear everybody is a refugee and how do they go on spending money and being fairly well dressed and well fed how do they'.

It is very strange, for the last two years everybody was wearing shoes with wooden soles there were no others to be had and now there are no others to be had nobody wears shoes with wooden soles they all wear leather shoes like anybody did and there are none to be had but everybody wears them. It is a pleasure that it is like that, quite a pleasure, almost a contentment.

And then in January 1944:

All one's friends are going up to Paris for a change. There are no trains but anyway all the time they all keep taking them.

On the third of February, Gertrude Stein's seventieth birthday, they went over to Belley and found panic because a drive was being made 'to round up the mountain boys and as everybody's boys are there it is rather horrible'. Everybody terrified, everybody ashamed because Frenchmen were arresting Frenchmen, everybody trembling, everybody crying, everybody listening, the telephone cut off and rumours abounding, 'rumours and rumours but some of them are true'. They were 'in the very thick of it now', and it was 'terribly the middle ages'.

It is funny why do the Germans wear camouflaged raincoats but not camouflaged uniforms now why do they. The first I saw was the other day, they went by on bicycles, and they reminded me of the chorus of the Tivoli Opera House in San Francisco, it used to cost twenty-five cents and the men in mediaeval costume looked so like these camouflaged coats, with sort of keys and crosses on them in contrasted colours. Oh dear, it would all be so funny if it were not so terrifying and so sad . . .

Ma foi it's long is what they say. Everybody in the country in France says ma foi, a nice mediaeval expression . . . that can mean yes or oh hell, or no, or just nothing . . . In this particular part of the world they have another thing, they say taisez-vous, or shut up, or shut it, and they say it as they are talking along about something and they say, oh shut it, and it is not to themselves, nor to you, it is of the facts of which they are speaking . . . they may say and the war is long and the Germans might be coming this way again oh shut up oh shut up and do you think it is possible that they will. This is a kind of sentence it makes, and it is enjoyable. Ma foi.

With her great vitality and zest for life how much she found even then to enjoy and translate into living language. When not writing she was reading and her taste was as catholic as ever:

So many books have been important to me, it is like the man who said about automobiles when someone asked him is that mark a good one, all automobiles are good, some might go better than others but they all go . . . Any book that I can read at all is important to me and I can read most of them . . . of course only English I cannot read any foreign language. I cannot lose myself in them, and so they are not books to me unless they are translated into English.[1]

She still had a large stock of English books bought up wherever they were to be had. Once they did not have time to hide these when Germans were suddenly billeted in the house, but they did not appear to notice them.

Every Friday afternoon the two women spent with a group of friends reading Shakespeare, *Julius Caesar, Macbeth, Richard III,* 'and what is so terrifying is that it is all just like what is happening now. Macbeth seeing ghosts well don't they, is not Mussolini seeing the ghost of his son-in-law . . .'

[1] *My Debt to Books.* Books Abroad, 1939.

The whole cast of the war in France is in these pages, occupying forces, Resistance, collaborationists, local officials, shopkeepers, farmers, men and women, children, the old and the young. Gertrude Stein records their feelings and their actions, contemplates and comments on them, but seldom judges, although she criticized the French for not understanding this twentieth-century warfare of attrition and still wanting 'nice eighteenth century fighting'. Usually, in her wide knowledge of human nature, she was tolerant. 'The young are strange', she says, contemplating the wildness and the courage of the boys and girls of the maquis. She had been talking to the local bank manager whose daughter was a student at Grenoble, thinking that as Grenoble was now a centre of resistance and reprisals, he would be keeping his girl at home:

> Oh no, he said, the young are not like that they say, this is their war, that we do not understand, their professors can be shot as hostages, their comrades mixed up in aggressions, their windows blown out and all the rest, but after all it is their war let us alone it is our war, and said the father there is nothing to do but to let them alone, I guess it is their war.

She also made the terrible discovery that this young generation never talked about its own future. 'There are no futures for this generation . . . and so naturally they never think of them.' And she observed that nobody imagined this war to be a war to end wars. The exploits of the 'young men in the mountains' delighted her. They raided the rich and the *collabo* and the profiteers but left the correct government price for the goods they took. 'Around here', she remarked, 'it is getting to be just like Robin Hood.'

Meanwhile the radio, which they had managed to keep, gave ever more thrilling news of American landings in the Pacific. 'We cannot help wondering how the American commentator can speak so quietly about all that, shows he is no Californian,' and they began to wonder 'if or where or when or if the Americans will be coming soon, well will they'.

There was so much geography in the war that she found all the places in her detective and adventure stories particularly interesting, and she wished she knew more foreign languages because she was so much impressed by the different ways nations began their broadcasts—'the English with this is London or the B.B.C. home service, always part of a pleasant home life, the Americans saying with poetry and fire, this is the voice of America and then with modesty and good neighbourliness, one of the United Nations, the French, Frenchmen speaking to Frenchmen' . . . In the first war, she said, it was the camouflage that was nationally characteristic, but in this war the heading of the broadcast. 'It is that a nation is even stronger than the personality of any one, it certainly is so nations must go on, they certainly must.'

Rumours were more frequent and upsetting than ever, but the American women had obtained Swiss passports of protection, 'the Swiss are very comforting, they really are'. But in spite of Russian and Allied victories, *ma foi* it was hard to go on waiting.

> Spring seems to find it impossible to come, we are all getting sad, this is the middle of March, neither spring nor the end of the war can come.

However by Easter everybody knew that the end was coming and pretty nearly everybody had forgotten about the Germans, 'everybody forgets very quickly but nobody forgets quite so quickly as the French, and although the Germans are still here they have pretty nearly forgotten them and they only think about Americans . . .'

Once more there were a great many German soldiers in the district and Gertrude Stein observed that as they were now weak and brutal instead of strong and brutal they were more hated than before. And then came May with lilies of the valley, nightingales and the bombardment.

> It is darkest before the dawn at least we all hope so, we are all terribly worried these days, alerts and airplanes and everybody wondering if everybody in Paris and Lyon are starving and indeed it is not impossible because with all the transport cut what can happen to them.

In the country the food situation was better than before, for everything remained in its own locality, 'and the quantity of food that the fields of France can produce cultivated by a few oldish men and women and young children is perfectly extraordinary'. And of course the farmers liked to sell as much as possible to the inhabitants so as to have less for the Germans. Clothes were a different matter. Good French tweeds, clothing and linen were all giving way, and Alice Toklas, who had earlier implored American friends to send her a darning-egg and other implements of housewifery, was now tired of darning darns and darned darns.

Listening to the American radio now

> was just like being in a theatre with a romantic drama, the things we heard when we were young, Secret Service and Alabama and The Girl I Left Behind Me and Curfew Shall Not Ring Tonight and Shenandoah, they were real American voices talking American and from headquarters and here we are in the heart of the French country with near a hundred German soldiers right in this village and wire entanglements and little block houses all around the railway station and it is exactly like a novel or a theatre more theatre than novel, and very exciting, and will they ever come well anyway I have always been quite certain that there will be no landing until Rome is taken . . .

She had not long to wait. On June the fifth Rome was taken,

> Well that was yesterday and today is the landing and we heard Eisenhower tell us he was here they were here and just yesterday a man sold us ten packages of Camel cigarettes, glory be, and we are singing glory hallelujah, and feeling very nicely, and everybody has been telephoning to us congratulatory messages upon my birthday which it isn't but we know what they mean. And I said in return I hoped their hair was curling nicely, and we all hope it is, and today is the day.

By the third day everybody was making fun of the Germans who had begun to be polite on the day Rome was taken, and although there was still fighting all round them, girls were leaning out of windows singing the Marseillaise. It was a strange interval.

> It is a queer state living as we are all doing, you have no news except for the radio because there are no newspapers

> any more and no trains no mail no telephone and even going
> to Belley is impossible there are twenty-three barricades
> between here and there a distance of seventeen kilometres.
> As I say we live within the village completely within it, the
> Germans rush forward and back there are distant sounds of
> cannonading, some villages have been burned and that is all
> anybody knows . . .

By now, Gertrude Stein said, the Germans were like an ants'
heap if you put a foreign substance into it, and it was wonderful
'the Americans just chasing around France'. And: 'It is nice that
the forces of the interior the French are helping things along so
well, it makes all the French people content that they are taking
part and everybody is happy and gay.'

It was only a matter of days before the maquis drove the remaining Germans, railroad workers and a few soldiers out of
Culoz, and shortly afterwards the radio announced that Paris
was free. The Frenchman's voice cracked as he told the news and
the American woman's pen echoed his excitement, 'Glory halle-
lujah Paris is free.' Now out came the flags—many of the smaller
children had never seen a flag before—and all the other expressions
of rejoicing, and the American women found stars-and-stripes
ribbon for the children in a village shop, and Alice Toklas began
to type *Wars I Have Seen* and Basket was shaved by the local
barber in order to be elegant for the coming of the Americans.

But a more painful barbering was going on too.

> Today the village is excited terribly excited because they
> are shaving the heads of the girls who kept company with the
> Germans during the occupation, it is called the coiffure of
> 1944, and naturally it is terrible because the shaving is done
> publicly . . . It is as I have often said, life in the middle ages,
> it certainly is most interesting and logical it certainly is.

Happy or painful she continued to watch and to write about
every detail of the living round her as she waited for the climax,
'and now if I can only see the Americans come to Culoz I think
all this about war will be finished yes I do'.

On September the first, 'what a day what a day of days',
her wish came true. They went into Belley by taxi to do some
shopping and there were the Americans, and they held each
other's hands and 'patted each other in the good American way',

and they took a colonel and his driver back with them to Culoz
to spend the night. They talked and talked, 'and my were we
happy, we were, completely and truly happy and completely and
entirely worn out with emotion'.

Next day more Americans came, war correspondents this time,
and the talking went on. Even the first G.I.s in Belley knew who
Gertrude Stein was, and she continued her practice of finding out
all about them.

> . . . how we talked and talked and where they were born was
> music to the ears Baltimore and Washington D.C. and
> Detroit and Chicago, it is all music to the ears so long long
> long away from the names of the places where they were
> born. Well they have asked me to go with them to Voiron
> to broadcast with them to America next Sunday and I am
> going and the war is over and this certainly this is the last
> war to remember.

Thus ends the main part of *Wars I Have Seen*. One of the war
correspondents took the manuscript back to America with him;
two instalments were immediately published in *Collier's* magazine
and Random House brought out the book, Batsford publishing
in London the following year. Meanwhile the author continued
with the last chapters, still describing conditions and particularly
the Americans in France, ending with the return to Paris of herself, Alice Toklas and Basket. At the same time she wrote the play
about a French family and an American woman in occupied
France, first called *In Savoy* and afterwards *Yes Is For A Very
Young Man*, with the sub-title *A Play of the Resistance in France*.
Much of the material had been used in *Wars I Have Seen*, but now
she selected and condensed her experiences to produce a shapely,
tender little drama of human relationships and emotions. There
is plenty of action and the unusual dialogue lends itself well to
speech, the repetitions subtly building character and sustaining
atmosphere. It is unfair to the play to read a passage out of con-
text, but these lines explain the title. Constance, the American
woman,[1] is talking with the French boy Ferdinand on the terrace
of a château just after the armistice with Germany.

---

[1] In a letter to Lamont Johnson, a young actor who while touring Europe in
1945 secured the rights to the play from Miss Stein, she said that the character
of Constance was suggested by Clare Boothe Luce, whom she knew well.

Constance: Denise is very lovely.

Ferdinand: Yes.

Constance: And Henry really loves her.

Ferdinand: Yes.

Constance: Yes can be said too often.

Ferdinand: Yes.

Constance: Oh Ferdinand, don't be stupid and annoying.

Ferdinand: Constance, Constance, what can I say, what is there to say but yes, no does not mean anything, no not now, but yes, yes means something. Oh my God, yes means you, it means you, yes it does, you do not want it to mean you but yes it does. Yes, yes, yes.

Constance: (*very slowly*) Yes, yes is for a very young man, and you, Ferdinand, you are a very young boy, yes you are, yes is for a very young one, a very young man, but I am not so young, no I am not, and so I say no. I always say no. You know, Ferdinand, yes you know that I always say no.

Ferdinand: Yes.

Many weeks passed before news came of the Paris apartment and the friends were so frightened to think what might have happened to the pictures that by mutual consent they did not talk about it. In the middle of November, however, a letter came from an American friend, Katherine Dudley, a neighbour in the Quarter who had been for a while in a concentration camp. She had paid a visit to rue Christine as soon as possible after the liberation.

Fortunately as far as I could see all the pictures on the walls were unhurt though several of the small Picasso heads had been thrown on the floor.[1] We put them back in their places and none are harmed ... But it's a miracle that your collection is still there for about 2 weeks before the Boches left 4 men of the Gestapo came, demanded the key of the concierge who protested in vain that you were American. The young girl who is secretary in the Bureau Weil heard steps overhead, rushed up, banged on the door until they opened it, pushed in past them and asked by what right they were there—that the proprietor was American, that she had

[1] The pictures had in fact been left on the floor by their owners.

charge of the house. They tried to put her out but she stayed. They were lashing themselves into a fury over the Picassos saying they would cut them to pieces and burn them. 'De la saloperie juive, bon à bruler.' The big pink nude 'cette vache'. They recognised your Rose portrait—they had a photo of you with them—and the other Rose heads in the long gallery, 'Tous des juifs et bon à bruler.' The girl rushed downstairs to her office, telephoned the police and in 10 minutes there was the Commissaire and 30 agents before the door much to the excitement of the street. By this time they —the G.s—were trying on your Chinese coats in your bed-room. The Commissaire asked them for their order of per-quisition which they had neglected to bring with them and they had to go but taking the key with them. So she waited before the door until a menuisier could be found to change the lock.

Only some linen and a few small objects were taken, and the collection was saved. The Russian man too, who had always closed up the apartment when they went away for the summer and cleaned it ready for their return, had somehow weathered the storm and now set to work to restore the place to order.

Letters now poured in from Gertrude Stein's friends and gradually life resumed something of its old shape, but she and Alice Toklas were still 'so busy just being excited and being liberated' that they stayed where they were. It was not until December that the homesickness 'for a roast chicken and the quays of Paris' which had haunted Gertrude Stein during the darkest days of the occupation returned so strongly that they decided to make the move. She had given her car, which early in the war had been changed to run on wood alcohol, to the French Red Cross in Lyon, so the return to Paris was made in a local taxi. It was an arduous and sometimes perilous journey through the snows in an old charcoal-burning car with 'ersatz tyres' which burst every few hours and 'an ersatz jack' to change them with. They were on the road for nearly twenty-four hours and exceed-ingly glad of the American K. rations they took with them.

Once they were stopped by members of the F.F.I., two men and a woman who, alone of the three, carried a gun. These examined their papers and asked about all the packages which

shared the back of the car with Miss Toklas and a small maid—
they had sent most of their possessions by *camion*.

> 'Oh those,' I said, 'are meat and butter and eggs. Now don't
> touch them, they are all carefully packed, and enough to
> keep us a week in Paris. 'Ah yes,' he said. 'And this big
> thing.' 'That,' said Miss Toklas, with decision, 'is a Picasso
> painting, don't touch it.' 'I congratulate you,' said the F.F.I.,
> and waved us on.

They had left Culoz at midnight, and night fell again before
they reached Fontainebleau.

> So then it was the gates of Paris, and was it real?

In her excitement Gertrude Stein wrongly directed the driver,
but then:

> . . . there at last was the Rue Christine, and out we got and
> in we came. Yes, it was the same, so much more beautiful,
> but it was the same.

The last pages of *Wars I Have Seen* glow with happiness.

> Picasso had been impatiently waiting our return. He came
> in the next morning and we were very moved when we
> embraced, and we kept saying it is a miracle, all the treasures
> which made our youth, the pictures, the drawings, the objects,
> all there.

Paris, as she and Basket walked about it, was all there too, so
that everything which had happened since she last saw it seemed
just a nightmare. They had simply been away for a summer vaca-
tion and come back. Here were the same little shops with the
same proprietors and those which had been dirty were still dirty
and the clean ones were clean. The same little antiquity shops,
'with, I almost thought, the same stock of antiquities. It was a
miracle, it was a miracle.'
In this mood the architecture of Paris impressed her more than
ever before, 'it was no longer a background but a reality', and she
came to the conclusion that architecture was made for people
who go about on their feet. 'How lovely it all was and the quays
of the Seine.'

And as she walked she talked to everybody and particularly to the soldiers, 'who wander eternally, wander about the streets'.

And so we are back in Paris, yes, back in Paris. How often has Paris been saved, how often. Yes, I walk around Paris, we all walk around Paris all day long and night too. Everybody is walking around Paris, it is very nice. How many days are there in a week so nice? Very many, happily, very many.

CHAPTER TWENTY

'WHAT IS THE QUESTION?'

'You have to learn to do everything, even to die.'
Wars I Have Seen.

GERTRUDE STEIN settled down once more to her full and pleasant life in the rue Christine. She was thin now, but very handsome, and if her health gave her some trouble, her interests were unchanged and her enthusiasm was as whole-hearted as ever. The preface that she wrote in 1945 for a Paris exhibition of the work of the young Spanish painter Riba-Rovira shows this well, and it is interesting to find her writing about painting again at the end of her life.

It is inevitable that when one has great need of something one finds it. What you need you attract like a lover.

I returned to Paris, after these long years passed in a little country side and I needed a young painter who would awake me . . . I walked a great deal, I looked around, in all the painting shops, but the young painter was not there. Yes, I walked a great deal, a great deal along the Seine where they fish, where they paint, where they walk the dogs (I am one of those who walk their dogs). No young painter!

One day, at a turning in the street in one of those little streets of my neighbourhood, I saw a man making a picture. I looked at him, at him and his picture, as I always look at everyone who does something—I have an insatiable curiosity to look—and I was moved. Yes, a young painter!

We began to talk for one talks easily, as easily as in the country byways, in the little streets of the neighbourhood.

His history was the sad history of the young of our time. A young Spaniard who studied at the Beaux-Arts at Barcelona; the civil war, exile, concentration camp, escape, Gestapo, prison again, escape again . . . Eight lost years. Were they lost, who knows? And now a little hardship, but even so painting.

Why did I find that he was he the young painter, why? I went to see his sketches, his painting; we talked.

I explained that for me, all modern painting is based on that which Cézanne failed to do instead of being based on that which he almost succeeded in doing . . .

And now, I found a young painter who was not following the tendency to play with that which Cézanne was not able to do, but who attacked directly the things which he had tried to do, to create objects which must exist, for, and in themselves, and not in relation to anything else . . .

In this preface Gertrude Stein does not mention Picasso. Although she loved the paintings that she had, there is no evidence of her being interested in his current work. She went far in her appreciation, but violence was alien to her and so of course were Picasso's Communist sympathies, although he said himself that this was the logical outcome of his whole life and work. Both rooted in freedom, living in the moment and using the stuff of daily life as the medium of their art, in their expression of it Picasso and Gertrude Stein had grown far apart. But their affection was constant, and in these last months of her life they saw one another often.

One of her very last pieces was about Raoul Dufy.[1] Repeating her favourite maxim, 'a writer does not write with his ears or his mouth, he writes with his eyes', she added, 'when I said that to Picasso, he said of course the mouths of all writers you can see it in the portraits are always tight shut and he pointed to mine'.

There is a great deal of nonsense talked about paintings, musicians and architects and writers do not talk about abstraction. They know perfectly well that everything they do is an abstraction, but painters because they have to use their eyes to work with labour under the delusion that they use their eyes to see the things they paint . . . but oh dear me, he does not paint what he sees, he paints what he is . . . Think of Dufy, think of any painter of course he is abstract, he abstracts the colours of which he is made and he puts them down in the light and shade of which he is made . . .

And so this is what life is and it is a pleasure . . .

One must meditate about pleasure. Dufy is pleasure . . .

[1] *Harper's Bazaar*, December 1949.

That is one of the things that we who abstract things have,
we are never bored we are always in a state of pleasure . . .
One must meditate about pleasure.

And so happily she did until the very end of her life.

Besides discovering the necessary new Gertrude Stein remained
faithful to what she had in the past found good and was as ever
energetic on behalf of her friends. She sponsored Francis Rose's
first post-war exhibition in Paris and also Pierre Balmain's first collection. She was a member of the reception committee for the visit
of the Negro author, Richard Wright, who had early praised
Melanctha; she toured Germany by air and spoke to groups of
American soldiers both there and in Brussels and Paris; she wrote
an account of the German trip for *Life*, worked hard at her libretto,
The Mother of Us All, which Virgil Thomson was eagerly awaiting,
and finally she turned to her last book, *Brewsie and Willie*.[1] At
the same time, hearing of liberties that the American University
in Biarritz proposed to take with the text of *Yes Is For A Very
Young Man*, she stopped—by means of a peremptory telephone
call from Miss Toklas—what was to have been the première of
the play. In fact, one way and another Gertrude Stein was very
much herself and thoroughly enjoying all the days of the week,
and to add to her happiness letters from America told her that
with the publication of *Wars I Have Seen* she was once more a
best-seller.

The only serious shadow was her distress at the imprisonment
of Bernard Faÿ. They were, however, able to write to one
another and she sent him parcels and he wrote, 'You have sent
me messages that are worth millions. I feel and enjoy from my
cell your affection and your vitality.'

Indeed her heart was warm now towards old friends and the
few relatives in America with whom she had kept in touch. On
October 27th, 1945, she wrote to her cousin Helen Bachrach:

Do send me a photo of yourself. I would kind of like to
know what you look like now . . . I suppose you have
nephews and nieces were any of them over, strangely enough
among the thousands of G.I.s who have turned up there

[1] Random House, 1946.

hasn't been a relative, the generations cannot quite have petered out can they have . . . Strangely enough one day I met a boy who had studied with Uncle Eph in Baltimore, and he was only in the late twenties, it was very sweet to hear him speak of him.

While continuing to entertain many distinguished people, she also had her G.I. salon. How little she had changed since 1917 when 'the Kiddie' fell under her spell at Nîmes! There used to be a section of her readers which liked to amuse itself by pretending to believe that there was no such person as Alice B. Toklas outside Gertrude Stein's imagination. William Whitehead, a young actor and writer in France with the American Field Service, had a cousin in New York who claimed this belief. Whitehead, finding himself in Paris, went immediately to the rue Christine where, not surprisingly, the door was opened to him by Miss Toklas herself. His uniform made him welcome and presently Miss Stein joined them, still in spite of cropped grey hair so like the Picasso portrait over the mantelpiece. The young man thought what a presence she would have had as an actress, and as for her voice, only second in Carl Van Vechten's experience to the golden voice of the divine Sarah, for him it was second to none. Her direct interest and kindliness drew him out and he was soon telling her about his background and literary aspirations. 'Bring me the poems,' she said, 'and I'll tell you whether or not you can write.'

On another occasion Bill Whitehead called just ahead of a contingent of army librarians. Three were expected, but he gave warning that there were nine earnest young men in the street searching for the number. Miss Toklas then confessed that the army invasion was sometimes almost too much for them. G.I.s and officers arrived at practically any hour to invite Miss Stein to the opera or pursue any other notion that came into their heads. Miss Toklas's firm protection of her friend had never been more needed. Whitehead witnessed how deftly room was made for these nine young librarians and drinks provided for them all, as they goggled at the room, mentally cataloguing everything, and Gertrude Stein conducted the conversation. He also noticed, in spite of her cheerfulness, how tired she was when at last, late at night, the young men went away. He did not know that Miss Stein was already gravely ill.

Occasionally in a letter to a friend she admitted a little *malaise* but always made light of it, with a complete absence of self-pity. She accepted old age and illness without sentimentality and without complaint and continued for as long as possible living fully and writing.

The heroine of the opera, *The Mother of Us All*, is Susan B. Anthony, and its theme the winning of political rights for American women. Some of the other characters are historical too, but she also, as was often her way, included friends in the cast. Jo the Loiterer, for instance, is a young man who once told Gertrude Stien about being arrested at his university for picketing and as there was no law against this charged with loitering. And so in the opera he sings: 'Anybody can be accused of loitering.' Gertrude Stein also brings herself briefly into the first act as 'G.S.' declaiming with the other characters that her father's name was Daniel.

Early in 1946 Carl Van Vechten handed the libretto to Virgil Thomson who enthusiastically decided to use it for the opera Columbia University had commissioned from him for the following year. *The Mother of Us All* was therefore not produced until May 1947, ten months after the author's death, when several performances were given and warmly acclaimed.

In this spring too Gertrude Stein finished her final work. 'Write about us they all said a little sadly, and write about them I will', the Epilogue to *Wars I Have Seen* begins. 'They' were the G.I.s and in *Brewsie and Willie* she fulfilled her promise. She had become a legend to more than the G.I.s, but this book, although 'that Stein woman' is mentioned, is concerned not with the Stein but the G.I. legend. She had finished writing her autobiography and except for the short message at the end of *Brewsie and Willie*, in which she speaks to Americans in her own person, Gertrude Stein completely submerges herself in her characters. These are a group of American army men and women in Paris directly after the war, and the book is written in the form of loosely flowing conversations in the G.I. idiom, Brewsie being the central thinker and talker.

How I hate that word job, said Brewsie. You're right, said Willie, you're right to hate that word, hate it good and plenty, but you can afford to hate it Brewsie, fellows like you dont need a job you just live, everybody's got to see to it you live and live you do but fellows like us, well we have got to have jobs, what you want us to do, nobody's going to feed us, you just watch them not feed us dont we know, no we got to have jobs, talk all you like and talk is good I like talk I like to listen to you Brewsie, but when we get home and dont wear this brown any more we got to have a job, job, job ... Yes but Willie, said Brewsie, that's what I want to say, industrialism which produces more than anybody can buy and makes employees out of free men makes 'em stop thinking, stop feeling, makes 'em all feel alike. I tell you Willie it's wrong ...

... You know, said Willie, what you make industrialism sound like, you make it sound like chewing gum. You chew and chew but it don't feed you, it's got a kind of a taste but that is all there is to it no substance. Have I got it right, kind of. Industrialism is like chewing gum.

And Gertrude Stein herself exhorts her characters not to be yes men or no men when they get back, but to go as easy as they can.

Remember the depression, don't be afraid to look it in the face and find out the reason why. If you don't find out the reason why you'll go poor and my God how I would hate to have my native land go poor.

Brewsie and Willie was published by Random House just before Gertrude Stein's death. A good, slightly sentimentalized television play has been made of it in America.

So this book too was accomplished and Gertrude Stein was pleased with it and still she went on writing.

They asked me what I thought of the atomic bomb, I said I had not been able to take any interest in it.

I like to read detective and mystery stories, I never get enough of them but whenever one of them is or was about death rays and atomic bombs I never could read them.

Secret weapons were dull and meaningless, she said, just

because they were secret, and machinery was only interesting to its inventors. As for the atom bomb's destructiveness: 'Sure it will destroy a lot and kill a lot, but it's the living that are interesting not the way of killing them . . .'

> They think they are interested about the atomic bombs but they really are not not any more than I am. Really not. They may be a little scared, I am not so scared, there is so much to be scared of so what is the use of bothering to be scared and if you are not scared the atomic bomb is not interesting.
>
> Everybody gets so much information all day long that they lose their common sense. They listen so much that they forget to be natural. This is a nice story.

With these characteristic words Gertrude Stein laid down her professional pen.

She admitted now, but casually, that she was tired, and her close friends knew that she was ill. This did not deter her from buying a new car, and she was sitting happily in it with Miss Toklas at the corner of a street near their apartment and Picasso's studio when she met him for the last time. It was not, he said, the kind of car that he wanted her to have, but perhaps it would do. He added characteristically that life was bitter and she, equally so, replied that for her it was not. So the painter and the writer smiled at one another as they had on and off for forty years, said their usual affectionate 'Au revoir, Gertrude', 'Au revoir, Pablo', and went their ways.

On June 14th came Carl Van Vechten's *A Stein Song*, his introduction to the volume of her *Selected Writings*.

> Gertrude Stein rings bells, loves baskets, and wears handsome waistcoats. She has a tenderness for green glass and buttons have a tenderness for her. In the matter of fans you can only compare her with a motion-picture star in Hollywood and three generations of young writers have sat at her feet. She has influenced without coddling them. In her own time she is a legend and in her own country she is with honor. Keys to sacred doors have been presented to her and she understands how to open them. She writes books for children, plays for actors and librettos for operas. Each one of them is one. For her a rose is a rose and how!

She sent him *A Message from Gertrude Stein* for the book and it was published by Random House just after her death.

In July 1946 Gertrude Stein and Alice Toklas set off south by car to spend the rest of the summer at a country house lent them by a friend. On the way Miss Stein became acutely ill and they were forced to return to Paris by train. At the American hospital at Neuilly the doctors found that she was suffering from an advanced stage of cancer. They held out little hope and in view of her age and condition were loath to operate, but she herself urged the operation and faced it bravely, although she had no wish to leave the life that she had loved and no comforting or troubling belief in a future one. She did not regain full consciousness after the operation.

Her last words are well known. 'What is the answer?' she asked, and when no answer came she laughed and said: 'Then, what is the question?'

In the evening of July 27th, 1946, Gertrude Stein's life came to an end.

The funeral service was held in the American Church and she was buried in the Père Lachaise Cemetery, her headstone, designed by Francis Rose, a large grey granite tablet bearing in big golden letters her name and dates and the names of the cities where she was born and died. Visiting her grave one early spring morning I watched a funeral taking place with ceremony while the *gardiens* of this great garden of death smiled and hummed, quite unoppressed. As she wrote in *Paris France*:

> And then the way they feel about the dead, it is so friendly so simply friendly and though inevitable not a sadness and though occurring not a shock. There is no difference between death and life in France and that too made it inevitable that they were the background of the twentieth century.

Through their splendour and their disasters Gertrude Stein remained faithful to her chosen country and her chosen century.

CHIEF PUBLICATIONS

Three Lives (1904–5)
   The Grafton Press, New York, 1909.
   John Lane the Bodley Head, London, and John Lane Co.,
      New York, 1915, 1920.
   John Rodker, London, 1927.
   Albert and Charles Boni, New York, 1927.
   The Modern Library, Inc., New York, 1933.
   New Directions, Norfolk, Conn., 1941.
   Pushkin Press, London, 1945.
   A. Scherz, Berne, 1946.
   Selected Writings of Gertrude Stein, edited Carl Van Vechten,
      Random House, New York, 1946.

The Making of Americans (1906–11)
   Contact Editions, Paris, 1925.
   Albert and Charles Boni, New York, 1926.
   Abridged edition, Harcourt, Brace and Co., New York, 1934.
   Selected passages, *Selected Writings of Gertrude Stein*, edited
      Carl Van Vechten, Random House, New York, 1946.

Tender Buttons (1910–12)
   Claire Marie, New York, 1914.
   transition No. 14, 1928.
   Selected Writings of Gertrude Stein, edited Carl Van Vechten,
      Random House, New York, 1946.

Geography and Plays (Introduction by Sherwood Anderson) (1908–
      1920)
   The Four Seas Company, Boston, 1922.

Composition as Explanation (1926)
   The Hogarth Press, London, 1926.
   In *The Hogarth Essays*, Doubleday, Doran and Co. Inc., New
      York, 1928.
   In *What Are Masterpieces* (see below).

Useful Knowledge (1915)
  Payson and Clarke Ltd., New York, 1928.
  John Lane the Bodley Head, 1929.

Lucy Church Amiably (1927)
  Plain Edition, Paris, 1930.

How to Write (1928–30)
  Plain Edition, Paris, 1931.

Matisse, Picasso and Gertrude Stein (1909–12)
  Plain Edition, 1933.

Operas and Plays (including *Four Saints in Three Acts*) (1913–30)
  Plain Edition, Paris, 1932.

The Autobiography of Alice B. Toklas (1932)
  Harcourt, Brace and Co., New York, 1933.
  The Literary Guild, New York, 1933.
  John Lane the Bodley Head, London, 1933.
  John Lane the Bodley Head, London (The Week End Library),
    1935.
  Random House, New York, 1936.
  Selected Writings of Gertrude Stein, edited Carl Van Vechten,
    1946.

Portraits and Prayers (1909–33)
  Random House, New York, 1934.

Lectures in America (1934)
  Random House, New York, 1935.

Narration (Four Lectures) (Introduction by Thornton Wilder)
    (1935)
  University of Chicago Press, 1935.

The Geographical History of America (Introduction by Thornton
    Wilder) (1935)
  Random House, New York, 1936.

Everybody's Autobiography (1936)
  Random House, New York, 1937.
  William Heinemann, London and Toronto, 1938.

Picasso—in French and English (1938)
  Librairie Floury, Paris, 1938.
  B. T. Batsford Ltd., London, 1938.
  Charles Scribner's Sons, New York, 1939.

The World is Round (1938)
  With illustrations by Clement Hurd, Wm. R. Scott Inc., New
    York, 1939.
  With illustrations by Sir Francis Rose, B. T. Batsford Ltd.,
    London, 1939.

Paris France (1939)
  B. T. Batsford Ltd., London, 1940.
  Charles Scribner's Sons, New York, 1940.

What Are Masterpieces (Foreword by Robert Bartlett Haas)
    (1935)
  The Conference Press, Los Angeles, 1940.

Ida, A Novel (1940)
  Random House, New York, 1941.

Wars I Have Seen (1942-4)
  Random House, New York, 1944.
  B. T. Batsford Ltd., 1945.

Brewsie and Willie (1945)
  Random House, New York, 1946.

Selected Writings of Gertrude Stein, edited with an introduction and
    notes by Carl Van Vechten
  Random House, New York, 1946.

POSTHUMOUS PUBLICATIONS

Four in America (1933) (Introduction by Thornton Wilder)
  Yale University Press, 1947.

The Gertrude Stein First Reader and Three Plays (1941-3)
  M. Fridberg, Dublin, London, 1946.
  Houghton Mifflin Co., Boston, 1948.

Things As They Are (1903)
  Banyan Press, Pawlet, Vermont, 1950.

Last Operas and Plays (including *Yes Is For A Very Young Man,
The Mother of Us All, Doctor Faustus Lights the Lights, Four
Saints in Three Acts*) (1917–46). (Edited and with an in-
troduction by Carl Van Vechten.)
Rinehart and Company Inc., New York, 1949.

THE YALE EDITION OF THE UNPUBLISHED WRITINGS OF GERTRUDE STEIN

Two: Gertrude Stein and Her Brother and Other Early Portraits
(1908–12) (Foreword by Janet Flanner). 1951.
Mrs. Reynolds and Five Earlier Novelettes (1931–42) (Foreword
by Lloyd Frankenberg). 1952.
Bee Time Vine and Other Pieces (1913–27) (Preface and notes by
Virgil Thomson). 1953.
As Fine As Melanctha (1914–30) (Foreword by Natalie Clifford
Barney). 1954.
Painted Lace and Other Pieces (1914–37) (Introduction by
Daniel-Henry Kahnweiler). 1955.
Stanzas in Meditation and Other Poems (1929–33) (Preface by
Donald Sutherland). 1956.

INDEX

Books and articles referred to in this Index without the author's name (e.g. *Accent in Alsace*) are by Gertrude Stein.